Routledge Revivals

The Three Rings

Originally published in 1963, this book covers one of the least known parts of Jewish history: the golden age of Jewish culture in Spain with the interaction of Jewish, Muslim and Christian cultures, the horrors of the Inquisition and the final banishment of the race from the Iberian peninsula. In the Middle Ages there were large numbers of Jews in most Spanish cities: financiers and statesmen, poets and musicians, honoured by the rulers of great cities such as Cordoba, Seville, Granada and Toledo. Their history ended abruptly as they were persecuted and dispossessed, the survivors scattered over many countries. This book tells this story and provides a fascinating record of their literature and art.

The Three Rings

The History of the Spanish Jews

Poul Borchsenius

First published in English in 1963 by George Allen & Unwin Ltd.

This edition first published in 2024 by Routledge
4 Park Square, Milton Park, Abingdon, Oxon, OX14 4RN

and by Routledge
605 Third Avenue, New York, NY 10158.

Routledge is an imprint of the Taylor & Francis Group, an informa business

© 1963 English Translation George Allen & Unwin Ltd.

The right of Poul Borchsenius to be identified as the author of this work has been asserted by him in accordance with sections 77 and 78 of the Copyright, Designs and Patents Act 1988.

All rights reserved. No part of this book may be reprinted or reproduced or utilised in any form or by any electronic, mechanical, or other means, now known or hereafter invented, including photocopying and recording, or in any information storage or retrieval system, without permission in writing from the publishers.

ISBN 13: 978-1-032-91121-2 (hbk)
ISBN 13: 978-1-003-56147-7 (ebk)
ISBN 13: 978-1-032-91125-0 (pbk)
Book DOI 10.4324/9781003561477

THE THREE RINGS

THE HISTORY OF THE SPANISH JEWS

POUL BORCHSENIUS

TRANSLATED BY MICHAEL HERON

Ruskin House
GEORGE ALLEN & UNWIN LTD
MUSEUM STREET   LONDON

FIRST PUBLISHED IN 1963

This book is copyright under the Berne Convention. Apart from any fair dealing for the purposes of private study, research, criticism or review, as permitted under the Copyright Act 1956, no portion may be reproduced by any process without written permission. Inquiries should be addressed to the publishers

This translation © *George Allen & Unwin Ltd, 1963*

Translated from the Danish
DE TRE RINGE
© H. Hirschsprungs Forlag, Copenhagen 1954

PRINTED IN GREAT BRITAIN
IN 12 ON 13 PT. CENTAUR TYPE
BY JARROLD AND SONS LTD
NORWICH

CONTENTS

I	The Three Rings	9
II	The Rings are Forged	22
III	Under the Crescent	39
IV	— and the Star	48
V	The First Nightingale	72
VI	Shadows of the Cross	82
VII	The Song Birds Tune their Lyres	94
VIII	No one like Moses	116
IX	The Cabbala	137
X	Thunder in the North	158
XI	Castles in Spain	169
XII	Reconquista	198
XIII	Isabella	216
XIV	Granada	228
XV	Ahasverus	240

I

THE THREE RINGS

ONCE upon a time . . .
That's the way all stories begin, and that's the way this story began, too, a very long time ago.

On wings of thought we fly backwards in time, century after century, until we come to the Middle Ages.

The world looked quite different in those days. For one thing it was much smaller. It was very difficult for the people who lived in Europe to leave their own countries. The route to America had not yet been discovered. Centuries were to pass before dauntless adventurers set forth across the seemingly endless, unknown Atlantic Ocean. And Russia was cut off by an iron curtain of impassable roads and barbaric peoples, so that only mysterious rumours came from that isolated country. In the south the Saracens held sway. They had been on the verge of swamping Europe; the crescent almost eclipsed the cross. And Christian Europe was armed to the teeth to combat her arch-enemy, Islam.

But the far horizon was not the only one which was restricted. Most European countries were imprisoned in the spiritual gloom of the Middle Ages; ignorance, superstition and fanaticism laid their heavy burden on people's minds.

There was only one country where things were different. Far down in the south-west corner of our part of the world, where the Spanish peninsula forms a bridge between Europe proper and Africa, the torch was about to be lit.

By one of the strange freaks of history, it so happened that the three great religions, Islam, Christendom and Judaism met

THE THREE RINGS

one another in Spain, each accompanied by its people, its culture and its special message. Spain was the setting for their clash and the resultant drama. They were on family terms with each other, even close family terms. Perhaps one could say that Judaism was the mother of the other two, or that they were half-brothers. The Jews had no doubt about the relationship and consequently gave them Biblical names, Ishmael, Edom and Jacob. Ishmael was Abraham's son by Hagar the handmaid whom Sara banished to the wilderness. And Islam emerged from the vast wilderness, so that it was natural to call it Ishmael. Esau became Edom the day he sold his birthright for a mess of pottage. In olden days the Jews applied the name to the Romans and later to the Christian church which in fact inherited the Roman Empire. And Jacob and Israel were one and the same. When Jacob fought all night with the angel for blessing, the Lord called him Israel, fighter with the Lord.

Similar faiths are the worst bedfellows. Already in the old Biblical tales we can read about how the three were obstinately opposed. And on this account we shall hear a lot more about bitter fraternal strife. It had momentous consequences, some of which have left their imprint on the world today.

But there was a long delay before it flared up in earnest. Many of the best minds in the three Spanish groups of peoples were receptive and tolerant of each other. They unlocked the door so that the three inspired and stimulated each other instead of quarrelling and causing destruction; they took from each other and gave of their best in return.

And it was this interplay of ideas that together brought the three peoples of the Iberian peninsula to a flowering whose like the world has not seen. For this reason we look on the Spanish Middle Ages as a mythical golden age in which the protagonists were either Mohammedans, Christians or Jews.

Almost a millennium ago the Spanish Jews told a story about this. By devious routes it spread from country to country and even reached us. But it left its traces behind in its wanderings so that we can follow it back to the place where it was first told. It is the parable of the three rings.

THE THREE RINGS

In 1778 the German poet and philosopher Gotthold Ephraim Lessing was waging a bitter controversy. He was exposed to venomous attacks by the orthodox church and the pietists. To be sure he had more or less asked for them, for Lessing was a major sceptic, of Voltaire's type, and he expressed his rationalist ideas incisively and uncompromisingly.

In the heat of controversy his ecclesiastical opponents had recourse to the state authorities. They managed to enlist their aid against him and he was subjected to strict censorship. To defend himself against these highhanded methods Lessing wrote his play *Nathan der Weise* (Nathan the Wise), in which he expressed his ideas about tolerance in religious matters. Since his youth he had known and admired one of the tales in Boccaccio's *Decameron*, the parable of the three rings, and it gave him the idea for his famous play.

The scene is set in the time of the Crusades. The great Saladin, the prince who conquered the crusaders and took Jerusalem, represents Islam, the Nathan of the title is Jewish and a number of Christians also appear. In other words all three religions figure in the drama.

Saladin wants to outwit the Jew, he needs his money and so he tries to lure Nathan into a trap. He asks him which of the three great religions, Islam, Christendom or Judaism, he thinks is the right one. But Nathan is not nicknamed the Wise for nothing. He sees through Saladin's guile and realizes that whatever answer he gives can be used against him and he will be cornered. Then the only way out will be to buy himself free and lose his money. But at the last moment he has a bright idea and tells Saladin the story of the three rings.

In days long past—so Nathan begins his tale—there lived in the East a man who owned a priceless ring which had been given him by one whom he loved dearly. The stone in the ring was an opal which gleamed all colours of the rainbow and it also had a magic power which made anyone who wore the ring and believed in it beloved of God and men. Therefore the man never took the ring off his finger and took steps to ensure that his descendants kept it for evermore. He bequeathed the ring

THE THREE RINGS

to the son he loved the most and decreed that he in turn should let his dearest son inherit it, and that this procedure should always be followed. And for countless ages the ring was handed down from father to son.

At last it reached a father who had three sons. They were all obedient and he loved them all equally. The father would not bring himself to choose between them, and in loving weakness he promised each of them privately that he would inherit the wonderful ring. But when he realized that death was approaching, he was sorely perplexed. What was he to do? If he let one of the sons have the ring, he would hurt the other two and he had not the heart to do so.

Finally he thought of a plan. He sent for a goldsmith in secret and ordered him to fashion two more rings. They were so like the real one that even the father could not distinguish between them. Then he summoned his sons to him, one by one, and gave each of them a ring and his blessing.

Scarcely was the father dead before the conflict started. Each of the sons appeared with his ring and claimed to be the head of the family, maintaining that his ring was the genuine one. But none of them could prove it.

Finally the brothers submitted the case to the judge for him to make a decision. The judge asked which of them had the ring's power and loved the other two more than himself. Ashamed, all three were silent. Then the judge laid down that each of them was the biter bit. Their father had obviously discarded the real ring, because he did not want to favour one son at the expense of the others. And he concluded by giving them a piece of advice:

'Each of you shall hold his ring to be the real one, and therefore you must compete to make the ring's power visible. You must show humility, tolerance and be devout. And if the stone's power manifests itself in your children's children's children, I summon them to appear before this court again after hundreds and hundreds of years. Until that time let a wiser man than I sit here and give judgment.'

THE THREE RINGS

Saladin was profoundly impressed by the Jew's wisdom and became his friend. And Lessing had given a fine expression to his ideas of tolerance between the different religions.

I have already mentioned that Lessing did not invent the parable of the three rings himself. It belongs to the class of itinerant fables, as do most of the stories we know.

For popular legends and tales are not dead. They live, and like everything living, they are constantly moving and developing. Mothers tell them to their children, they go down from generation to generation and form part of our invisible inheritance. They leap across frontiers, they are always making long journeys, we find the tales of our childhood in distant lands—like flowers whose seeds are carried by the wind and strike root wherever they find the soil which suits them.

But on their journey down the generations or over the wide world the tales alter, they change their form with changing ages and to meet the storytellers' needs. If we try to find the origins of such itinerant tales and parables, we feel as if we are holding a Chinese ivory ball in our hands. We open it, but inside is another ball, a little smaller than the first one and a different colour. This, too, can be opened and another ball appears. If we open that one, there is yet another inside. And so it goes on until at last we wonder how the innermost ball actually got there. It is the same with the story of the three rings.

Lessing knew it from the *Decameron*; it is one of the pearls in that brilliantly witty, daring mediaeval book. He follows Boccaccio fairly closely, except that the Jew was called Melchizedek and the ring had no supernatural power, it was only a beautiful precious jewel.

But in the case of both Boccaccio and Lessing, an undeniable shadow lies over the story. Both of them make the father procure two false rings, only one is genuine. In other words, the father deceives two of his sons; against his better judgment he pretends that all three rings are genuine.

This sounds wrong when we remember that the father is a symbol of God in heaven and the rings are the three religions

THE THREE RINGS

which show mankind the right way to salvation. Can God really deceive people? But both writers took the story as they found it. Mediaeval listeners did not attach much importance to such details. After all it was an innocent trick, and no holds were barred between Jews and Saracens. But otherwise in its original cleverness there is a breath of fresh air about the story.

We find different versions of the parable in various parts of Europe. Mediaeval monks and priests altered it openly, so that it ultimately passed into their religious propaganda. It becomes the story of a knight, who bequeathed his property to his eldest son. That meant the Jews who received the promised land. The second son inherited his riches, and the Saracens certainly laid great store by worldly splendour, but the youngest got the ring which had fabulous power and cured all illnesses. That was the Christian faith. In other versions Saladin is converted to Christianity and still others use the tale as moralizing exhortations to go on the Crusades.

We glance briefly at many of the Chinese ivory balls. Then we put them aside quickly; they are of no interest. But the more we come across and the deeper we probe into this lovely parable during its long journeyings, the more certain we become that it is fundamentally of Jewish origin.

Both Nathan and Melchizedek acted as long years of bitter experience had taught the Jews to act. As refugees they were defenceless in the face of the brutality, fanaticism and greed which were constantly unleashed on them. But nature teaches the persecuted to defend themselves and develop the special qualities they need. The Jews knew how to bow when the storm blew over them and they learnt presence of mind and ingenuity. The Jews became more wordly wise than their enemies.

So the story of the three rings provides a nice example of Jewish diplomacy. When the Jew was asked which religion was the true one, he avoided a direct answer which would only land him in trouble. In true oriental fashion he answered by asking another question. With subtle skill he told a parable which the prince was forced to apply to himself, so that he quite logically drew the conclusion the Jew wanted him to. Without his realizing it the questioner was baffled, the Jew gave him an answer whose purport he obviously did not understand until it was too late.

There are examples of this method in the Bible. Jesus used it when He was asked if it was lawful to pay tribute to the emperor, in the actual situation as crafty a question as Saladin's, full of pitfalls. And Jesus answered with the question:

'Shew me a penny. Whose image and superscription hath it?'

But the prophet Nathan is the classical example. Lessing did not call his Jew after him for nothing. The prophet has to convince King David of his guilt for Uriah's death. Instead of going to work like a bull in a china shop, Nathan tells the story of the poor man and his one ewe lamb which the rich man took from him. Everything went according to plan. David rose up and gave judgment:

'As the Lord liveth, the man that hath done this thing should surely die!'

And then quick as a flash came Nathan's answer:

'Thou art that man!'

David had judged himself.

Naturally we often find humour in the stories which tell of Jewish quick wittedness, or they simply would not have been Jewish. There is the story of the Mohammedan, the Jew and the Christian who were on a journey through the desert together. One day their provisions gave out and it was still a long way before they would reach human habitations. They had only one loaf of bread left and in the evening they agreed that it should not be divided between them. Next morning one of them should have the whole loaf so that he would have the strength to continue and fetch help. The man who dreamed the finest dream that night was to have the loaf.

The morning came and they told their dreams. The Christian was sure he had won. The devil had taken him to the verge of Hell, he had seen the glowing furnace and heard the screams of the damned. What dream could be finer?

But the Mohammedan surpassed him. The angel Gabriel had

THE THREE RINGS

seized him by the hair and taken him to paradise. There he heard gay music and saw lovely blue-eyed girls dancing. Was not that the most wonderful dream imaginable?

Then it was the Jew's turn. He looked at the Christian and said: 'I too dreamt that a devil took you to hell.'

And then he turned to the Mohammedan: 'And I saw the angel take you to paradise.'

He went on: 'So when I was certain that neither of you would come back, I got up and ate the bread.'

The story is an amusing example of Jewish wit. Once again the Jew triumphs because of his presence of mind, this time in a rather different field.

But back to the parable of the three rings. It can be traced back to about 1100, the time of the first of the big Crusades. It was set in Aragon in Spain and there were not three rings but two precious stones. There was no tension between the three religions at that time in the parable's place of origin; Judaism and Christianity alone were opposed to each other. This is how it runs:

'About 1100 King Peter of Aragon wanted to embarrass a Jew and asked him which religion was the best, the Jews' or the Christians'. The Jew gave the following answer:

'My religion is best for me. I was a slave in Egypt and my God delivered me in a wonderful way. Yours is the best for you, for it has brought the Christians great power.'

But the king held him fast: 'I didn't ask you which religion was best for you or me, but which is the best regardless of the man who professes it.'

Then the Jew asked for time to reflect. Three days later he came back, looking very excited. The king asked what was in the wind and the Jew said:

'I have been treated badly and I ask you for help, Lord King. A month ago my neighbour went on a journey. To please his two sons he gave each of them a precious stone. The next day the two sons came to me and asked me to tell them about the stones' different properties. I answered that no one could do

THE THREE RINGS

that better than their father who was a jeweller and therefore knew much more about the stones' nature than I did. But then they mocked me and ill-handled me.'

'Then they did wrong,' replied the king, 'and they deserve to be punished.'

'Right,' said the Jew, 'now let your ears hearken to what your mouth has said. Edom and Jacob were also brothers. Each one received his precious stone and now you want to know which is the best. Send a messenger to our Father who is in heaven. He is the great goldsmith who can tell you the difference between stones.'

That was how the parable looked in its first youthful version. A gentle smile shows for a second or two and casts a gleam of light on an important lesson: respect one another, whether you are Christian or Jew, you are both children of the same father. And children who grow up in the same house can certainly quarrel and fight, and be entirely different, but they still have something in common which they never lose. And in this way the tale was launched on its journey through the ages and different lands. Gradually the form changed and the two stones became three rings, but the idea was the same.

It was no coincidence that mediaeval Spain was the birthplace of such a parable. Here indeed people possessed the three rings, some owning one, some one of the other two. And to the man who honoured his particular ring it was his dearest possession.

It was only in the parable that the rings looked exactly alike and were impossible to tell apart. In real life each one was a different colour. But the same sun shone on them all, making them gleam and flash and vie with each other in beauty.

The Mohammedans, Arabs and Berbers who conquered Spain were called Moors. The name comes from the old Roman province of Mauretania in North Africa, present-day Morocco. Historically speaking, the seven or eight hundred years during which the Moors ruled in Spain is a relatively short period. But no country in the world approached Islam's genius in putting forth blossoms to compare with those it produced in Spain.

THE THREE RINGS

Proud monuments tell of the time—the red castle of the Alhambra at Granada, the mosque at Cordova and the Giralda at Seville to name only the greatest of them—but they are merely symbolic of the Moors' creations in the arts and the field of ideas.

Christianity's achievement in Spain is the incredible story of how a tree was struck by lightning and its broken branches lay strewn on the ground. Yet there was life in the timber and new shoots grew. Although it took nearly eight centuries, the tree ultimately spread its crown of foliage again, wider and prouder than ever, so that it finally covered both the old and the new world.

In 711 the Moorish conquerors defeated the Christian Visigothic kings so decisively that only broken fragments of the royal house and the nobility, in dire distress, managed to find shelter in lairs and caves in the country's most inaccessible mountains. For centuries the conquered Christian princes had to conceal themselves like glowing sparks in a fire banked with ashes during the night. But they survived; the sparks were fanned, given fresh fuel and became a blazing fire, the fantastic reconquest, the Christian victory which finally won the country back again.

Islam and the church, Moors and Spaniards. The two forged Spain's destiny and thereby laid the foundations of the present-day world, but in fact they did not work alone. Between them was Spanish Israel. The Jews had lived in Spain from time immemorial and in the Middle Ages there were large numbers of them in most Spanish towns. After a final assessment, there is no doubt that the achievements of the Spanish Jews stand comparison with the accomplishments of the Christians and Moors.

Generally their work was done quietly and secretly, but it was always the product of genuine talent.

And it was Jewish wisdom which told the story of the three rings. It has been forgotten and we had to make a lengthy search when we traced the stream back and finally discovered its source. This has happened so often. The world forgets what

THE THREE RINGS

it owes to the Spanish Jews. Today no one remembers that some of the most precious and indispensable values in our modern culture go back to them.

This is connected with the harsh fate which finally overcame them. The history of the Jews in Spain ended abruptly—they were driven out unmercifully and brutally, and scattered over many countries. During their misfortunes the memory of the great age they had lived through and the spiritual achievements they had produced, vanished. So we are only trying to make amends when we now set forth for those distant times to visit Israel's people in the Spanish Middle Ages.

All over the world, but especially in the Mediterranean countries, there are Jews of a different type from those we usually think of as Jewish. They have slim, graceful figures, with wiry strength, and their faces have pure regular features. There is a special refinement in their manner, a certain charming elegance and tact, a winning and engaging politeness. They are called Sephardic,[1] i.e. Spanish, Jews. Spain is called Sapharad in Hebrew and the name is found in the Old Testament.

Their appearance alone betrays their inheritance, stemming from their father's golden age in Spain. They formed an independent body there for so long that they evolved quite differently from the Babylonian branch they came from, these uncompromising strong Jews, who built a wall of rituals and ceremonies around themselves. Nor do they resemble the East European ghetto type; they have none of the cowed and suspicious quality which constant oppression and isolation had given the latter. They are living monuments of a golden age which has never been forgotten.

But in the country which once gave their fathers so hospitable

[1] A distinction is made between Sephardic and Ashkenazic Jews. Whereas Sapharad means Spain, the Jews called Germany Ashkenaz, the name of Noah's great-grandson. Probably they found a similarity between Somer, the name of Ashkenaz's father, and Germania. The Sephardic and Ashkenazic Jews are the two main branches of the Jewish people, each with its special rituals and pronunciation of Hebrew; the former grouped round the Spanish, the latter round the German, Polish and Russian stock.

THE THREE RINGS

an asylum, there are only dead monuments of those ancient days. Fortunately, stones can also speak, as anyone knows who has dreamed by the wall of the temple in Jerusalem or the village of Titus at Rome and seen the past rise up from the grave. Anyone coming to Spain in search of Jewish memorials inevitably goes to Toledo, Spain's age-old capital and the town which more than any other reminded Israel's people of the lost Jerusalem.

The Jews lived in Toledo for thousands of years; no other town during their exile made them feel so much at home. Moreover, they were convinced that its name came from the Hebrew Toledot, which means generation, in other words the town of the generations. And they found the town so old that they said 'God fashioned his beloved town Toledo before he created the world. Only then was the sun made and God placed it over the town like a crown with Adam as its first king.'

Toledo's *juderia*, the Jewish quarter, lies in the western part of the town. Here two synagogues from the Middle Ages are still preserved, Santa Maria la Blanca and El Transito. These were obviously not the original names; the former means St Mary the White, i.e. the immaculate virgin, the other refers to the ascension of the Virgin Mary.

The two names tell us about the fate which befell the Jews at the time of the Inquisition. Not content with compulsory baptism, the Catholic church also turned synagogues into churches. The latter usually had a better fate than the former. Today the two ancient buildings are neutral, neither church nor synagogue, but museum pieces, memorials of the ancient Jewish life in Toledo.

Santa Maria la Blanca is the world's oldest surviving synagogue. As its name implies, it is white and luminous, one large beautiful hall with five naves separated by four rows of columns. The columns' capitals are decorated with flower patterns whose details are carved in the stone with endless variations and cast a strange oriental atmosphere over the interior. El Transito is in the Moorish style, with no columns.

THE THREE RINGS

It has bare walls, broken high above by a frieze of flowers and stars, and a Hebrew inscription.

Such are the last remains of what was once one of the great centres where mankind's culture hibernated during the darkest centuries of the Middle Ages. Here beat a heart which sent fresh blood pulsing with new life all over the world. Here Israel lived and developed its finest qualities. The Christian kings of Toledo took Jewish financiers and statesmen into their service and raised them to the highest office. But first and foremost shine out names like Abraham ibn Ezra, Jehuda Alharisi and Jehuda ben Halevi, remote forgotten names, but those of scientists, widely travelled scholars, bohemians and poets, who made heavenly music when they sang.

Toledo—together with Cordova, Granada, Seville, Barcelona and many other Spanish cities—provided the setting in the ages when Jewish genius reached a peak scarcely surpassed in the classic Biblical times. If this epoch in Jewish history could be set to music, it would have to be to the proud rhythm of a bridal march, with the swift tempo of happiness and the sounds of cool rippling streams and bird song in springtime. There Israel tuned the instruments which had hung silent since its people lost Zion. And during this period of original creation, the Jews gave gifts to the world which we are still using.

That is why it is worthwhile to travel back and re-live those times once more.

II

THE RINGS ARE FORGED

FOR centuries catastrophes showered down on the Jewish State in Palestine. Nebuchadnezzar, Antiochus, Epiphanes, Vespasian, Titus. They are names which to Jewish ears have the same dull sound as the three shovelfuls of earth which send the coffin deep down into the confines of the grave at a Christian burial. Each one of them meant a whiplash over the beaten people which drove hundreds of thousands of them into exile. But it was the Emperor Hadrian, who, after the Son of the Star's unsuccessful revolt, drove the last Jews out of their inherited country. He put out the light which was not relit until May 14, 1948—more than eighteen hundred years later—when David Ben Gurion proclaimed the Jewish State of Israel on the soil of Palestine.

A whole people departed and went into exile. In this book we are not going to follow the main branch of Israel which emigrated to Babylon and founded the Talmudic culture. We shall travel with the numerous Jews who went westwards. Large hosts went wandering through the countries of Europe and North Africa. They only arrived gradually; the way was interminable. Families might easily take hundreds of years to reach their journey's end. Perhaps they found a town where they settled and stayed for two or three generations. Then they were driven out or heard of better towns and set forth on their journey again.

Many were prepared to wander until they simply could not go any further and Spain, where the sea formed the frontier, was the farthest point west in Europe. Old historians relate

THE RINGS ARE FORGED

that after Titus's destruction of Jerusalem Vespasian sent banished Jews to Spain, but we also know that Hadrian, who was a Spaniard himself, deported hundreds of thousands from Palestine and that many of them came to Spain.

There they found fellow countrymen, for Jewish settlers had lived in Spain since the dawn of history; in fact, no one knows when they first arrived. But more than a millennium before our calendar, ships from Tyre and Sidon sailed from port to port along the Mediterranean coast and among its islands. In the end they came right to the gateway of the world, today known as the Straits of Gibraltar, which led out of the land-locked Mediterranean to the boundless ocean. There stood the Pillars of Hercules, ready to warn rash seafarers against venturing forth where every kind of danger threatened. But the Phoenicians refused to be scared. They voyaged farther and founded the city, now known as Cadiz, but which they called Gadeira, which is Hebrew and means enclosure.

The first explorers had only primitive open boats, propelled by sails or oars. But the crews belonged to Shem's indomitable race, whose lot in the world's evolution was to carry the culture of the East westwards. All along the Mediterranean littoral the voyages of the Phoenicians can be traced by Semitic names, inscriptions and legends. Five hundred years before the foundation of Rome, political refugees from Tyre built Carthage, which they called Qarta Hadasha, i.e. the new town. The Romans called its inhabitants Poeni, the same word as Phoenicians, and their greatest ruler was called Hannibal, the Grace of Baal. However, if we try substituting the Hebrew word for God, Jah, for Baal, we get Hananiah. Changing the letters again, the result is Johanan, or as we say, John.

Spain's wealth beckoned. Great flocks of sheep grazed in fertile valleys; their wool was the finest anyone had seen. The dwarf oaks on the mountain sides were covered with a mass of small, shining growths from which the Phoenicians learnt to make scarlet, the precious colour, which competed seriously with Tyrian purple on the Eastern market. In Cadiz Bay there were shoals of tunnyfish, so delicate and so big that no one

THE THREE RINGS

had seen their like. Salted tunnyfish from Gadeira and pickled eels from Tartessus at the mouth of the Guadalquivir attracted the attention of expectant Greek and Syrian gourmets.

But that was not all. Far more important were the endless quantities of precious metals hidden in the Spanish earth, which made the Phoenicians the richest people in the world. Here was silver, inexhaustible deposits of silver, here was copper and tin, indispensable ingredients for the manufacture of bronze. From Almaden came cinnabar and quick-silver, from the coasts pearls and coral.

But even if the Phoenicians took wealth home from Spain, they gave something in return which was even more valuable —their religion and their culture. They taught the Spanish people how to write, as all Semitic peoples do, from right to left; they built lighthouses; they taught the Spaniards to make cloth, to weave and dye wool.

These first Semitic pioneers came from Phoenicia, Tyre and Sidon, but behind their towns, in the interior to the east and south, dwelt Hebrews, a closely allied people. They had the same language and in King Solomon's time there was intimate friendship between both kings and people in Jerusalem and Sidon. So the Hebrews followed the Phoenicians on their voyages of discovery.

We know from the Book of Kings that the people of Israel made lengthy sea voyages. King Solomon had two great fleets, one of which sailed from Ezion-geber on the Gulf of Agaba and the Red Sea, and went to Arabia and Africa. Possibly some of their crews accompanied the daring Phoenician seafarers who in the times of the Pharaohs sailed southwards round Africa and found the way to the Straits of Gibraltar. It was three years before they returned to Egypt via the Mediterranean. But Solomon also had a Mediterranean fleet, which, based on Joppa—present-day Jaffa—put in at ports far away to the west, Tartessus, for example, which some people believe was Carthage, but was certainly in Spain.

The Phoenician ships carried so much silver home from Spain that the ships almost sank under the heavy burden.

THE RINGS ARE FORGED

Israel's ships followed suit. The Book of Kings relates that silver 'was nothing accounted of in the days of Solomon'.

All these details are merely scattered sparks shining out of the deep gloom which separates us from the old days. But everything points to the conclusion that Jews have lived in Spain from time immemorial.

Whether they arrived sooner or later, we do know that the Jews felt at home in Spain. They had only said farewell reluctantly when they were driven forth from their country, but when the exiles from Judaea reached Spain after their long journey, they were confronted with a great deal which reminded them of what they had lost. Here towered the same massive peaks as in Judaea's brown mountains, here were the same great white sun by day and low-hanging starstrewn sky by night, as hung over Jizre'el Sletten and Galilee. From the mountain sides, vine-clad terraces overlooked the valley which lay bathed in silver rays at sunrise. Here grew the same fruits, the same wine as at home and there were the 'seven things'[1] for which Judaea was prized as a good country.

Everyone made the Jews welcome; they needed only a minimum of re-orientation to think and act freely. They never found a foreign land they understood as well as Spain. There they struck their roots.

When the last Jews left Palestine, the second of the three rings was being forged. The Christian church had its pioneers out all over the kingdom, following the precept of their Lord, who had ascended into heaven, to preach the gospel to all the nations on earth. Persecutors of the Christians tried to stop them but the church would not be cowed. Ultimately they conquered and became a political factor themselves. Then the young 'barbarian' nations on its boundaries were converted to the Christian faith in quick succession.

But there was one people which did not answer the summons. The Jews were inflexible and always remained constant to their old hereditary faith. Proudly conscious of their own

---

[1] 'A land of wheat and barley, and vines, and fig trees, and pomegranates; a land of oil, olive and honey.' Deuteronomy VIII. 8.

superiority, they looked down from above on the mass of heathens who now bowed down in multitudes before the one and yet three-fold God.

This stubborn resistance provoked both confusion and anger in church circles. As a result they proclaimed Christ's kinsmen accursed enemies. Those obdurate dissentients could easily be dangerous. The essential thing was to cow and above all isolate the Jews, so that they could not go forth and contaminate others. Especially in North Africa the church used its powers to exterminate 'the Jewish pest'.

The church there had early grown powerful; some of the mother church's greatest personalities were North Africans. Tertullian was one of them. He lived about 200 B.C. and was one of the keenest agitators against the Jews. A couple of centuries later the great Augustine followed in his footsteps. He gave new impetus to the streams of Jewish refugees on their way to Spain, but there, too, the church was already in power.

Old traditions maintain that the apostle James preached the gospel in Northern Spain and that Paul was active in the southern part of the peninsula. Perhaps there is some truth in them, at least as far as St Paul is concerned. In any case, it is certain that Christianity spread in Spain at an early date and that a well-organized, powerful church emerged. When the Roman Empire crumbled and collapsed, it was the church which survived. Here was a well-knit instrument run by bishops and priests, with enormous wealth and its own legal system, a state within a state. It was rapidly put to the test.

When the age of mass migrations came in Europe, there was a *Götterdammerung* of insecurity and horror; no one had dreamed of such terrors. Nations whose names the Southern peoples had never even heard of swarmed down from the dark unknown North and swept over the rich land like locusts. Behind them lay nothing but burnt towns and plundered provinces. The Vandals lived up to their name. Their only memorial when they disappeared from Spain was the word Andalusia, the smiling joyous part of the country they laid waste and gave their name to. The Visigoths drove the Vandals out. They

THE RINGS ARE FORGED

remained in Spain as the country's rulers until they in turn were ejected by the Moors.

But long before these violent events a couple of ancient narratives throw light on life in Spain. They only tell us scattered isolated details, but interestingly enough two of them deal with the relations between the church and the Jews.

As early as 306 an ecclesiastical council met at Elvira in Andalusia to discuss the mission to those Spaniards who were still not safely in the church's fold, including the Jews. All four of the council's decrees deal with the Jews; they are very strict and threaten anyone who does not conform to the church's law with excommunication. They also prescribe that Christian women shall not marry Jews and forbid farmers to ask Jews to bless their fields at seed-time and harvest time.

We see two aspects at work here. It is common knowledge that people do not protect themselves against imaginary dangers and the blusterer usually has good cause for alarm. Judaism may indeed have played a comparatively important role when the church armed itself against her. Mixed marriages naturally always implied the danger of Jewish infiltration into Christian families, so that it is understandable that devout Catholics were quite disturbed when they got out of control.

But there is something charming about the other glimpse of everyday life in those distant times which we get from the next decree. The Spanish farmers wanted to guard against nature's unpredictability as best they could. Of course they had asked the Christian priests to bless their fields, but some of them also called in the aid of Jewish rabbis. One never knows, so it is safest to be good friends with as many supernatural powers as possible.

Yet another picture is far from idyllic. The scene is the Balearic islands where countless Jews lived, on both Majorca and Minorca. One of their biggest communities was in the town of Magona in Minorca. Their leader was called Teodorus; he was a rich man and owned extensive plantations on both islands.

In 418 the church summoned the faithful on the islands to

a feast. A famous event was to be celebrated with all the pomp and circumstance it merited. St Stephen's leg had been found and this precious relic, which had healing power in addition, was to be transferred to the cathedral. Such an event stirred people's imagination and they streamed in from near and far to see the stoned martyr's earthly remains. The bishop, a fanatic called Severus, decided to fish in troubled waters. The Jews should be overthrown at one fell swoop.

He and his priests used the old time-honoured methods. They preached about the Jews who had stoned Stephen to death; now was the opportunity for revenge. Everything went according to plan; the people were inflamed and rushed in a fury to the synagogue, where the Jews had taken refuge. The defenders were unarmed, so that the battle was soon decided. The synagogue was set on fire and the Jews were given the choice of either hurling themselves into the funeral pyre or being converted. The bishop had a triumph, in that no fewer than 540 Jews were forcibly baptized. Teodorus was the first to comply; the others followed suit. But a small group of children refused to the last; they had fled to a hilltop and defended themselves by throwing stones.

Even here in history's grey dawn, two nightmare pictures gleam through like terrifying omens for the Spanish Jews; those of the council which enacted legislation about them and a militant bishop who believed that the ends justified the means.

For the time being the church had other things to think about than persecuting the Jews. The Visigothic kings were Christians, to be sure, but not Catholics; they subscribed to the Arian heresy which the church had proscribed at the celebrated synod held in Nicaea in 325. So the Catholic standard-bearers had enough to do to defend themselves against the heretics in power. There was great tension between church and state in Visigothic Spain for many long years.

For centuries the Jews enjoyed the benefits of this state of affairs. For it is a well-known fact that a minority, which the Jews nearly always are, is better off when the power is divided.

THE RINGS ARE FORGED

When two great adversaries are fighting to rule the country, small groups also carry some weight so that notice has to be taken of them. Both parties need them and court their favour. By skilful diplomacy they can procure many advantages and achieve safe living conditions. The danger does not become acute until the scales tip in favour of one side and one of the parties drives the other out. Then the new absolute rulers can settle with the small group which they suddenly discover had been a parasite on them. Then it can only hope for mercy—and that commodity was habitually strictly rationed.

The kings favoured the Jews; as heretics and unbelievers they were both in the same boat *vis-à-vis* the official church. The Jews increased in numbers and became prosperous, especially in Toledo, where the king held court. Spain was well on the way to becoming one of the Jewish exiles' most important centres. At the time no one could imagine that the Visigoths would treat them worse than any one else had done.

The Visigoths were a barbarian people in the true sense of the word. They never advanced beyond aping the culture they had conquered by force of arms and trodden underfoot, but never learnt to understand. Their history in Spain is one long saga of tumultuous events, conspiracies and regicide, oppression, demented avarice and desolation. Toledo witnessed incredible horrors when the tyrants seized the reins of power and were overthrown equally quickly, and ignominiously put to death. Kings followed each other in rapid succession and rare was the ruler who was allowed to die in his bed.

Opposed by sovereigns of such calibre, the Catholic church naturally emerged the stronger in the long run. It wove its web of intrigue skilfully and wormed its way into advantageous positions. It had plenty of time and it did not reach its goal until a hundred years had elapsed.

In 589 a big council was convened in Toledo. From all over Spain clergymen thronged to the capital; the streets teemed with Catholic dignitaries. Lengthy secret discussions were held; no one really knew what was going to happen, but everyone guessed that they were on the verge of momentous times.

THE THREE RINGS

When King Reccared appeared before the council and began to speak, everyone listened with baited breath.

There was a great sensation. The king solemnly forswore his Arian heresy and proclaimed that from now on the whole kingdom should profess the one true faith. The sceptre bowed to the crozier.

Naturally the council's proceedings were primarily directed against the Arian heresy, which it wanted uprooted, but the Jews were also defencelessly exposed to the church's hate. The country was no longer divided; church and state became one. Previously the council's decisions had only been binding on members of the church. Now the king subscribed to them too and they became laws binding everyone in the kingdom.

From that day Visigothic Spain became a theocracy whose philosophy was one church, one state. In reality this meant that the church decided everything. The Visigothic kings were elected and the prelates' votes always decided the outcome. If a prince wanted to be elected king, he could not succeed unless he enlisted the aid of the church. The church exacted its price and only supported the king who was prepared to be the pliant tool of ecclesiastical policy. Theocracy, or hierarchy, is the poorest and most evil of all the systems of government which have been tried on this earth. Misfortune and ruin have followed it like a shadow, and they did so in Visigothic Spain.

Gregory the Great did not believe in compulsion. Results obtained by force, he said, are not valid; they only breed bitterness and at the first favourable opportunity the compulsory converts lapse. In this connection he adjures the Christians to remember that the Jew is a witness to the truth of the holy scriptures and that his degradation shows that guilt is punished. Here he is referring to the most terrible of all crimes, the crucifixion of the son of God. But the Christian must also remember that the Jews are guardians of the Bible's original text and its interpretation. Naturally the church must strive to convert them, but it must be a voluntary process. The Jews should be free to follow their religion and be allowed to preserve their synagogues, but they are forbidden to proselytize

THE RINGS ARE FORGED

or own Christian slaves. And Christians must keep them at a distance. It is strictly forbidden to have a Jewish doctor, for he acquires physical and possibly also moral control over his patients and can influence them in undesirable directions. And lastly the state must never entrust the Jews with public office, however insignificant it might be.

There are details in these provisions which bear witness to a certain moderation. But both Gregory and his successors had difficulty in seeing that moderation was observed. In the Visigothic theocracy at least, the Pope failed completely. Here the church and also the king simply wished to eradicate what they called 'the accursed Jewish superstition and the Jews' pernicious power, which is an abomination to the Christians.' There was an occasional breathing space, but by and large the theme that Judaism should be rooted out and that no professed Jew might remain on Spanish soil runs like a red thread through Visigothic rule, from the council of Toledo to the victory of the Moors.

The first step was the social and economic degradation of the Jews. The ban on keeping slaves was a hard blow, for at the time slavery was the foundation of trade; it was literally impossible to practise agriculture or run plantations without slaves. But that was only the beginning; later steps went much further. Here are some examples of the decrees which poured out over the kingdom in an endless stream.

Jewish children were taken from their parents and brought up in monasteries or Christian homes. Converted Jews had to present themselves before the bishop in church on Christian and Jewish holidays, as a check that they not only held the Christian holidays, but also were prevented from celebrating the Jewish memorial days in the privacy of their own homes. If a Jew refused to hand over his children or slaves for baptism, he was punished with a hundred lashes and 'decalvation', i.e. the tearing out of his hair, in addition, his property was confiscated and he himself banished from the country. If a mother had her offspring circumcised, her nose was cut off. The most agonizing and ignominious punishments were devised.

THE THREE RINGS

All these provisions were painstakingly based on Biblical precepts. The Jews had to eat pork, because 'to the pure all things are pure'. The Jewish passover was forbidden, because St Paul says 'the passover is yours, Christ was sacrificed for your sake.' No one could celebrate the Sabbath or other Jewish holidays, because in the Book of the Prophet Jeremiah it says: 'Your new moons and sabbaths and annual feasts are an abomination unto me.' All these provisions can be found in the great Visigothic legal code, *Lex visigothorum*.

If it had been possible to eradicate Judaism by decree, not a single Jew would have been left in Spain; at any rate the decrees could not go any further. Naturally many Jews underwent forcible conversion, while others left the country and went back to North Africa or made for France.

But in spite of all the drastic measures the Visigoths did not succeed in uprooting Judaism. The Jews had lost their civil rights, their property was confiscated, their children were taken from them, they themselves were flogged, tortured, reduced to dishonour and contempt, and handed over to the clergy to deal with as they chose. But they continued to exist there and at heart they were still Jews.

The whole of this policy of violence resembles a hysterical fit. Although aimed at the Jews, it was also designed to cover up serious disorders in the Visigothic kingdom. Spain presented a spectacle of profound social decay; the country was slipping helplessly into chaos. The common people, the poor villeins and serfs, lived in direst need. The political situation was unstable; conspiracies and rebellions were the order of the day. Kings came and went. The common people were downtrodden and impoverished by the nobility. The only institution which towered above the confusion was the ever more powerful church.

To any intelligent observer, it was obvious that the Visigothic kingdom was moving rapidly to the edge of the abyss. It lay open to the first arrival. Spain was waiting for her conqueror.

He was already on his way.

THE RINGS ARE FORGED

In the early part of 622 an Arab merchant fled from his native town of Mecca. He had had revelations, seen visions and heard voices, and founded a new religion. This incurred the wrath of his fellow-citizens and he had to flee to save his life. The man was Mohammed and Islam dates its calendar from this event, which is called hegira (flight) in Arabic. From that day the movement spread with a speed the like of which the world has not seen. In a matter of decades, offshoots of the prophet's passionate surrender to God—Islam literally means surrender, i.e. to God's will—flowered in the countries of the East. Mohammed's warriors, spurning death, conquered old, renowned kingdoms; a new world power had come on the scene.

Mohammed knew the Jews well; there were many of them in Arabia. At one time the kings of the Yemen had professed the Jewish faith and in the rest of Arabia a good many towns and oases were exclusively inhabited by Jews, who introduced the date palm to Arabia. Islam contained a good deal of the Jewish inheritance and Mohammed had counted on the Jews being the first to follow him. But they were as little influenced by the new religion as they had been by the church. Mohammed acted cruelly in the face of this rebuff and many Jews fell victims to Islam's fanaticism.

But the prophet's successors changed this policy. Instead of persecuting them, they were tolerant, not only of the Jews, but also of the Christians. A famous *sura* in the Koran teaches: 'Do not fight him who has received the word.' Naturally both Jews and Christians had to put up with a number of restrictions in Islamic countries. They wore special clothes, paid heavy taxes, were excluded from public office, were not allowed to ride and a great deal besides. But within these bounds they were allowed to exist and practise their religion. Moreover, the Mohammedans were much stricter in theory than in practice. Both Jews and Christians enjoyed considerable freedom and— in the true Arabic way—hospitality from them.

Less than a hundred years after Mohammed's hegira, the host of Islam had covered the whole of North Africa. The

THE THREE RINGS

unique victorious progress only came to a halt when it reached the barrier of the Atlantic Ocean. So they called the country Maghreb el Aksa, the farthest west, Morocco in English.

Naturally Spain's Jews cast longing looks across the sea to the new power where their brothers enjoyed far better conditions than they themselves had. In their desperation they rebelled, but could not prevail against the armour-clad Gothic knights. So the last door was closed to the oppressed Jews. No, one was still ajar. They secretly sent envoys to North Africa and asked the leaders of Islam's victorious army for help. And help came before anyone expected it, to the great surprise of all, victors and conquered alike.

Now comes the story of the Moorish conquest of Spain, one of the great turning-points in mankind's long saga. It will be told as it has been handed down from generation to generation, with an intermingling of fact and fiction. We are well aware that the picture is drawn by folk-tales and ancient traditions, but we must not be so stupid and shortsighted as to condemn them out of hand. For countless generations they have lent their wings to popular imagination, and more often than critical researchers think, the myth, which in a flash enables us to conceive of the drama of days gone by and the mental climate behind events, is more real than many established facts.

The last of the Visigothic kings was called Roderick. He still occupied a fragment of North Africa; his representative, Count Julian, head of the Spanish garrison, was installed behind the strong walls of Ceuta. Following the custom of the time he sent his beautiful young daughter Florinda, or as the Spanish romances call her, La Cava, to King Roderick's court at Toledo, so that she could be brought up in a way befitting her station among the queen's ladies-in-waiting. This was the starting-point for what was the story of King David and Bathsheba all over again. The king saw the comely girl bathing in the Tagus (the place where La Cava bathed is still shown to visitors to Toledo). And this glimpse of a beautiful female body, scarcely concealed by a flimsy garment, decided Florinda's fate—and Spain's.

What the king could not achieve by tempestuous approaches, he took by force. Perhaps he counted on the proud count's daughter wanting to hide her shame, but he was mistaken. She sent a loyal page who galloped day and night across Spain to distant Ceuta to bring vengeance.

Count Julian hastened to Toledo. When he arrived he kept quiet about his plans and merely said that he had come to take the girl home. The evening before his departure, he was asked by the king to send him some hawks of a special kind, which he used when hunting. The count promised him hawks, the like of which he had never seen.

But on return Count Julian found the Saracen hawks less greedy for prey than he had expected. The old bird of prey, Musa, as the Moors' chieftain was called, certainly listened to Julian's enticing descriptions of the fair rich country which would be good to own and plunder, but he suspected treachery. Could he believe the man who had been his enemy for so long and now promised to lend him his ships in order to cross the straits?

Finally Musa's desire for booty and conquest was stronger than his distrust. In 710 he sent one of his chieftains, the one-eyed Tarik, off on a small expedition to reconnoitre Spain. He came back loaded with booty and told Musa that the country was virtually defenceless. Encouraged by this promising beginning, Musa risked an army of 7,000 men. In the early summer of 711 Tarik landed on the rock which still bears his name, Gebal Tarik, Gibraltar, and on the plains of Guadalete he met King Roderick who had hastened southwards with his Gothic horde to repel the invasion.

Legend never tires of the subject of the unfortunate king, 'the last Goth'. The so-called Tower of Hercules was in Toledo. Everyone knew that it concealed the secret of Spain's future; it was hidden behind a massive iron door and since Hercules's day every Spanish king had put his own new padlock on it. Roderick too went to the tower, but instead of adding another padlock, he determined to break the locks of past centuries and unveil the secret his predecessors had gone to their graves without finding. The king's councillors talked with him for days and tried to dissuade him, but in vain; the king's decision stood firm.

Roderick forced his way through the door; inside the tower he found a massive chest, on the lock of which was written: 'He who opens me shall see strange things.' The king hoped that it was full of gold, but when the lock was broken all he saw was a bit of canvas with pictures of Arab warriors. Suddenly, inside the cramped tower, a vision appeared of a battlefield, where Moors and Christians were fighting for dear life. The Christians retreated, the sign of the cross was overthrown and the royal flag of Spain trampled underfoot. Among the fugitives the king saw a crowned warrior. His back was turned so that Roderick could not see his face, but—he rode on King Roderick's white charger Orelia and wore his armour and helmet. In the heat of battle he was thrown off his horse and disappeared, while Orelia galloped madly away without a rider.

King Roderick must have shaken his head incredulously at these sinister omens when he saw how few enemies he had against him at Guadalete. He himself commanded 80,000 Gothic warriors; Tarik had brought reinforcements, but disposed of barely 12,000 men. When the battle began, Tarik shouted to his men: 'The enemy is before us, behind us the sea. By Allah, your only hope is courage!'

The battle raged for seven days. On the last day a division of Roderick's army went over to the enemy. That decided the issue; the Spaniards' morale was broken. The Moors cut down the foe and Orelia galloped riderless over the bloody battlefield. No one found a trace of the king.

Tarik had won Spain in a single battle. A raid had turned into a conquest of universal historical significance. Although Tarik had only one eye, he used it to such purpose that he immediately saw the possibilities of his victory. Without waiting for further directives, he divided his little army into three divisions and boldly attacked the Visigoths' key points. The Spanish towns fell at the Moors' feet as when a man shakes a plum tree in September. An army of 900 men took Cordoba; the worm-eaten kingdom crumbled wherever the Moors advanced. The Spanish Jews hailed them as liberators, they supplied provisions and acted as guides for the conquerors.

Tarik himself advanced on Toledo; in his train he had a Jewish division under the command of Kaula-al-Yahudi, i.e. Kaula the Jew. The Visigoths' important personages had fled from the town. Its surrender was the work of the Jews. An old Jew was lowered down over the walls in a basket; he promised Tarik to open the town gates if the Jews were given religious freedom. Tarik agreed and the next day he moved into the Visigoths' capital.

A flood-tide poured over Europe. That year the world's destiny hung on a thread. The Pyrenees did not halt the Moors; the way to France lay open. Bordeaux fell; the rich plains of Central France beckoned; now the Moors dreamt of making the Caliph master of the world.

But providence has seen to it that excessive ambition is punished. Before the Moors could cross the Loire, a French army stood in their path. Charles Martel met them between Poitiers and Tours. He dammed the tidal wave of Islam; the cross triumphed over the crescent in the week-long battle.

But Spain was won. And yet, not won. The Moors never entirely subdued their new land. Roderick was called the last of the Goths, but a few years after the flight from Guadalete, there were rumours of two Gothic kings hiding in the mountains of Asturia with small groups of brave men. One was called Pelayo, 'the hero who saved Spanish Christendom'. Together with a body of exiled knights and squires he held out in the inaccessible mountains.

Thirty Christians inflicted a crushing defeat on the heathens at Covadonga. Probably it was one of those guerilla battles in the mountains where a handful of men is in a position to inflict terrible damage on the enemy's serried ranks; where boulders

THE THREE RINGS

are rolled down the slopes and no arrow misses its mark. But to the beaten Christians Covadonga was not merely a battle, it was a miracle. There the spirit of reconquest awoke, the renowned *reconquista*, which seven or eight hundred years later won Spain back for the cross.

But until then Spain was the country of the three rings.

III

UNDER THE CRESCENT

THE Moorish victors nearly lost the newly won land. Arabs have always found it difficult to unite and subordinate themselves, and it was not long before bitter disputes split Spain into fragments. The Arabic tribes from the Orient and the Berber warriors from North Africa were in perpetual conflict; the chieftains and emirs waged regular war with one another and impoverished the unfortunate country. More than four years were to elapse before a pure coincidence brought order into the chaos.

Some of the feuding chieftains heard of a young prince, Abd al Rahman, who had had a romantic history. In Damascus, his family, the celebrated Omayad dynasty, had given the Arab empire fourteen caliphs before it was overthrown in a revolt by the Abbaside family. The new Caliph was nicknamed the Slaughterer and the title fitted him. He pursued the unfortunate surviving Omayads unmercifully and murdered them all; everyone who came into his grasp was flogged to death. Only one man, the youthful Abd al Rahman escaped his vigilance; after countless adventures he reached North Africa where he went underground.

There he received an invitation from Spain to come and win himself a kingdom. That was the signal for him; he came, he saw, he conquered. After an eventful campaign, the exiled young prince made his entry into Cordoba in the year 756.

No one had counted on the young Omayad prince being more than a kind of pennant fluttering over the army of a few independent tribal chiefs until they had satisfied their lust for vengeance and won enough booty, and no longer needed him. Too late they discovered that they had set a golden eagle free. During the thirty-two years of his reign, he united Arabic Spain and laid the foundations of the Moorish culture which was to flower during the next 800 years.

Abd al Rahman means the servant of the merciful God, but he showed no mercy to his enemies. His mortal foe, the Caliph in Damascus, intrigued and tried to overthrow him; he raised the Abbasides' black standard in Spain. Abd al Rahman put down the rebellion with a firm hand. He had the heads of the leaders of the revolt cut off and embalmed, and a label with the dead men's names was tied to their ears. The heads were put in a sack and sent to Mecca, where the Caliph resided. He was not normally nervous, but when he saw the gruesome greetings pour out of the sack, he burst out involuntarily:

'Allah be praised, who has placed a sea between him and me!'

The greatest danger threatened Abd al Rahman when Charlemagne of France formed an alliance with a party of disgruntled chieftains in Spain. The plan was that they should incite a rebellion and that the Emperor should advance into Spain with an army. If everything had gone smoothly, it would have been all up, not only with Abd al Rahman, but also with Islam's rule in Spain.

However, there were snags. The Spanish traitors did not stick together and the Emperor only had time to draw up his army outside Saragossa when he received bad news about a hostile invasion back in his own country. He had to retreat over the Pyrenees at full speed. The main army made a lucky escape through the narrow mountain pass, but the rearguard, under the command of the legendary Count Roland, were cut down by Basque mountaineers. That was the celebrated battle of Roncesvalles, about which so much has been sung and so little is known.

Abd al Rahman built the proudest kingdom in Europe; he ruled it with wisdom and strength, but never shrank from cruelty and treachery. Personally, he was a lonely man. Everyone feared and avoided him, and he surrounded himself with an enormous bodyguard of mercenaries. And it is not a happy fate to sit on a throne which is supported by sharp swords and spearheads. There is a melancholy poem by him, in which he compares himself to a date palm which was dug up in the Far East and taken to a foreign land where it tried to strike root.

A series of strong rulers followed in his footsteps, but they would not have been Arab sovereigns if they had not been forced to be eternally on their guard against endless revolts and self-willed temperaments among their high officials. The Moorish saga in Cordoba teems with accounts of intrigues, conspiracies and all kinds of amorous adventures. A good hundred years after the first Abd al Rahman, the whole kingdom was on the point of dissolution owing to internal strife, but just when the outlook was darkest, quite unexpectedly one of history's greatest ruling geniuses, Abd al Rahman III, came on the scene. He reconstructed the kingdom and raised Cordoba's power to brilliant heights. Under him Moorish culture acquired the splendour which is always remembered.

Abd al Rahman III ruled in Cordoba for fifty years (912-62). Out of a scattered divided kingdom he made an entity; the rebels yielded and gave themselves up; towns opened their gates to him. He went calmly about his sweeping work of reconstruction. Never beaten in war, his real inclination was for the work of peace. He travelled everywhere, intervening in affairs large and small with that mixture of iron will and generosity which was characteristic of him. He was so liberal, polished and noble that his contemporaries were never tired of singing his praises. This exceptionally gifted personality will always stand as the greatest of all Spain's kings, both Mohammedan and Christian. He will also be associated with the most glorious days—full of pageantry and steeped in beauty—of one of the most brilliant kingdoms the world has ever seen.

In Abd al Rahman's time Islam's centre shifted from east to west; Cordoba became a new Damascus or Baghdad. To such an extent that he took the title of Caliph.[1] He ordered that the

[1] Caliph means representative, i.e. of the prophet.

THE THREE RINGS

Friday prayers in Spain's mosques should be read, not for Emir Abd al Rahman, but for Abd-al-Rahman-an-Nasir, the Deliverer. It was not an empty title.

There was no town in tenth-century Europe to compare with Cordoba, 'the bride of Andalusia'. Squares and bazaars were filled with wares from all over the world; nothing was so rare or precious that it could not be bought there. Travellers flocked to it; all kinds of people travelled the roads through Spain to Cordoba, princes and ambassadors, merchants and pilgrims, students and poets. Even on the journey they were given some idea of the luxury which awaited them. The Caliph had installed comfortable inns or *manzils*, where they could stay free of charge. But once they arrived, they could scarcely believe their eyes when they saw all the splendour, palaces, mosques and gardens, and the swarming, boundless population, the shouting, bustle and din, and everywhere delicate works of art with strange arabesques and columns and colours.

The most majestic and magnificent building was the mosque, on which great princes squandered enormous fortunes for centuries. Originally a Roman temple to the God Janus stood there. In the customary way the Catholic bishops built a Christian church on the site of the temple as early as the time of the Visigoths. After the Moorish conquest, it was divided into two halves; in one of them the Christians held their services, in the other the Mohammedans. But the first Abd al Rahman bought the Christians out and began the great work which was later continued by his successors.

In Constantinople the Christian Santa Sophia was turned into a mosque. In Cordoba the opposite happened. The Christian re-conquest rapidly saw to that and Islam's most beautiful mosque is today one of the loveliest Christian churches in existence. But we can still glimpse Islam's impress on it, and we have so many mediaeval accounts of mosques that we have some idea of the vanished days when Islam's faithful knelt among the countless columns and professed their faith in the one God and his prophet.

At midnight the muezzin's call sounded from the top of the

minaret: 'God is great. It is better to pray than to sleep!' Two hours later he renewed the cry and at four o'clock he raised a lantern on the end of a pole and said: 'Day is breaking, let us praise God!' At the fourth prayer he raised a white flag and the fifth prayer was at midday. When the evening star came out, he summoned them to the sixth prayer, and at nine at night announced the day's last prayer. When the faithful came to divine service, they passed through the mosque's forecourt. The floor was decorated with porcelain tiles over which fresh water streamed and washed their feet after they had left their shoes outside. Women were not admitted, the only exception being the Caliph's wife who prayed on behalf of all women.

But there was something in this mosque which no one who had once ever been there ever forgot. It was not the twenty heavy bronze doors, nor the wonderful stones which bedecked the walls, porphyry and jasper of every beautiful colour, or the lovely mosaics or the air which was perfumed with incense. No, it was the twelve hundred columns which supported the mosque's arches and roof. It was like entering a forest at its densest point where tree trunks are all that can be seen. This was a forest of marble whose end no one could see. The eye followed long rows of columns back into semi-darkness, where more rows of columns emerged; faint rays of light came through the windows and cast a pale glow on columns and yet more columns. Men felt insignificant in the face of the neverending repetition and their minds were open to mystical experiences.

In Abd al Rahman's time two flags flew by the side of the pulpit in the mosque. They signified Islam's triumph over Judaism and Christendom. The Koran had been victorious over the Old and the New Testaments. Here the almnedian called out his salem, when the mosque was filled with white-clad worshippers. The Caliph came to the mosque from the castle by a secret passage and sat on a raised throne. All knelt in prayer; the mosque was nothing but columns and kneeling men. The priest read the day's sura from the Koran and concluded by summoning them to prayer. The faithful prostrated themselves on the floor and an echo from thousands of voices rang out under the arches:

'La ilaha illa 'llahu muhammadun rasulu 'llahu.' (There is no God but God and Mohammed is his prophet.)

But the mosque was only one of many buildings. At the time Cordoba had half a million inhabitants and was full of palaces. The wealthy families had hundreds of magnificent houses and the Caliph himself owned a whole series of famous residences, the Palace of Flowers, the Lover's Palace and the Palace of Pleasure. They lay in lovely gardens down by the Guadalquivir's rippling stream, where flowers and golden oranges shone between dark-green leaves.

More beautiful and still more marvellous than all Cordoba was the Caliph's summer palace outside the town, Az Zahra, The Flower, called after his favourite wife. For forty years the Caliph spent a third of the country's revenue on Az Zahra. Two thousand workmen and three thousand beasts of burden toiled there every day; six thousand stones daily were hewn for the buildings. In a moment of euphoria the Caliph gave the order simply to remove a mountain which cast a shadow on his golden palace. He was forced to moderate his wish, but all the trees on the mountain were felled and replaced by a forest of almond and pomegranate trees, which in spring, were covered with a mass of brilliantly coloured blossoms. There was nothing in Spain which excited such admiration as Az Zahra. But today it has gone; everything has disappeared and not even the site of the summer palace is known.

In this brilliant city the contents matched the framework. Cordoba was a spring where all the fine arts flowed. The Caliph himself was a discerning patron, who took scholars, artists and thinkers under his wing. At a time when the rest of Europe lay sunk in apathetic ignorance and barbarism, all branches of the sciences were honoured at Cordoba; there were found the most capable doctors, geographers, astronomers and mathematicians. And the torch did not burn only for the few. People of all classes honoured literature; it was said that poetry was the common man's normal speech. All kinds of handicrafts flourished; potters, silk weavers, glassblowers, jewellers, swordsmiths and leathermakers were celebrated; they ranked far above the craftsmen in other towns.

Yes, the Moors in Cordoba's caliphate towered high above all the others at the time and countless students took wisdom and inspiration home with them. We have only to think of the words in European languages which began with 'al'. They come from Arabic and each of them covers wide areas of knowledge and ideas: algebra, alchemy, almanach, alcohol, to name only a few examples. It is sarcastically said of alcohol that the Arabs discovered it, produced it (for medicinal purposes), gave it its name—and then left its future to the Christians!

Nevertheless the Moors' direct influence on mediaeval Europe was smaller than one would imagine. This was mainly because although they so outshone everyone else that they were immeasurably greater, they did not *lead*; they had no following. Middle-men were needed, people capable of transmitting Arabic culture. This was where the Spanish Jews came in.

Like his predecessor and namesake, the great Abd al Rahman also recorded his private thoughts, so that we catch a glimpse of the price of greatness. When he died, a diary was found among his papers in which he had carefully noted down in his own handwriting the days in his long active life when he had been completely happy and free from care. They were fourteen in number.

His son and successor, Hakam, was a man of peace, who was content to consolidate and develop his father's work. He preferred to let others run the government and withdrew to Az Zahra to study his books. He was something of a poet and scholar, and books were his passion. No difficulty and no expense were too great when it came to procuring copies of books for Cordoba's libraries. Wherever they were in the world, they had to be bought and brought back. His messengers went as far as Cairo and Baghdad on the lookout for books old and new. A vast treasury of books was assembled in Cordoba;

THE THREE RINGS

it was stated that the royal library alone contained 400,000 volumes. But the royal collector was not content with merely buying, he read his books and made numerous notes in them.

The Omayad dynasty reached its zenith when its sun was about to set, and its end was full of incredible romantic adventures. One of the most remarkable men in Spanish history was responsible for it, the man, who at the height of his power, rightly called himself Almanzor, the victorious. From his early youth he set great store by and relied on his lucky star. Once as a student he was enjoying himself with friends, and burst out in a moment of gaiety:

'You can choose what you want to be when I am minister.'

They entered into the spirit of the joke and divided Cordoba's highest offices among themselves. Only one of them played the fool and asked to be carried backwards through the streets of Cordoba, tied to an ass. Later he got his wish; Almanzor was not the sort of man to forget.

He was of distinguished lineage, descended from one of the genuine Arab families which had taken part in the conquest of Spain for Islam. But he was not rich, and only advanced through his exceptional talents, his will-power and quite incredible instinct for the skilful and ruthless exploitation of every possibility. He made a career for himself and revealed incredible qualities. He was given insoluble problems which he proved able to master. This gave him access to the court, where the Caliph's favourite wife fell in love with him and became his lover. He used her callously and calculatingly; he threw her out when she had served her purpose and had become an embarrassment. But before that she brought up her son, the new young Caliph, according to his advice, and turned him into a helpless, vacillating creature, who never became more than an empty shadow. Almanzor produced him on ceremonial occasions and displayed him in oriental splendour, but in reality the minister was the absolute regent of the country.

Almanzor won his name in victorious wars; he was a great strategist. The Christian states in northern Spain were completely defeated in Almanzor's time; he led his army throughout the country, as far as the north-western corner where he laid waste the holy city of Santiago. Christian captives carried the famous bells back to Cordoba where they were hung up as lamps in the mosque. Centuries later Arabic prisoners of war had to carry them the long way home.

He never stopped working. 'Rulers cannot sleep', he used to say to his doctor, who advised him to spare himself. He led the country further along its distinguished cultural path and acquired brilliant battle honours, and newly won wealth into the bargain.

When he died, the kingdom collapsed. Destruction and dissolution followed on the heels of greatness and prosperity. From then on the crescent was on the wane in Spain. In the frightful anarchy of civil war a Berber horde conquered Cordoba in 1013. The town was plundered and burnt. The proud caliphate was split into no less than twelve small states —at one time thirteen—which were in permanent civil strife and watched each other suspiciously. They owed their comparatively lengthy existence less to their own strength than to their enemies' weakness.

The powers which would drive the Moors out of Spain were not yet ripe and assembled; that was to take 400–500 years. But it was in this period of decline, full of humiliations for the once proud Moors, that their culture had its Indian summer and shed its finest blooms. The rose smells sweetest just before it withers.

IV

— AND THE STAR

THE Moorish conquest of Spain meant the beginning of a new era for the Jews. Persecution vanished as rapidly as the Visigoths and tolerance and freedom took its place. The new authorities were clever enough to see how useful the numerous Jewish communities were and gave them good material conditions. The Jews quickly learnt to adapt themselves. They spoke Arabic, not only with the Moors, but also among themselves; they took Arabic names and followed the manners and fashions of their environment. But individually they preserved their status and felt that they were Jews—if one hand was Esau's, the voice remained Jacob's. Naturally, it took a long time for them to recover their strength after the terrible oppression they had been subjected to. They did not really come into the limelight until the time of Abd al Rahman III, but then their great age began in earnest.

Characteristically enough it was the government services which first called on the Jews. Here they were especially qualified; they were intelligent, adaptable and had the necessary knowledge of languages. As long as there were Jews in Spain, they provided the country with a long series of prominent statesmen, ministers, diplomats and financiers. Perhaps the first of them was also the greatest; in any case he occupies a central place in his people's destiny and pioneered the way for new ages. He was Hasdai ibn Shaprut,[1] who entered the service of the great Abd al Rahman.

---

[1] The middle name of *ibn*, which we come across often, is the Arabic form of the Hebrew *ben*, meaning son.

— AND THE STAR

He came from a rich and highly cultivated home in Cordoba. His father was called Isak and was highly thought of in the Jewish community; he won his name as a patron of scholars and poets. But he took especial care of his son's upbringing and finally saw him develop into one of the time's best educated men. From his childhood Hasdai was familiar with Hebrew and Arabic; he learnt the suppressed Spanish dialects, and, something quite exceptional in Arabic circles, he knew Latin, the literary tongue of the Christian world. But he was also a doctor and won early renown for discovering a universal nostrum against all known diseases. All this wisdom was housed in a mind which vibrated with the urge for action, but was counter-balanced by commonsense and a practical skilful grip on things.

No wonder that his fame spread widely. It also reached the palace and the great Caliph noticed him. He made him his personal physician and with that Hasdai's fortune was made. The Caliph saw him daily and became more and more interested in the highly gifted young Jew. Soon he entrusted him with other than purely medical tasks and before long he was one of the Caliph's nearest, most trusted favourites. He was promoted by leaps and bounds. Hasdai was appointed minister of finance, but he achieved the final honour when he was nominated to conduct Cordoba's foreign policy. Time soon showed that the Caliph had made a shrewd choice.

There were international problems enough to watch and the Caliph at Cordoba had serious dangers to combat. Perhaps the greatest was to the south, from his Mohammedan co-religionists, especially Egypt, which found it hard to tolerate Cordoba's independence. But a constant danger threatened from the north. The Christian principalities, Navarre and Leon, had long fought with each other. Now they formed a league against the arch-enemy in the south, which also promised difficulties. But as it turned out, Hasdai mastered the problems.

The danger of attack from North Africa and Egypt was great. To ward it off, Hasdai approached the Emperor in Byzantium, who felt threatened from the same direction. In doing so, Hasdai unwittingly opened a door through which cultural currents from the ancient world reached Western Europe. The first fruits came in the form of an embassy from the Emperor Constantine in Byzantium. Among the valuable gifts he sent the Caliph, was a magnificently produced manuscript, a Greek work about botany, especially medicinal herbs, which excited the keen interest of the inquiring Caliph and his personal physician. But unfortunately, they could not read it, because it was written in Greek. The book's fate became a typical example of how deep the split between Eastern and Western culture was in the early Middle Ages, but it is equally significant that a Jew bridged the gap.

There was not a single man in Cordoba who understood Greek. Hasdai sent messengers all the way to Byzantium to ask for help. The Emperor then ordered a monk called Nikolaos to journey to Cordoba, where he set to work and translated the book into Latin. Next Hasdai provided the sequel by translating it into Arabic. The work was worth the effort. Copyists set to work and soon the book spread to north and south in both Latin and Arabic translations. It became of fundamental importance to medical science. This was only one of the many occasions on which Hasdai united the interests of statesman and scholar.

Hasdai became famous for his diplomatic skill when he averted an impending conflict between Spain and the new German Empire. The Caliph had been so imprudent as to write a few words in a personal letter to the Emperor Otto which were insulting to the Christian faith. They were very ill-received and the Emperor sent an embassy with his answer in which he gave Islam as good as he got. The leader of the embassy was the abbot Johan von Görtz. In a roundabout way he got in touch with Hasdai and let him read the letter secretly. Both of them understood that the consequences might be unforseeable if Abd al Rahman saw it.

The situation was precarious, but Hasdai coped with it immediately. In Cordoba he set the delaying tactics department to work and they managed to hold up the matter long enough for an urgent letter to reach the Emperor in Germany. He let himself be persuaded to write a new letter which was couched in more moderate terms.

So the affair ended peacefully. Later abbot Johan commented on the events and praised the clever Jewish diplomat; he said that he had 'never met a man with such an acute intelligence as the Jew Hasdai.'

Hasdai celebrated his biggest triumph over the Christian princes. Rebellion had broken out in Leon and the King, Sancho the Fat, sought refuge with his grandmother, Queen Tota of Navarre. This clever, beautiful woman had recently been at war with Cordoba, but nevertheless she had the idea of asking Abd al Rahman to help Sancho. She wrote to the Caliph and asked him to send a doctor who could cure Sancho of his terrible obesity (he had not got his nickname for nothing). People who sought medical assistance in those times found that the best available was in Arabic countries. And naturally she asked for military aid at the same time.

The Caliph sent Hasdai to Pamplona, the capital of Navarre. No one was better suited for the task, seeing that he was both doctor and diplomat. In addition to which he could negotiate with the Christian princes in their own language. He immediately began to give Sancho medical treatment and the cure proved effective. Diplomatic negotiations also made progress; Sancho was willing to relinquish ten frontier fortresses if the Caliph won him his throne back.

But Hasdai wanted more than a few fortresses. He told the Queen that she and King Sancho must go to Cordoba in person to conclude the negotiations. Queen Tota knew what that meant. No one—not even princes—came before the Caliph without throwing themselves on the ground at his feet. The proud lady shrank from such a humiliation, but Hasdai was too strong and clever for her. As a contemporary poet puts it, she finally gave in, persuaded by 'the charm of his words, the strength in his wisdom, the force of his cleverness and—his thousand tricks'.

Arabic Spain witnessed an unforgettable sight. Surrounded

by grandees and priests the Queen set out from Navarre on the journey to Cordoba. Behind her came Sancho supported on Hasdai's arm. The Caliph received them at Az Zahra and confirmed Hasdai's promises. With Arabic help Sancho won back his kingdom in a brief campaign, but the ten fortresses belonged to Islam. And countries re-echoed far and wide with praise of Hasdai's skill; he had outwitted the 'Swine'. Neither Jews nor Mohammedans eat pork, so they used the nickname swine for their Christian neighbours.

But if we really want to understand Hasdai, his success and his victories are not the most relevant factors. Behind his urge for action and energy, lay a deep love of knowledge and art. In this respect he lived in a fortunte age. Everywhere in Moorish Spain there was a spiritual renaissance; all the arts and sciences were in flower. The Jews were infected by it; they too were deeply affected by this renaissance. And now Hasdai championed for his fellow Jews. He gave the impetus to the new era of Jewish culture, which began in his days.

For in his innermost mind, in the heart of his being, he was a Jew, fast rooted in Israel's culture and deeply attached to his faith. We are fortunate enough to possess an episode in his life which throws a light on this side of Hasdai's great personality. It is a remarkable story.

Embassies from distant lands frequently came to negotiate with the mighty Caliph. When Hasdai received them in his capacity as Foreign Minister, he took every opportunity of asking if they had any news of his fellow Jews who lived in dispersal. He was especially interested in the countries of the Orient, the Byzantine Empire and distant Persia. In this way he heard about the Kingdom of the Chazars in the present-day Caucasus or Southern Russia, where the kings professed the Jewish faith. This touched the innermost fibres of his being; he began to take vigorous action and set about collecting all the available information about this incredible land. The picture was gradually painted for him and wonderingly he realized that it was really true; a Jewish kingdom did exist.

In the East, the time of mass migrations took place later

than in the West. The Chazars were of mixed stock, but had a strong Mongolian element; they were nomads and in the course of time came into contact with widely different peoples, including scattered Jewish colonists.

Islam's great agressive campaigns forced them to look northwards, to the Caucasus, the steppes by the Caspian Sea and between the Russian rivers, the Volga and the Don, until finally their empire stretched as far as the Crimea.

They developed such an explosive force that the Byzantine Emperor felt threatened and laid plans for blocking their advance. He unleashed the church on them. If its missionaries could convert the Chazars, it would be a triumph for the church, but also—and especially—a political victory and a relief for Byzantium. But here the Greek church met an adversary it had never had to fear before. Judaism, otherwise so despised, won victory's palms.

It was the story of the three rings all over again; here too, in the world's farthest corner, the three religions were found. Islam stormed northwards and the church had long been an important factor by the Black Sea. But Jews had lived there from time immemorial; their colonies, large and small, spread over the country like a network.

Naturally, what happened was the result of a lengthy process; on their wanderings the heathen Chazars met peoples who professed the three religions, so that they were influenced by them. We only know the story from old legends, but even if it simplifies and dramatizes events in the usual way, it certainly conceals a solid core of truth. This is how it goes:

Once upon a time the Chazars had a king called Bulan. In a dream God promised him that he would win honour and power. When Bulan actually did win great victories, he decided to say farewell to his idols and seek the true God. But where was he to find him? He asked those who said they knew him, but they gave different answers. The Byzantine missionaries praised the Christian faith, the Caliph's envoys sought to win him for Islam and the Jewish wise men spoke of the Law of Moses. The king became more and more uncertain and

THE THREE RINGS

hesitant, but he found a way out. When visited by a Christian missionary, he asked:

'If you were to depart from your own faith and had to choose between the Jewish and the Mohammedan teaching, to which of the two would you give the prize?'

The Christian answered: 'In that case I would choose the Jewish faith, because the Jews were once singled out by God to be his people. Only later did he disown them for their sins.'

Then the king summoned a Moslem and put the same question to him. The answer was again that the Jews' faith was the next best. The Moslems rejected the Christians' teaching, they ate unclean meat—pork—and worshipped the work of men's hands (he meant images of the saints).

Now the king assembled the Christian, the Moslem and the Jew and ordered the Christian and the Moslem to repeat their answers. Then he made his decision: 'You both admit that the Israelite religion is the oldest and most worthy of reverence; therefore I choose Abraham's faith.'

So it came about that the King of the Chazars embraced the Jewish religion. The great majority of the country's distinguished nobles followed his example. Later the kings bore Jewish names, such as Obadiah, Hezekiah, Manasseh, Isaac and Moses.

The first Jewish kings of the Chazar kingdom are obscured in the semi-darkness of the fabulous past, but the country's great age lies in broad daylight. It is strange to see a well-run kingdom blossom among nomadic tribes which were half or even wholly barbaric. Trade, prosperity and strength flourished there. The country was favourably situated. The main caravan route from Asia to Europe ran through it and the Chazars became skilful merchants. There was busy traffic with Byzantium, the Chazars exporting fish and furs.

But the most remarkable thing is to hear how the Chazar kingdom became an asylum for religious refugees. These ancient kings carried out the traditional Jewish ideas of religious tolerance and gladly gave shelter to people who had to leave their own countries for religious reasons. Their high court was composed of seven judges; two Jews, two Christians, two Mohammedans and one heathen.

When Hasdai heard of the Chazar kingdom, he was at the height of his career and was feared by both the Emperor in Byzantium and the Caliph of Baghdad. It dawned on him that he had found 'the remnant of Israel', descendants of the ten tribes driven forth from the Holy Land by the Assyrians in Biblical times, who were a never-ending source of fantasy in Jewish legends. Hasdai decided to communicate with them.

Such a task was by no means so easy in his days. Hasdai sent a trusted envoy, a man called Isaac, to Byzantium and asked the Emperor to give right of way so that he could travel through the Empire of the East to the Chazar country. The Emperor was not particularly willing to do this. Dangerous consequences might result from the establishment of relations between the mighty Jewish minister in Cordoba and the Jewish king in South Russia. He pigeon-holed the affair and put Isaac off with digressions and delaying tactics. In the end he came out with an answer: the journey along the Black Sea was dangerous and difficult; the Emperor could not accept responsibility for it.

Hasdai did not give up. After fresh negotiations he succeeded in pioneering a way through the Slavic country we now call Bulgaria and finally the envoy from Cordoba arrived with Hasdai's letter.

The letter still exists. It is a long communication in Hebrew, full of interesting information, but first and foremost it is a human document. We can see a heart beating behind the words; there are not many texts which catch the feelings of the Jews in the dispersion so vividly.

Hasdai begins by telling of the happy conditions in which he and his fellow Jews live in Sapharad (Spain). The great king is merciful to them; the country is fertile, rich in springs, rivers and reservoirs; its agriculture is flourishing, corn, oil, fruit, wine and spices; everywhere one sees gardens, and silkworms spin precious silk in abundance. Merchants from distant lands came with their wares; the king amassed great treasures the like of which have never been seen before, and foreign princes sent gifts and tokens of friendship. And it all passes through Hasdai's hands.

But—he continues—now he has heard of the Chazar kingdom and that its king shares his faith. So he asks if it is really true that there is one place on earth where there is a kingdom where Israel, which is enslaved everywhere else, is self-governed and not subordinate to anyone. The letter concludes as follows:

'If I learn that this is the case, I shall not hesitate to renounce all marks of honour, resign my high office, leave house and home, and wander over mountain and valley, travelling by land and sea until I come to the place where my king lives. If it is vouchsafed to me to see his greatness and Israel's happy life under his rule my soul will brim over with thanks to God, who has not withdrawn his mercy from his people. But I still have one prayer in my heart, that I could yet hear about the last times and the Messiah's coming. We of the diaspora listen spellbound when it is said: this people has its own kingdom—but we lack even the shadow of it.'

The exiled people's longing is clearly expressed in the Spanish minister's words. He was at the height of his power, surrounded by flattery and fawning subordinates, but deep down none of it really mattered to him. A Jewish statesman who conducted the foreign policy of a Mohammedan country and constantly had to be in the company of Christian diplomats could never breathe freely, his whole environment was against him. Not to mention the eternal insecurity he felt. No floor is as slippery as the court's, envy and intrigue lurk in the background, especially where the Jews are concerned. Religious fanaticism could be whipped up as soon as a favourable opportunity presented itself.

Hasdai's statement that he is ready to leave everything and travel from one end of the world to the other is made from the depths of a wounded soul. He would only feel at home with 'his king'. Only then could he say farewell to duplicity and ambiguity; there he would be free of all insecurity. And there he could hear the secrets of the eternally expected Messiah.

— AND THE STAR

The dream did not become reality. Hasdai received an answer to his letter. We have it too; it is one of the most distinguished sources of our knowledge of the remarkable Jewish kingdom. But shortly after the letter arrived, came other news, ominous bulletins that Russian tribes were invading the Chazar kingdom. Soon afterwards it collapsed. Hasdai ibn Shaprut died about the same time.

Exiled princes from the Chazar royal house came to Spain and settled in Toledo. Their stories later stirred the imagination of a great poet; Jehuda Halevi retold them, setting in motion new spiritual currents. Right up to our own day, Mongolian features of the so-called Eastern Jews remind us of these 'proselytes for righteousness' thousands of years ago.

We are at one of the milestones in the history of the Jewish people. When the Romans smashed the state, the emphasis shifted to Mesopotamia, Persia and Egypt. Out there in the Orient Judaism was reorganized; there it found itself after the devastating catastrophes. The Talmud was compiled in the countries of the East; there the great personalities were active, the learned scholars flourished and the people lived its quiet, everyday life. There were Jews in all the other countries, including distant western lands too; we ourselves have followed the large group which made for Spain. But they lived on the periphery; their drama was enacted on a remote provincial stage. For many centuries up to the year 1,000 the colonists spread eastwards where their centre lay; the light came from the East.

There is a secret hidden in the Jewish people, a riddle many have pondered over. How it is that this people, of all others, is able to stand firm; what kind of constant will to live sustains it? It is like a tree which is torn up by the roots from its original soil and never afterwards finds a permanent home. But against all probability it is ready to adapt itself and flower anywhere in the world. There are other peoples who were forced to decamp and find new places to live. The age of mass migrations has many examples, as have the big emigrations of more recent times, even if they are on a reduced scale. But all these peoples have lost their individuality when their background was different. They simply disappeared or became other nations. Naturally they gave strength to other peoples who imbibed their language and culture, and were themselves enriched in the process. But the wandering people remained aloof. Only the Jews were able to remain Jews, it is the unique factor in their destiny. However often they had to roam on and change towns, they always took their religion and their culture with them, and remained the same people.

One of the explanations—if not the vital one—we find in Israel's ineradicable need always to create a centre for themselves. Somewhere or other in the world a central point grew up where the old traditions were preserved. From it strength and renewal streamed out to the people in the dispersion. They gathered the sundered together so that they could become one again. But this centre shifted sometimes and moved to a new place, as changing ages and conditions demanded, yet it always remained the source of strength for Israel.

It was one of these great movements which took place in Hasdai ibn Shaprut's day. The old centre in the East withered away, but simultaneously a new day dawned and everything was made ready for the construction of the new centre.

Islam built a bridge from East to West; the newly won empire stretched from Persia to Spain. A man could travel from Baghdad to the foot of the Pyrenees without being confined by frontiers or changing cultures and languages; Islam's world was a whole. The stream went westwards; Abd al Rahman's Spain acted as a magnet both economically and culturally. On the Jews too. They made the long journey in vast numbers and came to Spain, where they found the doors wide open. Hasdai was the man who was responsible for this.

Men living in the midst of the stream of events only discern the various details, but cannot see them in historical perspective. This was so with Hasdai ibn Shaprut. Fascinated by the news from the Chazar kingdom he looked eastward and dreamed of shifting Israel's future thither. But his dream had no root in the world of reality. On the contrary it was Hasdai's destiny to lead the stream the opposite way, from east to west. With him the great epoch of Hispano-Jewish culture began. One might say that when Israel's culture withered in the East, he dug up the roots and planted them on Spanish soil. The Jews were to feel more at home there than anywhere else since Biblical days.

It was something of a new mass migration which got under way. And the long journey was not always free of dramatic experiences which were later remembered and handed down to children and grandchildren. The stories were also improved on now and then. Many chose the sea routes. But conditions in the Mediterranean were very disturbed; we have already heard of the tension between Spain and Egypt. Abd al Rahman had his reconnaissance ships out on the open sea on the look out for Egyptian pirate ships, and many bloody encounters resulted. This was forcibly brought home to one of the men who later assumed an exalted position among the Jews in Spain.

Four learned Jews were on a journey from the academy at Sura in Persia. The school was in a period of decline, as were all the Jewish schools in the East at the time. Now they were sent out into the world to collect donations from their fellow Jews. They had only sailed a short way into the Mediterranean, when one of Cordoba's pirate ships caught sight of them. The Spanish captain gave the order to pursue them; he overhauled the foreign ship, boarded it, and enslaved the four Jews. He sold two of them in an Italian port, but the other two remained on board. They were Moses ben Hanoch and his young son. Moses' wife was dead; he had remarried and his young bride, a woman of great beauty, had accompanied him on the journey; she was captured along with the two men.

The pirate captain did not sell any of the family; he had other plans. No sooner had he seen Moses' wife, than he fell passionately in love with her and decided to instal her in his harem. Meanwhile she had seen through his plans and determined to cross them at all costs.

One day she was sitting on the after deck with her pious,

rather unworldly and naive husband. In as light a tone as she could, she asked him if those who perished at sea also shared in the resurrection of the dead. Moses did not suspect anything and quite mechanically recited one of the Psalms in the Old Testament: 'Even out of the depths of the ocean will I deliver them.' Without a word his bride jumped up, hurled herself overboard and disappeared among the waves.

Moses was inconsolable in his sorrow. He scarcely noticed when they arrived in Cordoba. According to their custom, Cordoba's Jews immediately bought him and his son free. But the two kept themselves to themselves; neither of them had any real interest in life after the terrible disaster. They lived quietly, in direst poverty. Only a coincidence drew public attention to them.

One day, Moses, clad in his threadbare, tattered clothes, entered the ante-room of the synagogue where Cordoba's Chief Rabbi, Rabbi Nathan, was lecturing on the Talmud. He was a learned, devout man, respected by everybody. When the lecture was over, he was to go to another hall in the synagogue and occupy the judgment seat. The room was already full of people waiting for their cases to come up. They had to wait a long time that day.

The lecture dealt with an involved passage in the Talmud, about which opinions were strongly divided. Some of the students put questions, others objected and the discussion began to wax hot. No one noticed the poor foreigner who stood modestly near the door. But Moses ben Hanoch had earlier been engrossed in the very problems which were now being discussed so eagerly. He could not resist asking for permission to speak and as he spoke he revealed so much learning and wisdom that everyone in the hall gazed at him spellbound. Nathan realized that this man was someone out of the ordinary.

He tested him by asking him certain prescribed difficult questions and Moses constantly showed his brilliance.

Then Nathan went and opened the doors to the courtroom, so that the people could see Moses from both sides. He pointed at him and shouted: 'This poor man is a great scholar and I want to be his disciple. From today I am no longer judge in Cordoba, he alone is worthy of the judgment seat!'

So it came about that in the course of a single morning Moses ben Hanoch became the leading man in Cordoba's Jewish community.

When the pirate captain heard of this change in Moses' fortunes, he was annoyed that he had sold him too cheaply and wanted to have the deal cancelled, but the Caliph intervened. He had also heard of Moses' promotion and it fell in line with his own plans, so he put a stopper on his captain's mercantile tendencies.

For Abd al Rahman was well informed about the Jews in his kingdom through his Jewish minister. He also knew of the intimate relations there had been between them and Jewish cultural centre in the East. Whenever difficulties or knotty questions in religious matters arose, the affair was referred to the great eastern scholars; no decision was taken until they had heard from them.

The great Spanish Caliph looked on this practice with a critical eye. He wanted to free his kingdom from outside influences. His relations with Islam's eastern kingdoms were tense and his policy was directed towards creating a strong independent government in the West. Therefore he wanted his Jewish subjects to have as few obligations in that quarter as possible; his Jewish policy was aimed at making Cordoba's Jews spiritually independent. Here Hasdai worked in close cooperation with his sovereign.

Now, by pure coincidence, an important scholar of the calibre of Moses ben Hanoch had come to Spain from the East. That was the signal to go to work. Hasdai began to build an independent Spanish academy for Jewish studies and appointed Moses to run it.

Everything was done to give the new Jewish centre the best equipment possible. Valuable books and manuscripts of the Talmud were brought from far Baghdad; they cost enormous sums, but nothing was too dear. News of the great undertaking spread rapidly from country to country and scholars streamed towards Cordoba from all over the world to share in it. There was a place for all of them. Young students, hungry for knowledge, went to Cordoba from North Africa and the rest of Spain, and filled the halls of the newly built academy to bursting point. It was not long before Cordoba negotiated with the eastern Jewish teachers' schools on an equal footing. And when this happened the West was ready to take over.

Here Hasdai found an outlet for his Jewish feelings. The Spanish Jews had long looked up to him as their great man and given him the title *Nasi*, which means prince. Now he set the crown on his life's work. Like the Caliph he was a great patron of studies and the arts and took an interest in poor scholars and writers. He introduced new branches of study into the academy's curriculum and summoned scholars from distant lands. He had become a rich man and he generously lavished his fortune on his beloved academy. It repaid him with great happiness, but it also gave him difficult problems to contend with. As is well-known, the Jews are great individualists, and the Spanish Jews were no exception. They supported their own views obstinately and we hear of bitter disputes between scholars at the academy.

Hasdai attached great importance to the recently introduced science of language, or grammar, as they called it in the Middle Ages. A great deal happened in this field in Cordoba. From his boyhood years Hasdai had known one of the age's best known grammarians, Menahem ben Saruk. He had been secretary to Hasdai's father, Isaac. When Isaac died, Menahem journeyed to his home-town, but Hasdai called him back to Cordoba, as soon as the school was established. Incidentally, it was Menahem who wrote Hasdai's letter to the Chazar king, so we can thank him for one of the most important historical documents we own from that remote period.

For many years Menahem worked on a big Jewish dictionary and he concluded his life's work in 960; he called it *Mahbereth*. It was the first of its kind. It contained all the words in the Bible arranged according to the very primitive linguistic system Menahem knew. It was far from complete. He did not even know that every word in Hebrew can be derived from a root of three letters. Nevertheless, *Mahbereth* had far-reaching significance for both Biblical and linguistic studies among the Jewish communities for long ages.

At first the book brought its author little happiness. At roughly the same time as Menahem finished it, another philologist, the far more gifted Dunash ben Labrat, came to Cordoba from Fez in North Africa. He began his Spanish career by criticizing and insulting Menahem's book in the most pitiless way, at the same time dedicating his own books to the great patron Hasdai with obsequious toadying verses.

Hasdai was not insensitive to flattery. An undeniable shadow falls over our picture of him when we hear of his treatment of the man who had been his father's servant and known him since childhood. After all, Hasdai himself was a favourite, who owed his position to the Caliph. So it was natural that he, too, had favourites and at times based his decisions on personal rather than objective considerations. Menahem was to find this out. The new favourite's malicious talk made an impression. Menahem fell into disfavour and finally received a violent visit from Hasdai's police.

Soon afterwards Menahem died. His disciples agitated stormily against Dunash and sought to clear their master's memory. In any case it is established that modern Hebrew linguistics have their origin in Menahem ben Saduk's work, however ephemeral and limited it was.

The dispute continued for many years. We must remember that Hebrew is the holy language; the profoundest questions of existence are bound up with understanding it correctly. Therefore philology is a kind of divine worship. Rabbi Jonas, who continued Menahem's work, felt equally that he was summoned by heaven to it. To him Hebrew grammar was the queen of all knowledge; it provided the key to the holy words in their purity and holiness. 'I have worked so industriously on it night and day,' he said once, 'that I have used more oil in my lamp than others drink wine.'

Cordoba's Jewish community was shaken by serious conflicts

on many occasions. Hasdai and Moses ben Hanoch died about the same time; the forest's two biggest trees had been felled. This meant that a new leader of the Jewish community in Spain and a new Chief Rabbi of Cordoba would have to be elected at one and the same time. This led to great dissension.

Moses left a son behind, Hanoch, who was a learned Talmudist of the quiet, pious type. He had a dangerous opponent in Joseph ben Abitur, an unusual man, gifted and highly educated, with a sound knowledge of Arabic philosophy. Things went as they usually do in such circumstances. The majority of the community were for Hanoch. He had nothing like Joseph's stature in intelligence and wisdom, but people knew that with him there would be no departure from the traditional and customary, so that they would avoid exhausting mental acrobatics.

Both partners made great efforts to get the Caliph to support their candidates. Strange stories are told of hundreds of coaches with magnificently clad Jews driving out to Az Zahra every day and seeking audience. The Caliph, who had considerable humanistic interests, naturally favoured Joseph, but in spite of his personal leanings, he was compelled to recognize the wishes of the majority of the community. And Joseph had to hear his royal friend say these words to him:

'If I were as little honoured by my Moors, as your Jews honour you, I would leave the country.'

Joseph followed his advice; the rest of his life he roamed homelessly through the world. But in his misfortune he showed that his character was pure gold. In spite of the harsh fate he had to endure, he was not bitter; he learned resignation. A few years later new intrigues at Cordoba gave him a chance. But he said no, he did not want to return unless it could be on spiritual grounds.

At the time Cordoba was on the verge of disaster. The Berbers entered the city in 1013 and laid it waste. That meant the collapse of all the Jewish institutions which had been built up in the city. Strangely enough it turned out that this frightful disaster had salutary effects. Hitherto Spanish Jewry had been far too centralized. All the Jews who mattered were collected in Cordoba where the academy was, and the Caliph had the cultural centre in his hands. Now they scattered to the four winds. The Jews had to flee for their lives; they settled wherever they found fresh security. Statesmen, spiritual leaders and merchants spread to many towns. New small Jewish centres grew up in every corner of the peninsula. It did not take long before news was heard from places which had never housed Jews before.

Samuel ibn Nagdela was still a young man in his 'teens when he had to flee from war-ravaged Cordoba. He had been one of the great hopes of the Jewish academy, where he engrossed himself in Jewish studies and became highly versed in the Talmud's learning. But his was a many-sided talent; nothing human was foreign to him. He made an intensive study of Arabic literature and philosophy. In addition he was a linguistic genius, for he mastered at least seven languages; later in life, as a minister, he wrote a panegyric of his emir and translated it into sonorous verse in all seven languages. For he was also a poet, although not a great one.

In Cordoba he had been on the way to the heights of fame. Suddenly he found himself a poor refugee in Malaga, where he had sought refuge. But Samuel always knew how to adapt himself to circumstances. He succeeded in setting up a small spice shop in which he spent the day, leaving the evening and nocturnal hours free for reading.

But opportunity sought him out. His shop lay near the vizier's palace. A favourite slave girl from the harem occasionally came to shop there; she was struck by the young intelligent Jew and found out that he practised calligraphy. Now it was her task to keep the vizier informed about what happened at the palace when he was away travelling. She had the idea of getting Samuel to help her. She told him what the letters should say and had him write them in his decorative handwriting.

The vizier was startled by the letters; they were written in classical Arabic and had the most beautiful characters, almost like decorative drawings. When he returned home, he sent for Samuel. They had not talked to each other for long, before he realized to his astonishment that here was a young man whose intelligence and culture were on quite a different plane from what one would expect from a grocer. That was the turning point in Samuel's life. From that day forward he was the vizier's private secretary.

Samuel might have been made for the post. He approached the finer points of policy with remarkable sensitivity, on top of which he was very adaptable when dealing with different kinds of temperament, in short, the born diplomat. The vizier recognized Samuel's unusual qualities and allowed himself to be guided by him more and more. However, the vizier fell sick. The emir at Granada—Malaga was in the small state of which Granada was the capital—heard that his illness was taking a fatal turn; he sent a message, expressing his sorrow at losing so capable servant. But although dying, the vizier was honourable enough to admit what he owed to his secretary. He let the emir know that the honour for the success which had followed him belonged to his secretary, and urged the emir to take him into his service.

Habus—that was the emir's name—was in a difficult position, because he had to choose a new vizier. His subjects were divided into two parties, Berbers and Arabs, and they were bitter rivals. If he chose a vizier from one of the groups, he would have trouble with the other. In this situation Samuel seemed to be heaven-sent; he belonged to a third nation and was neutral in Islam's internal conflicts. It was particularly this fact—naturally in conjunction with the necessary abilities—which so often raised the Spanish Jews to the highest office. And so Samuel was formally nominated *katib* or vizier. That meant that all the political and military authorities in Granada were subordinate to him. For twenty-eight years, right up to his death, he occupied this powerful position, he was able to navigate among the many clashing influences with skill and flexibility, and avoided stranding his ship on treacherous rocks in dangerous situations.

— AND THE STAR

There were many who could not forgive him his Jewish birth and faith, which he never made any secret of. Once when he was passing through the streets in the emir's train, a fanatical Mohammedan sprang forward, showering insulting remarks on him. Habus was furious; he ordered the man to be seized and instructed Samuel to have his tongue cut out. However, Samuel let him go free and gave him money in addition. Next time they met, his former insulter, overwhelmed with gratefulness, stood and blessed his benefactor. In astonishment Habus asked the vizier what had happened. Samuel answered: 'I cut out his evil tongue and gave him a good one instead.'

The times were dangerous. The small Moorish states in south Spain were in perpetual civil strife; it needed great skill and experience to come through them unscathed. Nor was there any lack of internal difficulties. When Habus died suddenly, Granada was on the verge of civil war and Samuel needed all his statesmanship to steer the country through the struggle over the succession.

Two parties were striving for power. The minority supported Habus's eldest son, Badis, but by far the most, Arabs, Berbers and Jews, favoured a younger son. Samuel knew perfectly well that it could cost him his position and his life, yet he opted for Badis and put himself at the head of the minority.

Everything indicated that he was lost, for the people already paid homage to the youngest pretender to the throne. But Samuel risked everything on a daring gamble. He went to him and dared to speak out; he explained how wrong it was to scorn the right of the first-born which was honoured by both Jews and Arabs. The completely unexpected happened; the young prince renounced the crown and withdrew. A bloody civil war was avoided.

Badis never forgot what he owed to Samuel. Otherwise he was a weak character who devoted himself entirely to pleasure. So long as Samuel procured money for his excesses, he cheerfully left the affairs of state to him. In reality, Samuel was king in Granada. It sometimes happened that Badis flared up in a sudden despotic fit; then he wanted to see blood. However, Samuel knew how to curb him.

Once the emir of Seville—the neighbouring state to Granada—made a surprise attack on a border province, and slew all the Berbers he could lay hands on. Badis frothed with rage and gave orders to reciprocate by killing all the Arabs in Granada. Samuel had to use all his influence to restrain this wild lust for vengeance. He warned Badis that it was senseless to make the innocent die for others' evil deeds, and said that it would only set off a perpetual chain reaction of bloody vengeance. To be on the safe side he secretly had the Arabs in Granada informed of what was afoot and he succeeded in averting the disaster.

Naturally, during all these years his path wound along the edge of the abyss. He was the despot's favourite and nothing is more insecure than to be dependent on a weak capricious character. Samuel's Jewish origin made him particularly vulnerable. A rich, fanatical nobleman tried to overthrow Samuel. He was one of the Arabs of whom it was said that 'they hated the Berbers and despised the Jews'. It was intolerable to him that the government was in the hands of a Jew. He went to Badis and demanded that Samuel be killed, but Badis answered:

'If I followed your advice and sacrificed my faithful servant, I would be delivering myself into the enemy's hands.'

Samuel himself described the episode in a poem in which he called the man Haman, the name of the Jews' arch-enemy in Queen Esther's days. There were many Hamans at the court with daggers hidden up their sleeves, but Samuel enjoyed the emir's complete confidence. In addition he had a special ability to win people over; it was literally true that he not only disarmed his enemies, but also turned them into friends. An Arabic poet once admitted that Samuel had converted him into a secret worshipper of the God of the Jews and that he observed the Sabbath.

In Samuel's day, Granada was known as the 'Jewish town'. Naturally the town where he governed acted as a magnet to the Jews, who came to Granada from near and far, and settled.

And he saw to it that they had good living conditions. In return they loved him and showered him with marks of honour. He was elected the Jewish *Nagid*, which means prince, the same title as *Nasi*, and the Jews in both Spain and North Africa looked on him as their spiritual leader.

He was not so only in name. Throughout his life, he only breathed freely when he sat poring over his Jewish books or stood in the pulpit, reading from the Talmud. He became a very rich man, but like Hasdai ibn Shaprut put his money at the disposal of Jewish cultural life. He bought expensive books and manuscripts, and provided poor students with everything they needed. He constantly had hordes of scribes at work, copying the Bible and the Talmud.

There was one field in which he overshadowed the great Hasdai ibn Shaprut. He was not only learned and a patron, but also a poet. Unfortunately, most of his writings are lost. We know that he tried to re-write Biblical books, including the Psalms, Ecclesiastes and the Book of Proverbs, but we possess none of his books. On the other hand, we have several poems, which he wrote while he was on campaign with the emir.

He wrote one of them the night before a battle. It is an exhortation to his son Joseph and it is very typical of him. He advised the boy to lead a pious life, increase his knowledge, be friendly to others and not to be content to rest on his father's laurels. It shows no little spiritual strength that he could sit and busy himself with moral precepts in the middle of the campaign, and put them into classical Hebrew verse.

But it is not as a poet that we remember him. His contemporaries were highly critical of his poetry; the far more talented poet Solomon ibn Gabirol criticized him harshly and compared his poetry to the icy snow on Mount Hermon's summit.

But he pioneered the way for great divinely gifted poets. With him the golden age of Hebrew literature really begins. It was said that 'in mighty Hasdai's days the birds began to twitter, but in Samuel ha-Nagid's time the notes rose to a jubilant peal.' We shall go into that later.

THE THREE RINGS

When Samuel died, it was quite natural for his son Joseph to take his place; he became both vizier and *Nagid* automatically. Apparently he was well prepared to take over these two high offices. His father had given him a thorough education; he was well versed in all the sciences and arts, both Jewish and Arabic. He followed in his father's footsteps as a patron, acquired knowledge painstakingly and protected scholars. No one could deny that he was a capable man.

But there was one thing he lacked. In the course of a long life his father had learnt that a Jewish minister in a Mohammedan country was forced to act carefully and be modest and unobtrusive. Joseph, however, had never known poverty, so that power and wealth were something natural to him. What his father had toiled for and won step by step, his son was born to. So he lacked experience and common sense, as the sons of important men often do. Without thinking about it he was arrogant in his conduct and acted imprudently, for example in filling appointments, to which he unceremoniously preferred Jewish friends and relations.

The results soon showed. A whispering campaign was started against 'the Jewish vizier'. Disappointed Arabs who had been overlooked revenged themselves by saying that Joseph made fun of the Koran and hated Islam's faith. He believed neither in his father's nor any other God. He was about to make himself a dictator; he already dominated the emir completely. Badis was drunk as usual and easy to lead. Joseph surrounded him with spies and his every word was reported. Conspiracies began to flourish. People were only waiting for a favourable opportunity.

It came. A neighbouring emir invaded the outskirts of Granada. The Berbers were in the majority in Granada. The rumour circulated that Joseph had allied himself with the Arabs and summoned the enemy to the country. Now he wanted to murder Badis and proclaim himself as his successor.

That was the spark in the gunpowder barrel. The capital was in an uproar. A furious mob burst into the vizier's palace and harried it with fire and sword. Joseph hid in the cellars. He blacked his face and hoped that he would escape unrecognized. But the people discovered him and stabbed him to death. His corpse was dragged through the streets and hung up on one of the town gates.

Joseph's vast irreplaceable library was burnt. Then it was the turn of the other Jews. The Jewish quarter was stormed and 1,500 families rendered homeless. The Jews in Granada had been powerful and rich, and Jewish wealth has always beckoned.

Cordoba fell. Now Granada followed. The Spanish Jews had to seek new regions in the peninsula.

V

THE FIRST NIGHTINGALE

IN Spain the Renaissance began in the tenth century. This sounds surprising to anyone who was brought up in the belief that this mighty rebirth took place in fourteenth- and fifteenth-century Italy. But it is nevertheless a fact that the revival of antique culture—and that is surely what we mean by the Renaissance—began four hundred years earlier, first and foremost in the Iberian peninsula. The sources which once flowed in Hellas and Rome, were frozen and covered by the snow and ice of oblivion. Now a springtime of the spirit began to melt them; the stream awoke to new life and started to clear itself a path. Then it hurried forth down the river-beds made by the Arabs and Jews and found its way to Europe.

Anyone visiting North Africa today finds it hard to imagine that those backward countries house the descendants of a people who were once Europe's greatest teachers of all the sciences. Dim memories of their culture's dawn in lovely Andalusia still live in their minds and there are some who dream of hoisting the prophet's green flag over Granada's cathedral once again.

But everything was quite different in the great Caliph Abd al Rahman's day. Then the level of Arabic spiritual life began to rise as never before or since. Not only natural science and mathematical studies, but also philosophical ideas, theology and poetry started to flower. The old forgotten treasure from the ancient days was unearthed and stimulated new ideas. The same thing happened to Jewish cultural life. Both the Jews and the Arabs were fertilized and inspired as a result, so that they

THE FIRST NIGHTINGALE

developed their own distinctive character in overwhelming richness.

And not only that, they gave it away, they handed it on to mediaeval Europe. Slowly the new life penetrated into that part of the world, which was half-asleep mentally speaking, and roused it. And here it was—for reasons we shall see later—primarily Jewish scientists and writers who acted as intermediaries.

Around the time of the first Crusade the poets began to sing in Spanish Israel. A joyful chorus of song-birds—as they called it even then—rang forth. The first nightingale to utter his trills in this happy lyrical age was Solomon ibn Gabirol. He was also the first of the Jewish poets whose light shone into Europe's dark age; his world of ideas brought inspiration to Christian Europe in a most romantic way.

His parents were among the refugees from Cordoba in that catastrophical year 1013. He himself first saw the light seven years later. At that time they lived in Malaga. Unfortunately, long periods of his life are hidden in obscurity. Only now and then does a ray of light shine through and illuminate details of his sad life history.

It was genuinely sad. For we know enough to realize that Gabirol's life was a tragedy from beginning to end; fortune indeed had not smiled over his cradle. He was quite small when fate's first harsh blows struck him and rendered him homeless, killing his parents and brothers and sisters. He never knew the security and happiness of a parental home; on the contrary, the orphaned boy had a miserable childhood and had to fight against want and adversity. In his early youth he spoke of himself as 'a lad of sixteen, but with as much experience as an old man.'

Young as he was, he had known bitter sorrow, but even then his poetic talents broke through and he learnt to seek comfort in the arms of the Muse; there he found a place where he could weep and air his sufferings and complaints. Right from the first he struck the note which sounded in his song throughout his life. If we were to characterize his mentality and his song in literary terminology, it would probably be labelled a mixture of *Sturm und Drang* and *Weltschmerz*.

And yet it is not accurate to place him in that category. His remarkably complicated mind was far more profound. If he had only housed melancholy and bitter tears, he could easily have liberated himself and found the solution in malicious irony and sarcasm about the meaninglessness of life.

But this young poet dared to look stern realities in the face; he knew full well the hopeless longings for unattainable goals, the transience of all happiness, and shattered hope. He did not shun them and try—like so many other poets—to forget everything else when a young girl's eyes smiled on him. No, his innermost longing was fixed on him who is 'Israel's guardian, who sleeps not nor slumbers'. Among all the self-contradictions and improbable contrasts his mind contained, his faith was ultimately based on the incomprehensible God, in spite of everything.

His youth was spent in Saragossa, a town which teemed with Jewish intellectuals, writers, philosophers and scholars. But he felt lonely among them. He himself was largely to blame for this. His sensitive, touchy disposition aroused animosity among the majority of people he came into contact with. Everywhere he suspected ill will and envy. With his sharp tongue and cutting wit he attacked again, hitting out right and left, so that everyone avoided him. The inevitable result was that he isolated himself—and fresh bitterness gnawed at him.

But he did find one friend in Saragossa, a celebrated Jewish astronomer, Jekutiel Hassan, who at the same time was a highly trusted official at the emir's court. He took the young poet under his wing and Gabirol repaid his noble patron with brilliant poems; he clung to him and thanked him with youthful exaggeration in both sentiments and diction; at last he had found some security in life.

But that was not to be either. Jekutiel was murdered during one of the frequent court revolutions which ravaged the Moorish emirates. It was as if Gabirol's heart was shattered; the strings of the lyre which had uttered such sweet music

THE FIRST NIGHTINGALE

burst into a piercing discordant shriek and bled from a hundred wounds. We hear of all this in his poems, which lament of wrong and violence, and hopeless despair staring him in the face.

It was remarkable that a poet with such a hypersensitive mind did not founder in the darkness. In the midst of the whirlpool there was an anchor which held, for he tumbled into the fold, the faith in and surrender to God's inscrutable will. All this happened when Gabirol was nineteen years old.

The shadow of his great sorrow fell over the rest of his life and his unbalanced mind was none the better for it. He had a sharp eye for others' faults, shortcomings and ridiculous sides, and he never kept quiet about them. This ended as one might expect. There was growing animosity against him and finally he was formally expelled by the leading members of Saragossa's Jewish community.

The exiled young poet roamed homelessly about and toyed with the idea of leaving ungrateful Spain and going to the Holy Land. He was unable to make the journey, we do not know why, but we do know that he reached Granada, where he settled for the rest of his short life.

Once again he found a highly placed benefactor. For it was in Granada that Samuel ha-Nagid lived. He knew Gabirol's family from Malaga and took him under his wing. But the friendship was very uneasy; the young poet could not control his unstable mind, not even *vis-à-vis* this highly placed friend of the muses, when good behaviour would certainly have paid him. Gabirol did not try to master himself; his mind was like a shifting April breeze which cannot be directed. So sometimes we find exuberant panegyrics, in which he praises Samuel in lofty tones, and soon afterwards the exact opposite, lampoons, in which he belittles him with sour animosity, and in proud self-confidence compares his own poems with his friend's. He it was who scoffed that Samuel's poems were as cold as the eternal snow on the summit of Mount Hermon.

Gabirol was never free of conflicts in his lifetime. Every time we hear of his behaviour, it is in conjunction with disputes with others. His constantly shifting mind projected him into them, but there were other more deep-seated reasons. All his life he had to fight his way through spiritual crises and serious doubts. The solutions he found were often a long way from Jewish orthodoxy. Therefore official Judaism turned from him; the rabbis warned people against him and branded him a heretic.

As we can see, a stormy, unhappy life was Gabirol's lot. It was also a short one. There are sources which say that he did not reach thirty, but it is most likely that he lived to be fifty. Even his death was dramatic. A third-rate Mohammedan poet envied his poetic genius and murdered his more successful rival. He tried to cover up his tracks and buried the corpse under a fig tree. But—says the story—from that day the tree began to bear an enormous quantity of exceptionally sweet fruit. These extraordinary circumstances aroused suspicion. Workmen dug under the tree and found the vanished poet's corpse. Police investigations were made and the murderer found. He was punished by hanging.

It only fell to Gabirol's lot to work for a few decades, which makes us marvel all the more when we see how much he managed to produce. He was a brilliant poet and he went far beyond narrow Jewish frontiers.

An intricate mind shapes bitter hours for its possessor; it also hides riches. With Gabirol they emerged in the form of a many-sided talent. Two of the names he was given, point in widely different directions. On the one hand he was called 'the Jewish Plato', and it is true that Gabirol was one of the most original philosophers among both Arabs and Jews in the Middle Ages, 'a poet whose poetry is dedicated thought and a philosopher whose ideas flame up in a poetic flash of lightning', they said of him. On the other hand he was known as 'piety's nightingale'. They were thinking of the wealth of psalms and liturgical poetry he poured out and which have never been forgotten—to this day they are sung in the synagogue.

As with all great poets his verse flowed forth in profusion. In contrast to the strained and artificial products of many of

THE FIRST NIGHTINGALE

his forerunners, it came from a mind which was full to the brim with ideas and beauty. He knew it himself; he was proud and self-confident, and never hid his light under a bushel. 'I am the prince of song and verses are my servants—I am the singing poet's harp',[1] he said. There is something obviously superior in his poetic technique; the strophes seem to form themselves; one looks in vain for a trace of difficulties overcome. The work is fully developed and complete. Gabirol was—we can certainly say—the first poet since the days of antiquity, who was not the slave of the art of verse, but its master.

It follows that such a rich and complex mind did not always immerse itself in melancholy and spiritual conflict. For all his biting scorn, he had a lot of warmth and he would not have been a real Jew, if his poetry was not shot through with humour and wit. His wing-song is famous far beyond Jewish circles. He was invited to a banquet, but the wine ran out and the guests had to make do with water. Then Gabirol stood up and composed the long witty song on the spot. In order to understand it, we have to know a little about the language.

With brilliant humour he calls the wine 'seventy'; the Hebrew letters in the word *jajin* (wine) have the numerical value 70. But water is superior; it is called *majim*, and the total is 90. This is how the verse begins:

> The wine runs out—o fearful torment,
> the eye weeps—with tears of water.
> Seventy is full of youthful fire,
> but Ninety drives him away.
> So runs the song! The glass cannot ring,
> When it is only filled with water, water, water!

[1] It is always difficult to appreciate Hebrew poetry, when one is forced to reproduce it in translation. Goethe said that true poetry is what remains behind when the poem is turned into prose. Perhaps we can go further and say the essential in the poetry must be able to survive a translation from mediaeval Hebrew to modern West European languages. But obviously there are things which require explanation. In the short verse translated here Gabirol uses the Hebrew word for singer, *shar*. Prince is *sar*, so that a subtle but untranslatable pun is made.

And the poem continues in the same vein, with every verse ending in the refrain: water, water, water!

Everywhere in Gabirol's works we find examples of genuine Jewish humour. He is gentle but acute in several epigrams. Here are two examples:

'How do you show that you have had a good upbringing? By having patience with those who have not.'

'The eye of a needle provides ample room for two who love each other, but the whole world is not large enough for two who hate each other.'

Once he learnt that a quite unimportant writer was plagiarizing him and passing the results for his own. But Gabirol answered by comparing himself to an ever rolling stream. It keeps on flowing and does not get angry, even if one or another wretched scribbler draws a bucketful of water from it.

But the light vein is a rare one; it is only a gleam of sunshine in the wealth of heavy reflections which most often occupy his mind. The fundamentals of Gabirol's poetry are melancholy, gloomy sadness and impotent defiance of the unchangeable Fates. His poems are always clear; imagination is not allowed to go astray on bypaths; it is controlled by a clearly considered philosophy of life. He struggles with the great problems of ideas; however gloomy and sinister they seem, he is never afraid to bring them into his poems, so that we find both troubled doubt and fumbling attempts to justify God's inscrutable ways.

The solitary poet never knew earthly love and domestic happiness with wife and children; we have only a single love poem by his hand. He circled round the eternal problems of the riddles of the universe and all his love was devoted to his God and his people. We look into a lacerated discordant mind, but the battle ends with both audacious doubt and lofty ideas kneeling in prayer, when we listen to his songs, which touch our hearts too.

That is why so many of his religious poems are still alive

THE FIRST NIGHTINGALE

among the Jewish people and are used in both the Sephardic and Ashkenazic liturgy, for example a famous elegy on the great day of atonement. He wrote all kinds of religious poetry including hymns, penitential prayers and laments, and painted the people's hope for the future and longing for the age of the Messiah as vividly and in the same brilliant colours as they always appeared to exiled Israel.

Yet it is not as a poet that he is most important. Many of his works are just as much philosophy as lyrics. The best known are called *Kether Malkut*, which means 'The Royal Throne', and *Mibhar ha-Pennim*, 'Selected Pearls'. But the book which is considered his philosophical masterpiece was in prose, *Mekor Hayim*, 'The Fountain of Life', first known in a Latin translation, *Fons vitae*.

The Jewish philosophers wrote their books in Arabic. Since they lived in the Arabic cultural circle, it was natural for them to address their immediate environment. Later the works were translated into Hebrew and Latin. For this reason 'The Fountain of Life' came out under Gabirol's Arabic name, Avicebron. To this the book owed its remarkable destiny. We say that 'books have their fates'; the one which befell Avicebron's masterpiece was really fantastic.

It was a long time before his own people took any notice of the book. It aroused the great interest in Arabic circles, but even more in Christian Europe. No one there dreamt that the author of the celebrated much discussed book was a Jew, otherwise it would probably not have become the classic for mediaeval schoolmen which it did. Everyone supposed that Avicebron was an Arabic-Christian thinker and the great schoolmen, Albert the Great, Duns Scotus, even Thomas Aquinas himself, drew plentifully from its inexhaustible spring.

It was to take eight hundred years before the secret was disclosed. As late as 1846 someone came across a Hebrew transcript of *Fons vitae* among other Hebrew manuscripts in the National Library in Paris. The discovery gave rise to a great deal of research and the result was that scholars all agreed that this basic book for mediaeval Christian theology was written by the Jew ibn Gabirol.

What was it that made *Fons vitae* so significant? In it Gabirol rose to become a mediaeval counterpart of the great Jewish philosopher Philo of Alexandria in the first century B.C. It was Philo who made Greek philosophy known in Eastern countries and prepared the way for the blend of Neo-Platonic and Christian ideas which were characteristic of the early Church's theology. And now a thousand years later came another Jew and took Graeco-Arabic philosophy to Christian Europe.

'Ideas are like the wind which bloweth where it listeth; and thou hearest the sound thereof, but cannot tell whence it cometh, and whither it goeth'

—to quote a famous passage from the Gospel according to St John. Nevertheless it is interesting to seek out the hidden, unnoticed ways by which ideas travel. As it turned out, Avicebron was really only repaying the Christian church an old debt. Many centuries before his time Christian scholars had rescued the old Greek philosophers' works and translated them into Syrian. This was the model which passed into Arabic translation. Then Avicebron found them and via *Fons vitae*, sent them back to the Christian church which had completely forgotten them.

Philo and Avicebron had similar destinies. Neither of them found a hearing among their own people, but both of them had a strong influence on the Christian church, Philo on the early church, Avicebron on mediaeval Christian theology. Only later, by devious routes, did Avicebron acquire importance among the Jewish people.

We may as well take a brief look at his philosophic ideas, since we shall meet them again. For him God is absolutely the first and he is wholly spirit. How then was the world created? To answer this question Avicebron had recourse to the doctrine of emanation. Emanation means a flowing out; the world flows out from God. First will, then reason and lastly soul. From the soul the suprasensible world flows out and that con-

THE FIRST NIGHTINGALE

tinues to the visible, the sensible world. Avicebron called this the Macrocosmos, the great world. But creation took place in the same way, through will, reason and soul, in Microcosmos, the little world or mankind. This is to repeat that there is harmony between the little and the big worlds.

Thus life's great decisive basic law is that mankind stems from the source of life, from God. One line goes from God to men. But a line also goes in the opposite direction, from men back to God. Here we are at the centre of Avicebron's ideas. Mankind aspires to the God from whom he came. The stronger this longing is, the more spiritual man is. The important thing is to follow this striving; a man must drown himself in God, meditate on him and be absorbed in him. This—we call it contemplation—is the way to God, from the sensible world to eternity. These were the ideas which mystics took up and developed into a grandiose system in the so-called Cabbala. Not until that time came did the Jews understand what they owed to their great son.

That was how ibn Gabirol strove to find the truth and a solution to the riddle of existence. His own people shunned him, and the church thought that he was a Christian philosopher on the threshold of the Occident and with access to the schoolmen. For centuries his ideas streamed forth, but he himself was unknown, forgotten by his own people, wearing a mask for the Christians, until a pure coincidence tore off his Moorish-Christian persona and everyone saw that the philosopher Avicebron and the devout Jew Solomon ibn Gabirol were one and the same.

He was one of mankind's great men. A Faust in his broodings, a mind which aspired to clarity, indomitable and proud in adversity, a gifted poet and a devout believer, he was great in all these fields. No wonder that his successors said of him:

> High song is Solomon's.
> He is like a king, sublime and great.

VI

SHADOWS OF THE CROSS

THERE is an old Hebrew book dating from the middle of the fifteenth century. The author's name is Joseph ha-Cohen and the book has the extremely expressive title *Emek Habaha*, which means 'The Vale of Tears'. At first glance it seems to be as dry reading as a telephone directory or a time-table. It is an interminable monotonous recapitulation of old events and yearly reviews. But if we look at it more closely, we soon discover that *Emek Habahah* is a terrifying book whose pages are steeped in tears and blood. In fact it recounts all the massacres of the Jews from the dawn of history until the author's lifetime. It is hair-raising reading. Not so much that the author laments vociferously and uses rhetorical devices to make an impression. No, the gripping thing about the book is the depressing monotony, in which these endless appalling episodes merge into one long threnody. It is nearly always the cross which casts the dark shadows.

The year 1096 covers many pages in *Emek Habahah*. It was the year in which the First Crusade started and it became one of the Jewish people's darkest years.

A longing for the east was constantly burning in the minds of Christian Western Europeans. Their minds hankered after the holy places where God's son had lived, where He died, was resurrected and went to heaven; once they had been the cradle of the one true faith. So devout men took staff in hand and wandered on interminable paths; they endured hardships, hunger and want; they fought with robbers, and caught fevers and diseases they had never even heard of. Many of them disappeared and left no traces, but those who returned had exciting stories to tell of the journey and the great moment when they knelt in Bethlehem and at Christ's grave.

With the course of time this longing changed character. At first it had had a purely religious emphasis, but later acquired political overtones. Naturally this was connected with Europe's growing power and the massive resources which were being assembled in the Christian countries. These powers strove for liberation and employment. Here the new disturbing reports from returned pilgrims came in useful.

It was said that the Saracens desecrated Christ's grave and dishonoured His holy memory; they insulted Christian pilgrims, great numbers of whom fell victims to Mohammedan fanaticism. Some embroidered on the chronicles still further and claimed that the Eastern Jews were even worse. The church was the great martyr and it was terrible that Christ's grave was in the heathens' possession. The rumours flew far and wide and a cry for vengeance rose to heaven. Christianity must cast off the yoke and liberate Jerusalem, the centre of the world!

At the synod held in Clermont in 1095 all the newly aroused powers were concentrated when Pope Urban II gave his famous speech exhorting princes and people to unite in a mass crusade to the Holy Land. The unanimous answer from the vast assembly resounded under the sky: *Deus lo vult!* (God wills it). No other speech has had such tremendous consequences.

Once the movement was started, there was no stopping it. It flew from country to country. The flame spread like a forest fire and set people's minds ablaze. Kings and feudal overlords, knights and citizens from the towns and farmers in tens of thousands left house and home and, wearing the sign of the cross on their arms, went to wage war on the heathen.

The armies streamed together; they were a motley mixture of all kinds of people and they were activated by the most varied motives, the lowest side by side with the most sublime. Here genuine religious longing met the urge for deeds of prowess and the thirst for the rich booty which beckoned. The

THE THREE RINGS

church promised forgiveness of all sins and remission of Purgatory's flames to everyone who took the field. So pure adventurers and common criminals seized the opportunity to settle their future and simultaneously slip away from places which were haunted by unpleasant memories.

The army moved off. It so happened that the people of the East were in bitter internal strife, so that Islam was in one of its weakest situations. The opportunity could not have been more favourably chosen, even by a trained calculating Prussian chief of general staff. Consequently, the first assault succeeded and the kingdom of Jerusalem was consolidated. But in the long run the situation was hopeless. When Islam saw the danger and rallied, things went badly for the crusaders. When that brilliant statesman and general, the great Saladin took over the command, everything collapsed.

The only remarkable thing is that the Christians were able to cling on to the Holy Land as long as they did. Jerusalem was in their possession for nearly a century and the last base, Acco, held out for another century. The ruins of the crusaders' mighty castles in Palestine still remind us of the superhuman efforts Christianity made to hold on to the country.

Europe's people were activated by a great idea. It dominated them for centuries; even after the collapse it was able to dominate international politics for countless generations. Right down to modern times echoes of the Crusades sound in the minds of the Western peoples.

The Crusades literally revolutionized Europe. They made the church powerful and even more influential than before, but they also marked a sharp change in people's everyday life. Merchants followed in the warrior's footsteps; new trade routes and business connections with the East came into being; countless wares never seen before found their way to mediaeval Europe. Arabic culture made an impression and infected it; knowledge and art received completely new stimuli.

The results were even more pronounced for the Jews. Evil passions and inclinations were awakened and flared up; they made their mark on every single branch of Jewish life and can be traced to this very day. They decided where the Jews could live, what their social and political status should be, they determined their literature, in fact they penetrated the Jewish character and spiritual life. In every respect for the worse.

It began with blood and fire. There had been bad omens. Many crusaders had sworn to revenge Christ's blood on the Jews before they went to war. They found it outrageous to let Christ's oldest enemies stay alive behind the front, while they themselves risked life and fortune in the battle with the heathens.

It was not the organized divisions of the army which did the damage. They marched from northern France down the valley of the Rhine in orderly fashion, under strict discipline. Their commanders could be bribed to guarantee the Jews' safety. Not for nothing does a Jewish proverb say that a hammer of gold opens a heart of stone. But the loosely assembled mass, which if anything, set out quite haphazardly, wild to see blood and win booty, was uncontrollable. In addition the rumour spread among them that striking a Jew conferred forgiveness of sins—quite apart from the fact the Jews had gold.

The responsible authorities did what they could to prevent pogroms. They warned the Jews, they concealed them, they defended them. But it was all in vain when the cry of 'hep! hep!' began to ring out.[1] Every kind of terror struck the communities in the Rhineland. The Jewish districts went up in flames in Speyer, Worms, Mainz, Rüdesheim, Cologne and Trier, and the Jews were senselessly murdered.

They had to choose between baptism and death. By far the most chose death. Page after page could be filled with bloody tragedies from those evil days, so shameful for the Christians. There were enough sheep to point out the Jews in Mainz. The bishop had hidden them in his palace, but wild hordes of irregular crusaders forced him to deliver them for baptism or

[1] 'Hep! hep!' was the classical cry when the Jews were persecuted. It may stand for *Hierosolyma est perdita*, Jerusalem is lost. Or perhaps it is the Schwabian pronunciation of 'Hab, hab', which means give, give, i.e. tax to the Holy Roman Empire. It is said that the Jews answered with the cry 'Jep, jep', i.e. *Jesus est perdita*, Jesus is lost.

death. Then they chose to go the same way as the defenders of Massada a thousand years before. The parents killed their children and afterwards themselves. Eleven hundred people lay dead when the attackers forced their way into the palace.

The crusaders moved on. Their path can be followed by their bloody footsteps. Prague was ravaged; in the Balkans they cut down the Jews at Salonica. The high point came with the capture of Jerusalem. The surviving Jews were driven into the synagogue to which the victorious crusaders then set fire. Not a single Jew in Jerusalem survived.

Jewish historians coined a pun, a new name. Clermont, the town where the Crusade was proclaimed, means the mountain of light. The Jews called it Har Ophel, which means the mountain of darkness. They had good grounds for it.

After the Crusades, the Jews of Western and Central Europe lived in a constant state of alarm. No one knew when he might have his house burnt down over his head, while he himself was murdered by a raging mob or driven out onto the highroad with wife and children to look for a new place to live—if one could be found—or die in some casual ditch.

This does not mean that a perpetual state of persecution reigned. There might be long intervals of comparative peace and quiet. But the Jews had a permanent feeling of insecurity; in one place or another, usually not far away, lurked deadly peril. Even in times of apparent security it was clear that they were only tolerated, dependent on the whims of a prince who had the power to do what he wanted with them.

The Crusades were the Christian counter-offensive against the extreme wing of Islam's advance. Half a year previously Christianity advanced its lines a long step forward at the opposite end of the world-wide front, in Spain. Here the war between the cross and the crescent also had consequences for the Jews, but surprisingly enough of an opposite kind. In Central Europe the shadow of the cross was ominous and dangerous. In Spain it meant shelter and protection, at least in the first place.

The Moors never overcame the splintered and beaten

SHADOWS OF THE CROSS

remnants of the Christian royal house and its knights. They hid themselves and gradually came to power in the inaccessible mountains of northern Spain. The Moors were satisfied with having won the best part of the country, Andalusia, that smiling, delightful domain in the south. The Christians kept control of the mountain country; it was a rough, hard life, but it bred a healthy, tough race.

Here small principalities and kingdoms grew up; Leon and Castile, Navarre at the foot of the Pyrenees, Portugal on the Atlantic coast, Aragon and Catalonia to the east. They often fought with each other, but the Moors were their enemy number one. After endless wars, the direction became more and more unmistakable; it was southwards; the spirit was that of the Crusades and primitive, impressionable minds absorbed the church's inflammatory stories from childhood and called for war against the heathen. The spiritual centre of the re-conquest was the town of Santiago de Compostella in the north-western corner of the peninsula. The Catholic church has always had an incredible piece of luck on its side; whenever it has needed miracles, they have come almost on the hour. This happened at Santiago, too.

The name means St James and the story goes that the apostle James, one of the sons of Zebedee in the Gospels, travelled to Spain after the first great Pentecost and preached the gospel. When he returned to Jerusalem, he suffered a martyr's death and was beheaded, as we can read in the Acts of the Apostles. But his disciples concealed his body; they put it in a coffin and took it to Spain. There they buried St James in the country where he had been the first to preach the joyful message.

Many years later a pilgrim knocked on the bishop's door one night in what is now Santiago and related an extraordinary experience. He had lain on the ground sunk in prayer, when suddenly he heard angels singing and saw a new, unusually large star shining brightly in the evening sky.

The bishop realized at once that something strange was afoot. He ordered men to dig in the earth at the spot where the

THE THREE RINGS

pilgrim had prayed and in fact there lay a coffin containing a corpse, with its head severed from its body, and a document which said that the dead man was James.

The bishop did not delay; he built a chapel and later erected the famous St James's Church on the site of the chapel. The name Compostella came naturally from *campus stellae*, the field of the star. And once the story had begun to blossom, it received a new following; the place became one of the most famous shrines in Europe and pilgrims flocked there from every country. Now the Christians had a centre which could vie with Moorish Cordoba.

Once the seed was planted, popular imagination was ready to put forth new shoots, faithfully aided and abetted by zealous priests and bishops. The apostle appeared to the fighting Christian army; he rode on a white horse and carried a glittering golden sword which brought the Christians brilliant victories. Meanwhile, reality did not quite correspond to the vision. The Christians shuddered with fear and disappointment when Almanzor led his Saracens to Santiago and took the famous bells back to Cordoba.

But during this long bitter war there developed a Christian type of warrior whose like could not be found in any other country. We can reasonably refer to a special Spanish religion when we think about the development of the Catholic church during eight hundred years of implacable struggle with Islam. Religion and politics became one; the cross and the sword were to be worn at the same time; the Spaniards became the only Christian nation where the faith, so to speak, entered the people's blood for good and evil. It was an order of chivalry inspired by burning fanaticism, blind obedience to God's church, and an ice-cold and implacable hate for the heathen. There was no time left for effeminate pursuits nor to cultivate knowledge and the arts. A single goal beckoned; to rid the holy soil of the fatherland of the heathen plague.

Early in the eleventh century—around the time of the first great Crusade—the reconquest got under way. Strong, purposeful Christian kings united the kingdoms of Leon and Castile.

SHADOWS OF THE CROSS

At the same time as Christian Spain was strengthened, Moorish dominion began to collapse. It was precisely at this time that the once so mighty caliphate in Cordoba broke up and disintegrated. The fruit was ripe and the great King Alphonso VII of Castile reached out his hand to pluck it.

On May 25, 1085, he made his victorious entry into the Visigoths' ancient capital of Toledo. In a hundred battles and with skilful diplomatic manœuvres he had driven Islam's beaten army southwards before him. The cross-shaped sword triumphed over the curved sabre.

Naturally an omen appeared on that day. One of King Alphonso's most feared knights rode at his side. His name was Rodrigo Diaz, but everyone knew him as el Cid, the name countless Spanish folk tales and songs adorned their hero with. He was the bravest of the brave, a daring warrior who had been the protagonist in incredible adventures.

In the middle of Toledo's main street el Cid's horse stumbled. He felt it kneel for a moment and at once realized that it must be a sign of something miraculous. Just here was a mosque which had once been a church. El Cid ordered his squires to knock the wall down, when, lo and behold! a niche appeared and the king and his retinue saw to their astonishment that it concealed an ancient statue of Christ. But most remarkable of all, a burning lamp stood in front of the Christ. It must have been burning since the day, nearly four hundred years ago, when the Moors conquered Toledo and the priests managed to hide the holy statue of Christ. The new archbishop of Toledo purified the mosque on the spot and rededicated it to the Christian religion. Naturally it was named Cristo de la Luz (Christ of the Light). King Alphonso hung his shield on the wall of the church. It hangs there to this day.

People told a story about this image of Christ. We shall retell it, because it is characteristic of the atmosphere of mysticism which hangs over the age of the reconquest. It was an old custom in Toledo for people passing by to kneel and kiss its right foot. But a Jew wanted to revenge himself on the Christians who had murdered one of his friends. So he smeared poison on the foot of the image. The very next morning a woman passed by. As usual, she fell on her knees and bent her head to kiss his foot, but at the same moment, Christ drew it back, so that the woman missed the poison. Anyone can see that the story is true because Christ stands with his right foot drawn back to this day.

The fall of Toledo frightened Moorish Spain; everyone realized that danger was imminent. But the small divided kingdoms were unable to defend themselves against the victorious army of Castile on their own. They looked round for help and found it in North Africa.

A holy war, or Jihad, as it is called in Arabic, had been proclaimed there. A new Mohammedan sect sought to revive the original unadulterated faith and raged with fire and sword to purify and win power. They called themselves Almoravides, and their warlike prophet and great commander was Jusuf. He had founded the city of Marrakesh and conquered the country as far as Tangier from where he looked out on the Spanish coast.

The Spanish emirs still remembered the disasters caused by the fanatical Berbers; they had indeed devastated Cordoba. They also knew that it was easier to invoke the Berbers' aid than to get rid of them afterwards, but they saw no other way out. With heavy hearts they sent a message to Jusuf. Motamid, the emir of Seville, expressed everyone's feelings when he said: 'In spite of everything I would rather lead an ass in Africa than be a swineherd in a Christian Spain.' One more reference to the fact that the Christians ate pork, which was an abomination to the Mohammedans and Jews.

They did not have to ask Jusuf twice. He lost no time in transporting his army across the straits and advancing on the Castilians. A famous and bloody battle took place at Zallak in 1086. Since all three faiths were represented in the two armies, it was difficult to find a day on which to engage battle. The Mohammedans were not allowed to fight on Fridays, the Jews could not fight on Saturday and the Christians had to keep Sunday sacred. So they agreed to fight on Monday.

Jusuf won a decisive victory and the battle put a temporary stop to further Christian advances southwards. Islam won four centuries' respite in Andalusia, even if it was under a steadily waning crescent. But the victory brought the Moorish emirs little joy; they found themselves degraded to the status of humble servants of the Berbers. Jusuf founded a dynasty which ruled Arabic Spain with a firm hand for the next fifty years.

A new spirit set in with the advent of the Almoravides. The age of tolerance was over; now both Christian and Jew had to bow before Islam and profess themselves followers of Allah and his prophet. Yet it sounded worse than it was. The Almoravides could be talked over at this time.

The inhabitants of Lucena discovered this. This delightful little town near Granada had long been a centre of Jewish culture. Large numbers of Jews lived there, so many that it was called the Jewish town. They had been left in peace to establish themselves. Lucena's Jews were industrious and rich. The town housed a celebrated Talmudic school in which great teachers taught. The Jews used to call Lucena 'the town of poetry'.

Now a message came from Jusuf, ordering the Jews in Lucena to be converted to Islam forthwith. On quite original grounds. Jusuf said that in his lifetime Mohammed had made an agreement with the Jewish people. He promised them freedom of worship for the next five hundred years. If the Messiah did not come within that time, it would be a sign that the prophet had been right and the Jews should bow to his teaching. Now the period of grace had expired and the Messiah had not come.

The Jewish leaders in Lucena took the situation lightly. They realized immediately that Jusuf wanted their money more than their faith. They were right. Jusuf connived at letting them escape and go free merely against the payment of a fairly exorbitant ransom.

But when the Almohades succeeded the Almoravides in the middle of the eleventh century, it was another matter. Almohad means professor of unity and they were implacable champions of the strictest monotheism. They had conquered

THE THREE RINGS

North Africa and rooted out every other faith with fire and sword. The Jewish communities were annihilated and the Jews killed; the survivors fled or made the necessary profession of belief in Islam. When the Almohades came to Spain and ousted the Almoravides, they carried out the same policy. The synagogues went up in flames; the communities in Seville, Cordoba, Malaga and Lucena fell victims to their fanaticism.

Once again the Jews had to flee; the roads were thronged with them as they hastened away to save their lives and escape the ignominy of being forced to deny their faith and bring dishonour on the unutterable name.

In fact a door stood open for them in the Christian land to the north. It seemed scarcely possible. After all, the Christian kings were the Visigoths' rightful successors and the notorious Visigothic law with all its severe regulations concerning the Jews was still in force. Moreover, the Christians had regarded the Jews with suspicion and contempt for a long time. They had betrayed the country to the heathen and was there really any difference between Moors and Jews? The Jews spoke the same language as the Moors, they dressed like them and their whole culture bore an Arabic impress. The very fact that the Moors treated them tolerantly aroused suspicion.

But little by little the atmosphere changed. The kings of Castile, especially Alphonso VII, the conqueror of Toledo, saw that he could use them, particularly in the service of the state. Many Jews had received first-class educations; they could speak the Romance languages as well as Arabic; they were neutral in politics and were accustomed from childhood to acting flexibly and piloting their way through shifting and opposing interests. Jews began to appear at the court of Toledo; they were known as clever doctors, natural scientists and men of letters.

But first and foremost the king used them as diplomats and put them at the head of important financial undertakings.

It cost him the Pope's friendship and King Alphonso fell into disfavour at Rome. The mighty Gregory VII sent Alphonso letter after letter putting pressure on him to stop

Jews acquiring authority over Christians, in other words the old time-honoured Papal Jewish policy, 'It would be debasing the church and exalting Satan's synagogue', he wrote, 'if you encourage Christ's enemies, you deny Christ himself.' But nothing was farther from Alphonso's mind than foregoing the sympathy of useful citizens for the benefit of a Pope who lived so far away.

We must constantly bear in mind that the Spanish church was the most independent in Europe during the first thousand years after St Paul the apostle landed in Spain. It was only when Queen Isabella insisted on the Inquisition and King Ferdinand's inordinate greed was aroused that the Spanish church destroyed heretics. If Torquemada had tried to take the stage in the days of el Cid and King Alphonso he would have been strung up on the nearest tree.

Consequently the doors stood open for fugitive Jews in the kingdom of Castile. The majority settled in Toledo, which became the centre of Jewish life for many years. We have witnessed one more displacement of Israel's cultural centre.

It is usually asserted that the Jewish flowering in Spain coincided with the Moors' great age. This is not in fact true. Christian tolerance—limited and temporary as it was—gave them far safer conditions than their fellow Jews north of the Pyrenees. In the shadow of the cross the renaissance broke through to Spanish Israel. But Moorish culture had managed to stamp the Jews decisively and there was still room for Jews in Islam's eastern countries. The greatest of them all, Moses Maimonides, found refuge in Mohammedan Egypt.

The three rings were tightly interlaced.

VII

THE SONG BIRDS TUNE THEIR LYRES

※

SOLOMON IBN GABIROL was the first of Zion's singers in Spain. He handed down the harp to the next generation and the song rose and became a sonorous chorus whose voices sounded in harmony, the deep and plaintive side by side with the light, joyful and happy. Israel had never sung outside its father's land as it did in Spain in the age between ibn Gabirol and Jehuda Alharisi, but three great poets stand in the front rank and their voices still resound. There is something eternal about the best of their songs. There were two cousins, Moses ibn Ezra and Abraham ibn Ezra, and the greatest of all Israel's singers abroad, Jehuda Halevi.

Moses ibn Ezra (1070–1139) was the closest heir to ibn Gabirol. He came from a distinguished Jewish family in Granada; his father was a high official in the days of Samuel ha-Nagid. We know the names of the three other brothers who grew up at home with him, they were Isaac, Joseph and Zeharia. Moses went to the Jewish town of Lucena when he was quite young and was given a Jewish education at the celebrated school, but he did not neglect the study of Arabic culture and the old Greek philosophers.

There are so many long centuries separating us from these Hispano-Jewish poets, and when our curious gaze roams back through the ages, we usually discover to our disappointment that a veil of fog conceals most details of their lives and development. But Moses ibn Ezra is an exception. For long periods he and his young fellow poet, Jehuda Halevi, were in active correspondence with each other. A number of their letters have been preserved; they provide us with valuable intimate knowledge of this highly gifted man and his tragic lot in life.

Everything seemed so bright. Happy and carefree he sauntered lazily through life, which was a succession of joyful hours. Youthful dreams and longings filled his mind and out of his happy poet's heart he sang of all of them. He dreamed of a 'wonderful maiden's face, of flowing wine and the twittering of birds, of the stream which gently gurgles into the sea, of love's balsam and intoxicating delights and all songs celebrating life.' And he likes using all colours of the rainbow. 'The garden dresses herself in her gaily coloured robe, in her green woven skirt. The flowers swarm forth to greet the spring with a smile. But first steps the rose like a queen ascending her throne. It has burst the bounds of its bud and cast off its prison garb. And he is a miserable sinner whose desires are not satisfied with this glad message.' And he sings further of sparkling wine and rejoices over him who 'for a small silver coin buys so golden a drink.'

He was adept at composing the verse riddles, full of images and fertile invention, which were in favour as an intellectual game at gay contemporary banquets.

> Who is the sun's sister,
> but serves thee at night,
> as the palm reaches up to heaven,
> it shines like a golden spear,
> but tears run down its cheeks,
> because fire gnaws at its body.
> When it is ready to die, we behead it
> and put new life into it.
> I never saw anything else which
> laughs and cries at the same time.

The answer is: a candle.

The young poet only compared his candle to tears, but suddenly his life-enhancing song was stilled and only tears remained. It was the old story. He fell in love and could not have the girl. She was one of his elder brother's daughters and she returned her young uncle's love with all her heart. They dreamed the sweet dreams of all lovers and Moses sang of his joys in wonderful love-songs. But the father had other plans; he said no and gave her to another.

That was the turning point in Moses ibn Ezra's life; he felt as if his heart was broken. He could not bear to stay in Granada which had witnessed his happiness and deep disappointment. So he left, and for the rest of his life he was a homeless vagrant. He wrote home from Castile that for his beloved's sake he 'had come into the foreigners' net and become the guest of Edom', i.e. Christian Spain.

There the next blow struck. The girl did not survive her first child-birth. On her death-bed she sent a greeting to the man who 'for my sake drinks the bitter cup of exile: thou shalt remember the promises of thy youth, with thy loving hand thou must knock on the door of my grave.'

This greeting from the other side shook him deeply. Throughout his life he was lonely; his muse donned mourning and he journeyed through foreign lands. His happy life had become empty; now he saw only the ephemerality in all the things of this world—old age which creeps up unnoticed, faithless friends and blighted hopes.

Yet now we see what has happened so often before and since; blighted love incites the muses to bestow their favours on the rejected poet. In any case it is certain that after his deep sorrow, Moses ibn Ezra towered up as one of the great religious poets and his psalms and songs of penance have been sung in the synagogue for centuries. He joined the long series of Jewish *pajetanim* and became one of the greatest of them all. But this special word requires an explanation.

The Hebrew word *pijut, pijutim* in the plural, comes from the Greek word poet, but gradually it was used not of poets but of their song. So someone coined the new word *pajetan, pajetanim* in the plural, from the same root and applied it to poets who wrote psalms and prayers. These were the devout poets who for thousands of years gave the Jewish service the songs which became a permanent feature of the prayer-book

THE SONG BIRDS TUNE THEIR LYRES

and worked their way into the ritual for holy-days. The commonest form for a *pijut* is called *seliha*, i.e. penitential prayer; literally translated the word means devotion. The refrain taken up over and over again is a prayer for devotion. These prayers are sung more particularly in the period between the New Year and the great Day of Atonement.

Such words as *pijut* and *seliha* do not mean much to us today, but many of them are great poetry. They are examples of the song of the dispersal which patiently waiting poets taught changing generations to sing and console themselves with in sorrowful anxious times.

These old poets had the synagogue as their mirador. From it they looked out on the world which was filled with unrest and panic, and regarded them and their people as pariahs. To them the whole world was literally drowned in the waves of the Flood, with only a few mountain tops emerging from it. We follow them through their poems; they are onlookers, often victims but always passive, never taking part in the drama which so often ends in tragedy. But they are far-sighted, they always look forwards with a faith which never falters to the dawn they hope will come one day, when everything which now crushes them will collapse and they themselves triumph and endure.

That was the type of song Moses ibn Ezra learnt to sing. He became a gifted poet and was given the nickname Hasallah, the poet of penance. He was a master of formal beauty and it was said that 'he drew pearls from the fountain of thought'. Here is an example of his penitential poetry:

> A mere breath is man and his striving,
> his life fleets by like a shifting shadow,
> it speeds away like the flight of a bird
> without wings his years hasten past
> what he saves in his chamber crumbles and falls into ruins
> only his purified work
> accompanies him to the grave
> and beyond punishment and guilt
> God rises on the mercy seat.

THE THREE RINGS

Jehuda Halevi was born in the fateful year 1085, when the king of Castile conquered the town and made it his capital. His father was 'Samuel the Castilian', to all appearances a prosperous man, and the lad grew up in a wealthy home which gave him everything the heart could desire.

There was not a better place in the whole world for a young, receptive mind to grow up in than Toledo. Here East met West; the culture of Islam and Christian Europe. Everything which the East had to give the West in the way of wisdom and inspiration flowed to and was collected at the focal point of Toledo. Christian students came in droves from lands beyond the Pyrenees. Jewish scholars were there, translating the books of antiquity into Latin. But the lad also met strange individuals with Mongolian features, the last fugitives from the royal house of the Chazars, who had found refuge in Toledo. We can easily imagine how the youth sat avidly listening to the stories of the Jewish kingdom on the shores of the Black Sea, far, far away. Later he found the framework for his philosophical masterpiece in these fantastic tales.

All we know about his schooldays and further development comes from scattered passages in his books. But there is plenty of evidence that the Jewish teachers gave the boy a comprehensive schooling, in both specifically Jewish and general affairs. When the boy was adolescent, his father sent him to Lucena (this was before the Almoravides came to Spain and the school was still at its height). Moreover, Granada was quite near, so that Jehuda had another centre of Jewish spiritual life within his reach. Gradually he decided to study medicine and later in life he made his living as a doctor.

But there was one branch of art which was closer to his heart than all others and where he found everything as easy as child's play. Poetry was greatly enjoyed in Arabic culture and the art was practised and developed for centuries according to ingenious complicated rules. From distant times the Jews had an instinctive feeling for verse and they were willing pupils. They chose to translate the art into their sacred language, Hebrew, and poetry was an important faculty in the school.

Undoubtedly it was dearest to Jehuda. In Lucena he enlivened his dry Talmudic studies with his first fumbling attempts to float on the wings of song.

However, he did not have to fumble long; poetry was where his talent lay; Jehuda was hardly more than a boy when he revealed all his brilliant poetic imagination. What was more natural than to send copies of his poems to Moses ibn Ezra, who was still living in Granada at the time? He was certainly the greatest literary authority of the day and himself one of Israel's most original poets.

The older poet accepted Jehuda's youthful efforts and was immediately impressed at finding such early maturity in a young lad. His answer to Jehuda in the form of a poem has been preserved. In it we read: 'How can a boy in his early years —bear such a weight of wisdom—all his peers are greybeards—but he is in the spring of youth'. This exchange of compliments rapidly led to a close friendship which lasted all the years until ibn Ezra's death.

Jehuda Halevi was quickly drawn into a friendly circle of an unusual nature. His day was right in the middle of the golden age of Jewish cultural life; throughout southern Spain Jewish personalities were prominent in all spheres of mental activity. Youthful literary circles grew up in every town. One thing about the circle Jehuda entered makes a definite impression on us; its complete lack of mutual jealousy and rivalry. When there is talk of young poets and writers, we automatically listen for echoes of dissension. It usually accompanies them. But here we find nothing but harmony and friendship; there is an atmosphere of fresh air over their feelings and communal life. They said fine things not only to but also about each other. They express their mutual friendship in such a directly naive manner that we begin to think of school-girls' poetry books of later times. 'I set up my tent in your heart', one passage reads, and when Jehuda is to go on a journey, the far older Moses ibn Ezra, who otherwise could not be suspected of sickly sentimental feelings: 'Our hearts were as one. When you leave, they are cut in two.'

THE THREE RINGS

In such a circle Jehuda could breathe freely; his harmonious pure hearted nature suited it. He must have had a talent for attracting, almost magnetizing people. He found friends everywhere; everyone fell for his charm. Here was the counterpart to Solomon ibn Gabirol of the earlier generation, that prickly poet with the awkward, querulous disposition which always found him enemies. Jehuda's nature was gay, affectionate, happy and easily enthused; this showed in his eyes and made everyone smile again. We see this in his own early poems and there are echoes of it in the many poems which were dedicated to him.

It was not long before he was a kind of court poet to the Jews in Andalusia. No feast was held, whatever type it might be, unless Jehuda's muse was there to celebrate it. When people met to enjoy themselves, ideas flashed and gave him inspiration. For example in the elegant riddles which had just become the fashion. Two of them have been preserved.

> What is it that is blind, but has one eye,
> which men cannot live without,
> because it devotes all its life to clothing others,
> but itself is always naked and bare?

The answer is: a needle. The other one runs:

> Lucky lovers, learn our law,
> be as united as one, like us,
> even if separated a time
> we always become one again.

A pair of scissors, of course.

Not long ago an anecdote of the time was unearthed by chance. Jehuda is involved in the story and it shows us a glimpse of life among the young intellectuals of that distant time. Jehuda's circle used to meet in one of the palaces in Granada, where they discussed the themes and problems of the day in friendly fashion. This is the story, word for word:

THE SONG BIRDS TUNE THEIR LYRES

'We sat one day talking about the Creator and praising his wisdom, when a young lady came into the salon who was exceptionally beautiful and dressed in very good taste into the bargain. We were quite speechless with admiration and thought that here was the perfect illustration of what we had just been discussing. But just as we were watching her lovely features, the lines of her face and mouth, her beautiful figure and proud carriage, a terrible thing happened. She said a few words to one of her companions, and we heard a deep grating, disagreeable voice and unpleasant language. Our faces fell, but Jehuda broke the spell when he immediately retorted:
'The charm was broken by the very mouth which shaped it!'

Naturally the immediacy of an anecdote vanishes when it happened so long ago, but it tells us something which most of us have experienced, and the quick answer and the whole atmosphere gives some idea of the mixture of gay innocent youth and easily awakened enthusiasm and piety which prevailed in the leading Jewish salons in Granada some nine hundred years ago.

Many of Halevi's youthful poems are based on Arabic models. This is true of both his riddles and his songs about wine and friendship, but not so when he sings of love and marriage. Then he is wholly himself, i.e. he is a Jew. We should remember how much time young Jews spent in the company of Moors. It was quite natural for them to shower exotic favours on any girl they met who had inflamed their senses. After all, Islam's heaven is a paradise, full of lovely houris.

The Jews were receptive to outside influences in many other fields. But on this point they were slow to imitate. It is always dangerous to generalize, but there really is some truth in the belief that it is Jewish to be faithful in love. In any case it is certain that Halevi only loved one woman in his life; one could accurately give his love poems the generic title, 'To the only one'.

But she also set mind and senses on fire; one can literally feel how he quivered with ecstasy over her. She it is who gets an ode like this:

> If you send me a greeting when I lie in the earth
> even the grave's cold air will feel sweet.
> Perhaps when I am dead I shall hear
> your skirt rustle and your footsteps over me.

Naturally the celebrated poet was invited to weddings and equally naturally he had to honour the newly-weds in a song. As many as twenty-three such songs have survived the long years which separate us from him. They are as alive today as when they were first sung. He knew the lovers' sweet longings, tension and uncertainty before they know that their love is reciprocated and their impatient waiting to be united quickly. But when he hymns these eternal themes an unexpected idea sometimes springs forth:

> Soon ye will be united,
> your longing finds its goal.
> O approach my people too,
> thou gentle time of redemption.

Or words like these:

'Could my race but have the fortune to enjoy the same sweet freedom!'

At first glance it seems odd that the poet mixes national sentiments with something so private and intimate as the love and marriage feast of two young people. But this is when Halevi plucks one of his harp's most sonorous strings; the one which rings with sorrow for Israel's destiny, the lost country and the homeless people's wanderings, sufferings and longing for Zion.

Already in his green and carefree youth Halevi was the typical Jew in this respect. He was certain that love and family life should not be cramped and isolate themselves inside four walls, locking the rest of the world out. On the contrary, love

THE SONG BIRDS TUNE THEIR LYRES

spreads its arms and shelters those who roam homelessly abroad. In the most genuine sense of the word these Spanish Jews were patriots. They had lost their country and did not own any of the land whose guests they were. Yet ideas flew across many countries to the scattered tribes of their own blood and became a prayer for the great liberation and journey home at the end of time.

Thus his youthful years slipped by, golden years full of development and ideas. His rich, harmonious character took shape. He was remarkably free of all sourness and narrowness; he shows no trace of affectation. Naturally he could be youthfully arrogant in the pursuit of his talents, which were so far above the usual mediocrity. There are occasions when he proudly lets others see his consciousness of his own worth, which with other less well equipped brains is merely an exhibition of vanity.

Nor do we lack examples of impatience with fools who were so slow and hard put to it to understand his work, and were obviously an irresistible temptation to a highly gifted man. This is an example:

> Look, my light pierces down into the gloomy darkness,
> I bring gems up from the black earth,
> not till then can the foolish see them.
> But tell me, shall I cast my pearls before swine?
> Shall raindrops fall from the skies
> on the dry land where as yet no fruit grows?

But it is only the mood of a moment, an impatient grumble. In reality no land was dry to his bright, optimistic temperament; he was one of those who sows his seed in the morning and does not withhold it in the evening, to use a Biblical expression.

But the time came when he had to face the stern reality of life. He returned to his native city of Toledo, where he practised as a doctor. There he found 'the only one' and married her. We know that he only had one child, a daughter, who in due course bore his only grandchild, a boy, who was

THE THREE RINGS

also called Jehuda Halevi. Most of the other traces of his adult years have vanished. Rumours have it that he left Toledo later and settled in Cordoba, where he remained until he set out on his last celebrated journey.

But even if details are lacking, we know about his life and ideas. One great event overshadowed everything else. When he was eleven years old the First Crusade started. We can easily imagine what an impression the conquest of Jerusalem made on a young lad of his sensitivity and temperament. He felt like the rightful heir who sees two more distant relatives fighting for the parental heritage he himself could not push his claim to.

Then came the terrible news of all the evils which struck Israel wherever the crusader's army appeared. Grief over these sufferings aroused Halevi's poetic impulse and raised his genius to the heights. He was enlightened enough to see that deep down neither of the two main contestants cared about the Jews:

> Accursed be both of them
> whether they conquer or are conquered
> it is always woe to Israel.

He was saying bluntly that Israel was between the devil and the deep blue sea.

'I live between the scorpion and the snake. Edom is master in my halls [the crusaders in the Holy Land]; Ishmael's arm stretches into the kingdom of Edom [the Moors in Spain].'

That was the national elegy, the mourning song, Halevi taught his people to sing.

Here we stand at the gateway to the world in which Jehuda Halevi created his greatest work, the religious poems which are the crowning achievement of his lyric verse. When we listen to them, we hear the same tones as once rang from David's harp in distant times; in them he towers far above any other Hebrew poet since Biblical days. He felt deeply attached to God:

THE SONG BIRDS TUNE THEIR LYRES

> He who serves time is a servant's servant,
> only he who serves God is free.
> When others seek their fortune in the world,
> my soul breaks out: my lot is the Lord!

There is genuine religious experience behind verses like these:

> When I depart from thee, Lord,
> I die, even though I live,
> but if I hold thee tight,
> I live, even though I die.
> I always sought to be near thee.
> My whole soul called to thee.
> When I went to seek thee,
> I met thee on the way to me.

In such turns of phrase we find the essence of Judaism expressed and they could well stand as Jehuda Halevi's profession of faith.

Naturally, he was so genuinely a Jew that he implanted religious life in the midst of practical everyday life. To tell the truth the Jewish religion is more concerned with actions than ideas; it has a practical emphasis, whose ideological consequences take second place. Therefore Judaism makes more demands on practical behaviour than on theory and dogmatism.

But only one side of Judaism is rooted in the everyday and the present. There is another side, which is needed to make the picture complete. The Jew sees signs; heaven arches over the lowly earth, the heaven from which deliverance comes in God's hour. So we can say that Judaism is both a discipline and a hope. The Bible itself contains both the law and the prophets; the Talmud has room for Halaka with its legal provisions, but Haggada, which contains the stories, legends and visions is equally important. The two sides do not clash; they are friends, completing and supplementing each other.

But just as men vary, they divide themselves into the same two groups. Some find most in the law, others in prophecy. Moses Maimonides was the great, icily clear legal teacher, but

THE THREE RINGS

for Jehuda Halevi it was the prophecies, the lofty promises of coming deliverance, which struck sparks from his poet's mind. From them sprang the inspiration which made him sing like the birds, effortlessly, indeed almost without his knowing it.

In stormy times longings increase. They may take a wrong turning and lead men astray. The great Rabbi Akiba made a fatal mistake when he proclaimed the Son of a Star the Messiah, something for which he and the whole Jewish people had to pay dearly. When the dark shadows of the Crusades fell on Israel, the dream of a Messiah awoke with new force. Pious Jews had long looked forward to the millennium before Jerusalem's destruction—but the Messiah did not come in 1070. Of course, false Messiahs appeared on all sides and Jehuda Halevi's mind was passionately stirred when rumours of them reached him.

His hopes were dashed; the Messiah did not come in Halevi's day. There was nothing but disappointment, but disappointments did not cast him down. Perhaps they bowed his faith to the earth, but they did not break it. Something quite different happened to him, in which he was once again typical of his people. When the Messiah did not come, his longing for redemption blended with his love for Jerusalem, the passionate emotion which increasingly overshadowed everything else in his mind.

Time after time he sang of the holy city and declared his love for it. He did so in the words of the time, like a minnesinger hymning the lady of his heart's desire. It was a time of strong emotions. The crusaders set forth to win foreign lands and knights fought for the colours of ladies they had scarcely seen. It was love for love's sake, with no hope of requital. The poets sang of it, while the people listened spellbound. This was the kind of love which overpowered Jehuda Halevi. He was the troubadour singing to his beloved and Jerusalem was the goal of his desire. This was the Jehuda Halevi depicted in his famous poem.

The poet's task is to express what lives in the minds of the people, what many feel but cannot find the right words for.

THE SONG BIRDS TUNE THEIR LYRES

Love for Jerusalem—perhaps we should use the stronger word, passion—had lived in the minds of millions of Jews for generations. People needed a symbol, something external to look to. Jerusalem was the ancient capital, the centre of a great past, but also the eternal reminder of the lost and hope for a new future. The Jews have always felt this; from Jerusalem springs one of the sources which give the people strength, but no one has sung of it as finely as Jehuda Halevi. It should have been the Biblical singer who uttered the immortal words: 'If I forget thee, Jerusalem, then may my right arm wither.'

Let us listen to one of Jehuda Halevi's declarations of love for Jerusalem:

> My heart dwells in the East, but I have to
> live in the far far West,
> how can I worry about everyday trivialities,
> how live according to the Lord's precepts
> when Zion is in the toils of Edom and I in
> Ishmael's fetters?
> All Spain's beauty is but emptiness
> compared with finding the dust of the fallen
> sanctuary.

This proved to be more than merely the fine language of a poet. His desire was too strong for him and gradually the great decision to go to the holy city ripened in his mind. Personal sorrows played a part. His wife died and his daughter had married so that he was alone in the house. At the same time he missed his friend Moses ibn Ezra, who died in 1139. Perhaps that was the year when he wrote his wryly smiling epigram:

> One day I discovered my first grey hair.
> When I pulled it out, it began to talk:
> Now you think you're rid of me,
> but I have ten fellows who will soon make
> fun of you!

Before he left, he finished his work. He wrote the book which is considered his philosophical masterpiece. It is called *Kusari* and gives a coherent statement of his philosophy of life.

THE THREE RINGS

The title is an unusual pronunciation of Chazars. In the book all the remarkable tales he had heard about the exiled south Russian princes in his youth in Toledo stir in Jehuda's imagination.

So Jehuda Halevi tells in his own way about the heathen kings who longed to find the one true God. He makes representatives of the great religions visit the king and champion their particular faith. The philosopher expounds Plato's and Aristotle's systems, while the Christian and the Mohammedan also put in an appearance.

Last of all comes the Jew. Actually the king had not even thought of talking with someone from that ignominious downtrodden nation. Their lowly station alone must be proof enough that they were the object of God's wrath, but both the Christian and the Saracen had continually referred to the holy scriptures as proof of the truth of their religion. Consequently it was unreasonable not to listen to the people who had produced the holy books and guarded them so long. So it came about that a certain Jew was given the opportunity to explain and defend his faith before the king.

He began quite differently from the others. To the king's great surprise he by-passed all the proofs of God's existence and explanations of his being which fitted God into ideological systems. In amazement the king asked why. The Jew asserted firmly and calmly that problems of God's existence and the creation of the world should not be elucidated in a speculative way.

Instead he went to work practically. In the course of a long series of conversations with the king the Jew went through the whole of Israel's history; he spoke of the temple and the sacrificial service; he passed on to the holy Hebrew language and the geography of Palestine. He explained the creation—like Solomon ibn Gabirol—with the help of the concept of emanation, radiations from the godhead. All his ideas and expositions ended in the same way: 'Among the peoples Israel is what the heart is to the limbs'. God's heart beat in Israel; everything depended on the chosen people. All its suffering would cleanse and cure it.

THE SONG BIRDS TUNE THEIR LYRES

We know the result of the conversations. The king was persuaded and adopted the Jewish faith. Finally, the Jew said farewell and prepared himself for the journey to the beloved land, the heart of all countries. The king sought to dissuade him from the dangerous journey, but he stuck to his decision. When he left, the king bade him goodbye and said:

'God be with you and make your journey a success. May he give you everything you need out of his grace and mercy. Go in peace!'

This wise Jew is Jehuda Halevi himself. When he had written the last line of his book, he too took his pilgrim's staff and headed for Jerusalem. We must remember that at that time it was a journey from one end of the world to the other and that the holy land was in the hands of the crusaders, who had exterminated the Jews to the last man. In addition there were the difficulties and dangers of the journey, both from storms and pirates. Everyone advised the aging man against plunging into such an adventure, but he merely answered:

'Shall a mere body of dust stop a soul which is borne on an eagle's wings?'

Jehuda Halevi passed through Spain's cities, bidding farewell to his many friends. Everywhere his fellow Jews honoured him and were proud that the celebrated poet dared to set forth on the journey they dearly wanted to make themselves.

A great peace came over him when he took ship for Alexandria. Some of his greatest and most beautiful poems were written on the journey. There is the famous poem about the storm. Mighty waves formed. He got up and stood by the ship's side, looking out over the turbulent sea. His description of the power of the forces of nature and mankind's insignificance in comparison is full of vivid and gripping images.

In Egypt the Jews received him with the same jubilant enthusiasm that his Spanish brothers had shown, but Jehuda Halevi's only thoughts were of travelling on; he was impatient to reach Jerusalem. As soon as a ship was available he went aboard and sailed to Tyre. Then he wandered over the mountains of Lebanon as far as Damascus. There he settled and

THE THREE RINGS

waited a favourable opportunity to cover the last little stretch separating him from his beloved Jerusalem.

From that moment history loses sight of him. The last thing we know is that in Damascus—on the threshold of the Holy Land—he wrote the most famous of all his poems, the Zionid, the great poem which expressed all his longing for the beloved city.

Did he actually reach Jerusalem? History is silent on this point, but when it is dumb, fable begins to speak. It relates that he reached a point where he could see the towers of Jerusalem. Quite overcome he fell on his knees and began to recite the Zionid. Finally, he bowed his head in the dust of the road, weeping and praying.

At that moment an Arabic warrior galloped up on his noble steed. When he saw the elderly dusty Jew in the dirt of the road he spitted him with his spear. Jehuda Halevi saw Jerusalem—and died.

It is comparatively unimportant whether the story is historically accurate or not. The myth it contains is true; it expresses the idea of how a man like Jehuda Halevi should die. He was a man nearing his home.

Heinrich Heine rightly epitomized his life in his famous poem: 'When his soul left heaven, the Creator kissed him. That kiss re-echoed in the poet's mind throughout his life and vibrated in all his songs.'

Abraham ibn Ezra (1092-1167) was the third of the great Jewish poets at the time of the Crusades. He was one of the conspicuous rather shocking personalities the masses can love and therefore enjoy talking about. Abraham ibn Ezra usually did the unexpected. His mind was extremely colourful and his life story out of the ordinary. Small wonder that he early became a fabulous figure about whom stories were woven. It is worthwhile listening when popular imagination writes about its favourites; it catches the significant aspects. This is one of many anecdotes.

THE SONG BIRDS TUNE THEIR LYRES

The great Jehuda Halevi was sitting in his study, working on a complicated acrostic, i.e. a poem in which the first letters in each line can be read downwards and form a separate word or sentence. That day Halevi was uninspired and only made slow progress. Finally he ground to a halt at the letter R. Tired and dejected he put down his pen and—fell asleep in his chair.

An unknown wanderer entered his study. He glanced at the manuscript, understood the situation immediately, took up the pen and inserted the missing line in the poem. Then he withdrew, sat in a dark corner of the study and waited.

When Halevi awoke shortly afterwards, anxious to continue the verse, he saw to his amazement that the knot was untied. Now comes the point of the story; the great poet jumped up excitedly, called in his wife, showed her what had happened and burst out:

'Either an angel from heaven has visited me, or—it is Abraham ibn Ezra?'

So it was the last of the great poets who entered the poet's home in this way and soon became a close friend. Naturally the stories go further and improve on the tale. They say that Abraham ibn Ezra married Jehuda Halevi's only daughter and so became a member of the family, but this is certainly wrong. Presumably there is little factual basis for the whole story, but nevertheless it hits the nail on the head. For it expresses the indisputable truth that as a master of form Abraham ibn Ezra was not inferior to Jehuda Halevi himself, even if he never matched the greatest of the Hebrew poets in integrity and high inspiration. Although he lived in a time which was rich in great men, he was still one of the most original and interesting products of that remarkable cultural epoch.

He was born in Toledo, Jehuda Halevi's town. His father's name was Meir; he was of the same stock as Moses ibn Ezra, but came from one of the poor branches of that aristocratic family. The son suffered for it. He married without adequate means to keep a family and had five children in rapid succession. Four of them died early and the fifth, a son, called Isaac, later caused his father bitter sorrow.

THE THREE RINGS

Abraham ibn Ezra was always rather short of money; he was a typical example of the academic proletariat. He was not brought up according to the sensible Jewish tradition that intellectuals should learn a profession so that they can earn their daily bread and thereby gain a measure of independence. Instead ibn Ezra had to tread the thorny path to various wealthy benefactors' doors, knock humbly and wait until his patron was in the mood to listen to him and condescendingly offer him charity.

Fortunately, Abraham ibn Ezra was a man who could appreciate the comedy which can illuminate such grotesque situations in spite of all their unpleasantness. We still smile with him today when he tells how he knocked on a rich man's door one morning and was told: 'I'm afraid you can't come in now. The master is just going out riding.'

When he came again in the evening, the servant said: 'I'm afraid you can't come in now; the master is changing his clothes.'

Then he describes how unlucky he is: 'The stars must have conspired against me; everything I turn my hand to fails. If I had tried to sell mourning clothes, no one would have died as long as I was alive. If I dealt in candles, the sun would not set until my dying day.'

Ibn Ezra had a many-sided talent; he studied the most widely varying sciences. He was philosopher, mathematician, astronomer, grammarian, as well as interpreter of the Bible and poet. They were not merely so many hobbies which he dabbled in now and then. He did important work in all these fields. He had a remarkable degree of strength and sparkling genius, but at the same time a complex discordant mind, which constantly oscillated between extremes. Two natures strove for mastery inside him; one day he was a devout simple believer, the next a cold critic. Now he was serious, almost remorseful and broken-hearted, but just as suddenly witty and bitingly sarcastic. One day he sang pious psalms in the synagogue, on another he immersed himself in mathematical problems.

Abraham ibn Ezra was also very much of a bird of passage;

THE SONG BIRDS TUNE THEIR LYRES

he spent the last half of his life travelling in foreign countries. He was in the East at the same time as Jehuda Halevi journeyed thither. His son Isaac had gone there and his father heard grievous news from him. In Baghdad, Isaac had struck up a close friendship with another young Jew, but he was converted to Islam and the young ibn Ezra followed suit. This caused his father agonizing grief; he wrote despairing poems, which he tore up, about 'the dead son' and finally travelled the long road to Baghdad to snatch him away from error.

He was unsuccessful. All his attempts to persuade Isaac failed, but for a long time ibn Ezra stayed in the East where there had always been plenty for a Jew to study. He returned to Europe full of new bitter experiences, but also full of multifarious impressions. He did not go back to his native land. From now on he always had his pilgrim's staff near at hand, travelling restlessly from place to place until he found peace in the grave. But wheverever he went he sowed his seed and had so much genius and stimulus to give others that his visits were remembered for centuries.

The Italian Jews lived well materially speaking, but they were very backward intellectually. When the celebrated Spanish scholar visited them, they felt honoured and received him hospitably. Wherever he appeared, young men hungry for knowledge flocked to him. He went to Salerno, Mantua and Lucca. Everywhere people asked him to settle down and stay, but restlessness was in his blood and he hastened on. His discourse in Provence made such a deep impression that it was still being talked and written about 150 years later. He went as far as London where the Jewish community listened to him with awe, but he could not strike roots there either. He made his way back to the south of France.

Now he was an old man, over seventy. Finally, his longing for Spain became too great for him. Abraham ibn Ezra set out on his last journey. He crossed the Pyrenees, but died in a small town in Navarre.

His life was apparently fortuitous and unplanned, but he did have definite goals. He felt that he had a mission. Wherever he appeared, he told his fellow Jews of the newly-awakened spiritual life among the Spanish Jews. It was his vocation to work as a travelling teacher in the land of Edom and dispense knowledge from his rich store. All over Europe there were Jewish communities living in isolation and their surviving culture was liable to wither and be forgotten. To them came the foreign teacher and expounded the holy Hebrew language with a clarity they had never known before. It was like a revelation when he told them about the results achieved by philologers in Cordoba.

In spite of his restless wandering he had an impressive literary output. His muse followed him faithfully on his journeys and he showered his songs around him. He was given the simple nickname Hashar, which means singer, and his admirers said that 'he strengthened Israel's hands with song and words of consolation'. His poetry was first and foremost didactic. In skilful verse he constructed dialogues between God and the poet, in which he struggled with the highest problems and dared to tackle the riddles on the borderline of human understanding.

The Bible was always in his knapsack. He never tired of studying it and one great work of interpretation after another flowed from his pen. Abraham ibn Ezra made his mark on the history of Biblical research. We would be quite justified in calling him the first critic of the Bible. In his very first book he dealt with the Song of Solomon and demonstrated its worldly character. It consisted of love songs and painted a beautiful picture of love's longings and delights, but no sooner had he reached this point than he stopped and carefully went back to the traditional reading of the book, according to which it symbolizes the relationship between God and his people.

This is the method he constantly uses. Unperturbed by the customary conceptions he intrepidly attacks the difficulties in the Biblical texts. With great acuity he discovers self-contradictions and problems. Then he stops sharp with a 'here is something we do not understand' or 'the intelligent man will be silent'. In Abraham ibn Ezra's methods we find a striking example of the eternal clash between tradition and criticism, and his split mind made the ideal battlefield.

Seldom has such a divided mind been seen. He never managed to find terra firma, but was cast helplessly hither and thither by the two perpetually warring mental currents of faith and knowledge. His heart was divided in two and did not grow together. That was the price he paid for absorbing widely differing elements in his education, but it also meant that he had a uniquely fertilizing effect on later generations. Many centuries afterwards his books sparked off Spinoza's mind and set him working, to name only the greatest example of his significance.

Abraham ibn Ezra was a pathfinder, he himself did not venture on the paths he discovered. He was content to point out the way to coming generations.

Later, lived yet another important poet, Jehuda Alharisi. Like Abraham ibn Ezra he was always on the move and travelled in many countries. He it was who wrote the epitaph on the Hispano-Jewish golden age in these somewhat flowery, but expressive words:

'Now that Solomon ibn Gabirol, who wore the royal crown of poetry, its prince Abraham ibn Ezra, its general Jehuda Halevi and its prophet Moses ibn Ezra are all dead, the founts of song have dried up; the glorious age is over and God's angel has vanished. Never again were there such singers, never were such songs sung. We only glean what they left behind; we follow in their footsteps, but we cannot overtake them. The ancients had flour without bran, we have only bran without flour.'

VIII

NO ONE LIKE MOSES

'FROM Moses to Moses there was no one like Moses'. That is the inscription on Rabbi Moses ben Maimon's grave in Tiberias on the shores of the Lake of Genesareth. No stronger words can be used by Jews about Jews, but Maimonides—as he is usually known by a Greek transcription of his Hebrew name—marked the high point and also the conclusion of the Jewish golden age in the Middle Ages. The people used to call him 'the second Moses'. When he was put on the same plane as the actual founder of Judaism it was naturally not because he happened to have the same name, nor because he was a great philosopher and scholar, but first and foremost because he became Judaism's spiritual reformer and organizer. Favourite children have many names and one of them—the one he is usually referred to among the Jewish people—is Rambam, a contraction of the first letters of Rabbi Moses ben Maimon.

He was born in Cordoba on Easter Eve, 4895, according to the Jewish calendar, which corresponds to A.D. 1135. His father, Rabbi Maimon, was a *dayan* as were his father, grandfather and great-grandfather before him, not to mention a long line of ancestors who had filled this important office. The word *dayan* comes from the same root as the Biblical *din*, which means judgment. We have met it before in *beth din*, the courthouse, but in post-Biblical language *dayan* means judge, the man who conducted the local court in a self-governing Jewish community and was responsible for its life being led in accordance with Jewish tradition.

NO ONE LIKE MOSES

As a young man his father had lived in Lucena and studied at the famous Jewish academy, where many great teachers had taught. He was a highly respected man, who pointed to his family tree with pride. It was, in fact, framed in gold; it went right back to the celebrated Rabbi Jehuda Hanassi in the second century A.D., the man who edited Mishna and was himself descended from King David. Rabbi Maimon's spiritual pedigree was equally brilliant. His teacher in his youth was called ibn Migash and he was one of the forty-eight bearers of the tradition which had been handed down from teacher to pupil, starting with Simeon the Righteous, the last survivor of the great Sanhedrin in Jerusalem when the city was conquered by the Romans in the year 70. It was a distinguished, self-confident man who became the father of Judaism's guiding light.

The story goes that in a dream Rabbi Maimon was told by God to marry the daughter of a butcher who lived on the outskirts of Cordoba. It was quite unheard of for a learned man who was also inheritor of the office of judge in proud Cordoba to marry a girl whose father had never studied. The wise men taught that it was worth offering one's all to win a learned man's daughter. How could a woman who had not been instructed in the Torah from childhood bring up her children properly? In spite of his misgivings, Rabbi Maimon accepted the divine command and brought the girl home, but he was worried about what kind of a son she would bear him. The time came and just as Rachel in the old, old days paid for the birth of Benjamin with her life, Rabbi Maimon's wife died giving birth to her first child. The boy she brought into the world was Moses ben Maimon.

The story goes on to say how Rabbi Maimon naturally tried to give his son the best possible education, but unfortunately the lad showed but little love for or interest in learning. His father was most distressed. Would the butcher's blood prove stronger than the long line of brilliant ancestors? He tried to speak to the lad's heart; he disciplined him severely, but to no avail. For days on end Moses hid in the women's section of the

THE THREE RINGS

synagogue—it was empty on weekdays—weeping and pouring out his heart to God. One day his father was particularly desperate about the lad's dislike of books; he lost his head and blurted out: 'You are only fit for the lower things of life!'

It was too much for Moses, who had inherited not only his mother's gentle nature, but also his father's pride. He left home and disappeared. His father searched for him everywhere, but he had vanished without trace.

A year later a young man stood up in Cordoba's biggest synagogue. He preached to the community with his face almost buried in his prayer stole. His sermon was so clear and beautiful, so full of intelligence and rare learning that all eyes were glued on the preacher; everyone felt that they had never heard its equal. When the preacher concluded, his prayer stole fell aside and his face was revealed. Rabbi Maimon recognized his lost son.

The story is a good one and its drama effective, but it obviously belongs to the world of legend. The works which Moses wrote in his early youth alone show that he had not wasted the years in idleness. Nor do we find in later life the least trace of tension between father and son; until his father's dying day Moses had the deepest respect and affection for him. Far more probably Moses had a happy, rich childhood in a cultivated home; he grew up as the fortunate heir to the great spiritual treasure created by Hispano-Jewish culture in those years.

The real drama hit both home and boy when he reached his fourteenth year. In 1148 Cordoba fell into the hands of the Almohades and both Jews and Christians were given the choice of 'death or Islam'. Rabbi Maimon had to leave house and home with the utmost haste and flee from the city where his family had lived for many generations.

Later in life the old Rabbi was asked why the story of Israel's departure from Egypt in the Book of Exodus is in the present tense when one would have expected the past to be used for a description of such distant events. He answered that just as the Jews in the old days left the land of bondage with heads held high, later generations preserved the same proud bearing, as when Pharaoh pursued them. Degradation and persecution should never cow them. And Rabbi Maimon and his family travelled through Spain like exiled princes. Andalusia was devastated, plundered and ravaged by fire; there was hardly a Jewish home left where they could find refuge; bandits lurked by the roadside. But nothing could break their pride; Maimonides later called this period 'a school for courage'.

Rabbi Maimon had another son, David, by his second wife; Moses taught his younger brother and loved him dearly: 'my greatest happiness was to see David' he affirmed later. Now the two brothers were fleeing. They found no friends in those troubled times, but at least they had each other.

However, tradition does tell of a friendship of a quite unique type. In the course of his flight Moses came to Almeria. In the house, where he hid, lived a young Arab of the same age, who also came from Cordoba. He was Averroës, later the most famous of all Arabic philosophers; the Almohades drove him out because of his liberal attitude to the Koran. But it was significant for later times' assessment of the two great men that people thought that they had met each other as quite young men and in dramatic circumstances at that.

Young Moses refused to be cowed; he pursued his studies unconcernedly during the flight. He always had the Torah and the Talmud in his knapsack and he was insatiable where knowledge was concerned. Nothing human was foreign to this extraordinary young man. He became absorbed in mathematics, natural science and astronomy; he was keenly interested in the study of the flora and fauna in the parts to which his flight led him; he was alive to everything new. He learnt people's customs, languages and dialects, and studied medicine intensively—in fact it was during these years that he studied to become a doctor. Seldom has anyone absorbed so much as Maimonides did under disturbed and dangerous conditions.

But he was most deeply impressed by Israel's sufferings and misfortunes, merely because they clung to their hereditary faith. Moses began to feel that his vocation was to strengthen Judaism's proud edifice, which now was threatened on all sides by superior forces. During these years spent on the move he had already begun to conceive the works which would later set their mark on Jewish life and thought.

In 1160 the family reached Fez in North Africa. The Almohades were also in power there, but a temporary hiding place offered itself to the refugee family. The city might have been made for concealment. Countless narrow alleyways formed labyrinths in which it was impossible to track a fugitive. The exteriors of the houses were inhospitable, tightly locked and barred; the people were equally cut off, taciturn and withdrawn. Men as well as women wore a veil over their faces. The house where Rabbi Maimon lived with his sons is still pointed out in Fez to this day. It is a fine old house, but what the visitor particularly notices are the windows. They are fitted with cup-shaped decorations and open upwards, the idea being to study the stars through them. Both old Maimon and his son were interested in astronomy. Here, too, they were more occupied with heaven than earth.

Dark shadows fell on North Africa's Jews. The Almohades were implacable in their demand that everyone must bow to Islam or lose his life. Many Jews were martyrs, but the great majority attempted the difficult art of keeping a foot in both camps. Publicly they professed their faith in Islam and assembled in the mosque on the one day in the week prescribed by the law, but in their hearts they adhered to their hereditary faith and honoured all the Jewish customs in their homes.

Judaism's burning problem was always: what shall we do when we are faced with the choice of death or denying our father's faith? From the days of Queen Esther and the evil Haman it runs like a bloody red thread through Israel's history and nowhere was the choice more difficult than in Spain when the Inquisition held sway. But it was already deadly earnest in Fez and the whole of North Africa in the year when Maimonides lived there. Consequently the majority sought a compromise, so that at least they saved their lives.

NO ONE LIKE MOSES

But these *anussim* (the word means not free, for they were slaves of a foreign faith) had to pay for it with bitter mental suffering and pangs of conscience. We do not know what happened to Rabbi Maimon and his family; presumably they succeeded in staying hidden and escaped the frightful choice. But Maimonides got to know the problem from the inside.

He needed all his knowledge. Some enthusiastic rabbis sent a pastoral letter to the communities in North Africa in which they emphasized the fact that any form of recognition of Islam was apostasy. No exceptions or excuses were valid, even if a man had a sword at his throat. Nor should anyone come and say that he professed Islam with his tongue, but was a Jew at heart. They were apostates, excommunicated. Naturally this merciless pastoral letter heightened the unfortunates' sufferings, but then Maimonides took the stage.

'Thus speaks Moses, son of Rabbi Maimon, the Spaniard'. They are the opening words of his book 'Missive about Apostasy'. The language is sharp and clear, instinct with a feeling for beauty; the thought brilliant and penetrating; the point of view irrefutable in its logic and arguments from Biblical premises. When a man recognizes a strange religion under threat of death claims Maimonides—he is only an apparent apostate, wearing a persona which is forced on him. True apostasy takes place in the mind and is a matter of conviction. Clearly it is a fault, a sin, to act like the *anussim*, but it is not a mortal sin which casts them out into eternal darkness. The over-zealous law-lovers, who wrote the pastoral letter, should know that they might easily be guilty of mortal sin, unintentionally and unconsciously. When they cut off the unfortunate *anussim* from Judaism's tree like withered branches, they gave grounds for their own apostasy.

Maimonides laid down that brothers who erred were still brothers. A Jew may sin, but he is still a Jew, all the more so because Islam is not idolatrous.

He was realistic enough to see that only the very few are heroes by nature, and that the instinct for self-preservation is something fundamental in mankind. So he attacked this immeasurably difficult problem from the point of view of humanity. In a highly practical way he advised his brothers to leave the country which oppressed their consciences and find a place which offered them freedom instead.

It needed personal courage to advance such ideas. The people were nervous and angry, and the zealous might easily misunderstand and distort Maimonides' standpoint. But from the very beginning he showed that he stuck to his opinions.

It was not long before he himself was forced to follow the advice he had given others. Naturally people paid attention to him; reports of his learning and talent spread to ever wider circles. At last the authorities also began to take an interest in him. One day an informer whispered in the ears of the police that he was a converted Mohammedan. That was the last straw; no crime could be greater. Recently a man had been condemned to death on the same grounds and executed with agonizing tortures.

Maimonides was told of the danger at the last moment and the family left Fez in haste. Travelling by night and hiding by day they reached the port of Ceuta. There they found a ship which was actually sailing to Palestine. They embarked and sailed away.

The coasts of North Africa and Spain disappeared behind them and dipped below the horizon. Moses never saw the country of his youth again, but—as he had put it himself in his missive—'the world is great and wide'. There must be room for him too somewhere or other.

The sea voyage lasted over a month. One sabbath, when the first quarter of the journey was over, a terrible storm broke and the ship nearly foundered. Maimonides was the only man on deck when the hurricane was raging its worst. Later he wrote, 'on that day I found no one on the sea but God'. And he was overcome by the feeling of security he had when there was only God to trust in. For the rest of his life he fasted annually on the days of his departure from Ceuta and the storm at sea; they were two days worthy of remembrance.

On May 16, 1165, the ship anchored in Acco's roads; the

sorely tried family had reached the land of their fathers. But Palestine was occupied by the Crusaders, and Acco was their supply base and headquarters.

Perhaps Maimonides had hoped to find refuge in the kingdom of Jerusalem, the first Christian State he had ever seen. In his view there was nothing to hinder a Jew from living in a Christian country. For the Christians recognized the Bible, which they had got from the Jews. And Maimonides was in favour of tolerance. 'God wants men's hearts; he judges them according to the disposition of their hearts,' he said, 'therefore our song says: the devout from all nations on earth have a share in the world to come, so long as they recognize as much of God as he has allotted to them.'

But it was not long before he realized that he was a stranger in his own country. He shuddered when he saw that the Christians worshipped images and revered relics, while intolerance and superstition had a free hand. Only a handful of Jews were hidden here and there; in all Jerusalem he found four families who had survived the rooting out.

The family left Acco and by long detours—they did not dare to use the main roads—they reached the Holy City. They prayed by the weeping wall and made their devotions at their forefathers' grave by the Hebron. Then they hastened on. By slow degrees they reached Egypt, where they found shelter in Cairo's old quarter, the so-called Fostat. There Maimonides remained for the rest of his days; at last he had found a permanent home.

The Jews sensed that Egypt was an island in the midst of the stormy sea. The crusaders harried their brothers in Europe; only ruins of Jewish life were left, while in Andalusia and North Africa the Almohades shattered their remaining communities. But the stormy waves of intolerance and persecution did not reach Egypt. Countless Jews had lived in Egypt since far distant times and under Mohammedan rule they had been permitted to breathe freely to some extent.

In Maimonides' day Egypt formed an important centre between East and West, and Saladin's victory over the crusaders increased its prestige. Several Jews reached high posts in the government; one even became vizier. Maimonides rose in esteem during the many years he was allowed to live and work in the Pharaoh's ancient land.

Yet the first years were a hard struggle. Great sorrows struck him. He had only lived in Egypt a couple of months when the old father fell sick and died, but he still had David, his favourite brother, and the two stuck together. Together they set up a business dealing in diamonds. The family had probably converted their fortune into diamonds before they left Spain. It was the Jews' normal practice when they were driven out into the unknown; diamonds were easy to transport and hide.

David bore the brunt of the business; he was constantly away on long journeys. Moses was able to stay at home and do his literary work in peace and quiet. 'David ran the business; I lived a carefree life', he said.

But one day disaster overcame him. News came that David's ship had sunk, that he had perished and that the whole stock of precious stones was lost. So the family's capital was destroyed and the friends who had put money into the business also lost everything. Bankruptcy was imminent.

The catastrophe broke Maimonides. Grief and worries put him in the sick bed. It took a year before he was on his feet again and began to build up a new existence. He could easily have earned his and his family's daily bread—he had married in the meantime—by working as a teacher of the Torah, but it was against his principles to 'use the Law as a spade'. Instead he set up as a doctor and practised medicine for the rest of his life. He was soon well known and sought after. The great Saladin made him his personal physician and Maimonides' fame rose to the heights. A flattering offer came from Palestine. 'The King of the Franks in Ascalon', that is to say, King Richard the Lion Heart of England, offered him the position of personal physician. Maimonides refused—but it is interesting to speculate how events would have developed if he had settled in London and not in Cairo for the rest of his life.

Naturally he was a hard-working, painstaking doctor; he

applied himself to everything he took up with the same scrupulous care. Once he wrote to one of his disciples: 'You know yourself how difficult the medical profession is for the man who is conscientious and accurate and only makes a definite diagnosis when it is supported by good reasons or by experience.' He could have used these words as an epigraph for all the other spheres in his life.

But first and foremost he was the great Jewish teacher and thinker. The Egyptian Jews looked up to him and gave him the title *Nagid*, in other words he was their spiritual head. Nor was it long before Jews in every country heard about him. In the midst of his arduous work as a doctor he found time and gathered his forces for the monumental books which were his real life's work, the books which became milestones in the spiritual history of Judaism.

From his early childhood it had been Maimonides' aim to use the Bible and the Talmud to expound and explain the great Jewish basic principles, faith and life, to his people and his time. He was barely thirteen years old when he began his task. During the years of wandering he carried the heavy volumes with him wherever he went and used every free moment to study and meditate. We only know these first works from fragments and indications in Maimonides' later books, but it is impressive to think of a lad so young setting himself such a goal.

All the more so when we hear of the great teacher who had tackled the task some generations before Maimonides' day. He was the famous Rabbi Isaac Alfassi, who ended up as teacher of the law at the academy in Lucena. He reached the great age of ninety, but he needed a long life. For Alfassi set himself the task of going through the whole of the massive Talmudic literature, from which he extracted all the individual provisions and systematized them. The result was the so-called 'Small Talmud', one of the most famous books of the day. In reality, it was a labour which was almost beyond the powers of a single man, but Isaac Alfassi completed it. And now along came young Moses ben Maimon wanting to do it all over again!

THE THREE RINGS

But in order to understand the scope and importance of this labour, we must take a brief look at that massive, boundless book, which goes under the general title of the Talmud.

The Law of Moses did not contain ordinances covering every eventuality, nor was it always applicable to the cultural situation of later ages. Therefore it had to be brought up to date and interpreted. We find hints of such an attempt in the New Testament, which speaks of 'the tradition of the ancients'; these were explanations handed down orally and therefore they supplemented the Law of Moses. Later as these ordinances and discussions were written down, the Talmud, which means instruction or study, came into being.

It took several centuries to finish the work, so a differentiation is made between separate parts of the Talmud. The first written work is called Mishna, which means repetition; before it was written, it was taught by rote, the pupils repeating section after section until it stuck in their memories. Later, Mishna was followed by Gemara, which means completion. Mishna and Gemara together form the Talmud. The Palestinian Talmud, i.e. the version which was redacted in the Holy Land, was completed at the beginning of the fifth century. The Babylonian Talmud followed a century later. Isaac Alfassi systematized the Babylonian, or later, Talmud in his book. Maimonides tackled the Palestinian Talmud.

In Maimonides' day Mishna was a vast muddle, overgrown with interpretations, and the text itself was both obscure and uncertain. Three years after his arrival in Egypt in 1168, Maimonides completed the enormous labour and produced his Mishna Commentary, the first of his three main works.

It was the first attempt to make Mishna accessible to ordinary people. He paved a way through the tangle the books were in; he brought system out of chaos; he analysed the countless ordinances and simplified them with his clear rational treatment.

Certain parts of this Mishna Commentary remained in force during the next 800 years after its appearance, some have expired since it saw the light of day. First and foremost the famous thirteen principles of faith which devout Jews always read after morning prayer. It recognizes: (1) that the divinity creates life; (2) that he is only one; (3) that he is incorporeal and unchangeable; (4) that he is eternal and above time; (5) that it is a duty to obey him; (6) that all the words of the prophets are true; (7) most particularly the revelation through Moses; (8) that it is a duty to believe in the Law; (9) that the Law can never be changed; (10) that God is omniscient; (11) that his retribution is just; (12) that the Messiah will come and, (13) the resurrection of the dead.

The Mishna Commentary was only a beginning. When Maimonides had finished with it, he took on an even greater task. We have seen that the Talmud, in the form it took in Maimonides' day, was an endless labyrinth, a network of intricate, interminable paths into which only bold spirits, skilled in mental acrobatics dared venture. Now Maimonides conceived the plan of making a whole out of all this confusion, an architectonically complete and thought-out edifice which could stand as the spiritual image of Judaism. He worked for many years and reached his goal in 1180. His second main work, Mishne Torah, which means repetition of the Law or 'The second Torah', was completed.

Here we get to know Maimonides' religious attitude better than in any other work. First and foremost the cool, clear intelligence which creates order and a general summary. If anyone wanted to count how many hours industrious Talmud readers spent in making out the problems in the mammoth work the Talmud had become, he would reach an astronomical figure. Maimonides wanted to save them this endless superfluous work. In Mishne Torah he puts everything in order, he unravels the tangled skein and presents the results, so that they can be read quite simply and rapidly. All the time so saved can be used for something much more useful and lofty, namely in studying philosophy.

Maimonides put clarity of thought before anything else; he is the typical rationalist, in that rational understanding stands immeasurably higher for him than the experiences men have through feeling and intuition. Therefore he uses a sharp knife and cuts deep into all traditional religious attitudes. He rids the idea of God of everything which smacks of worldly conceptions. He declares total war on what is known as anthropomorphism, which means that men try to comprehend God with the help of images from human life. All such things only coarsen and falsify religion, claims Maimonides. We see the results—to take but one example—in his teaching about life after death, where he depicts the state as wholly spiritual, cleansed of all conceptions of heaven and hell and the resurrection of the body.

In an appendix to the book he covers ethics. He takes the commandments in the Law as his starting point. According to the Jewish view the Torah consists of a total of 613 commandments. There are 248 'Thou shalt's', the number of bones in the human body, and 365 'Thou shalt not's', the number of days in the year. These 613 commandments are called roots or trunks and from them spring all other commandments and ordinances.

Mishne Torah is one of the clearest books in world literature. Maimonides devoted all his energies to expressing himself so clearly that no misunderstanding was possible. He had an unusual gift for writing concisely; there is no irrelevant chatter here, everything superfluous is mercilessly pruned; the story alone is there, clear and transparent.

'If I can write the whole Talmud in one chapter, I will not use two,' he said about it. Of course that was impossible. On the contrary he had to divide the book into fourteen parts, each grouped around an important theme. That gave rise to the name it had in the vernacular: 'The mighty hand.' At the end of Deuteronomy we are told that after Moses no prophet arose whom the Lord knew face to face and that Moses showed his mighty hand to his people. Now Israel had a match to the first Moses and 'The Second Torah' was his hand. Here we have a brief amusing insight into the play on words and speech current at the time. Hand is *jad* in Hebrew and the word has the value fourteen—but that is exactly the same total as the chapters of 'The Second Torah'! And this name tells us something about how highly the book was esteemed.

It could rightly be called Maimonides' masterpiece; it is a unique landmark in Judaism's spiritual heritage, a complete expression of its every side. Not for nothing does legend relate that the night after the book was finished, Maimonides dreamt that his father came into his room and that he could just glimpse someone else behind him. Old Maimon pointed to the stranger and said: 'That is our teacher Moses, the son of Abraham.'

Maimonides was afraid, but Moses only said: 'I have come to see what you have accomplished.'

Maimonides pointed to the thick pile of manuscript and Moses went on 'May your strength grow greater!'

Jewish merchants came to Egypt from all over the world. They heard about the new masterpiece, bought the book and took it home with them. In the course of a few years it made a triumphal progress through every country where there were Jewish communities; it became the best-seller of the day. Enthusiastic letters of congratulation and thanksgiving flowed in from distant lands. Maimonides was honoured and admired. 'The second Moses' and 'Light in exile' were some of the simpler titles with which enthusiastic readers adorned the famous author. The book was read and discussed; soon it became a kind of oracle, a new *urim* and *tummim*. No single man's word had had so much weight in Israel since time immemorial.

But critics lurked in the background and gradually they dared to venture forth. For there were points in the book which invited criticism. Maimonides had been self-confident enough on several occasions to advance his own ideas on his own responsibility, without basing them on established authorities, which was the normal practice. Surely the man who substituted his own work for the Talmud was dangerous. Did not new, almost free-thinking tendencies emerge in the book? There were men who whispered that he was 'untruthful' and 'a falsifier'. This was the first quick blast of the hurricane which was to break loose later. But not until after the next great book, in which Maimonides advanced ideas which split Judaism to its roots.

For he still had not finished his task. Before the structure he dreamed of erecting could be called complete, a third storey was still missing. He had taken ten years to write the commentary and ten years to write The Second Torah. Now he used the next ten years to meditate and write *More Nebukim*, 'The Guide for the Deluded', his philosophical masterpiece which had such disastrous consequences.

We get an impression of its train of thought from the image with which Maimonides begins the book. The king lives in his castle—he writes—and around him live the people, some far out in the country, others in the city which has grown up in the shadow of the castle. Many people in the city never give the king a thought or cast a glance at his castle. But there are some who would like to see the king and speak to him; they ask the way to the castle. They have not all progressed the same distance towards it; many have only gone far enough to be able to see the castle in the distance. Some have actually entered the castle, but even they have not reached the goal. They wander through the corridors and halls, looking for the door which leads to the throne-room, for only there can they see the king face to face.

Then follows the explanation. The king is obviously God and the image describes man on every possible different stage towards him. Maimonides pours scorn on those who do not even reach the city with the castle. They are people with no religion, inferior individuals, to be counted as animals. The people in the city are those who are nearer to God. Some of them have gone astray and taken the wrong road; they never look up at the castle. But the many who seek the path to the king have not all gone equally far. The ignorant masses who merely follow the law can also glimpse the castle. But they at least are on the right path. Nearer still are the learned who eagerly study the Talmud; they are on the threshold, but still not inside. Only the philosophers who use all their industry to know God have arrived inside the castle. Then they knock on many doors and seek the one which opens to God himself. Only the philosopher succeeds in seeing God face to face.

Obviously the great majority of devout Jews were shocked at this caste system. Just imagine that the wise and learned who studied the holy books all their lives were excluded from knowing God and that only philosophy, metaphysics, led right into His presence! But that was precisely Maimonides' opinion.

In a foreword he wrote that the book was not for the ordinary reader, nor for those who merely busied themselves studying the Torah and the Talmud. It was aimed at those who wanted to go further.

In its first version *More Nebukim* was written in Arabic; it was only translated into Hebrew later. Maimonides intended the book to put Judaism's cause to the intellectual world; it would be easy to say that it was meant as an apologium. But it was more than that. Its real purpose was to show the way to those Jews who were in doubt after discovering discrepancies between the literal word of the Law and the teaching of the philosophers.

For Maimonides any discrepancy between revealed truths and the results men arrived at by using their reason was inconceivable. Both stemmed from the same divine source. Like his boyhood friend, the great Arabic philosopher Averroës, Maimonides was steeped in Aristotle's philosophy. In reality he felt that there were two ways of throwing light on the ultimate riddles; religious revelation and Aristotle's philosophy, or as we would say today; faith and reason. All Maimonides' efforts were directed towards creating harmony between these two, reconciling them so that they could ring forth together.

The result was that he impregnated Judaism with philosophy in order to make it unassailable by rational doubt, while simultaneously he made philosophy Jewish, he 'judaized' it. The Bible and Aristotle merged to form a still greater unity. Naturally he did not escape compromise in his attempt. In this he was more inclined to make concessions to philosophy than to religion.

THE THREE RINGS

Maimonides was convinced that he knew the truth in so far as man is now capable of knowing the eternal. It was his aim to help others who had the same difficulties and doubts as those he had had to combat. To this end he concentrated all his massive intellectual powers. But naturally the book bore the mark of his personal characteristics and as a result had an unfortunate bias.

Once again we meet—as in the first books—his one-sided intellectual attitude and tendency to rationalize. Anyone reading him feels lifted to ice-cold heights, where there is light in plenty, but no warmth. The heart's emotions and longings move into the background in favour of clarity of thought.

But Maimonides was a Jew and he maintained strongly that the whole of philosophy was hidden in the Torah. He explained this circumstance in a quite characteristic way. When Moses was on Mount Sinai, the Lord gave him the written Law, but he also taught his friend the oral law. When he alone knew and used it to interpret the written Law, no doubts could ever arise nor could there be tension between heart and reason. Naturally Moses handed this knowledge down to his successors, but during the people's dispersal and vagrant life, it was lost and forgotten. Now Maimonides came and brought it out into the light of day again.

Maimonides was typical of his time. In the Middle Ages scholars dreamed of finding a *'filosofia perennis'*, an evergreen lasting conception of life. He wanted the truth established once and for all, completely and definitely. He also loved system, putting truth in a lucid form, so that it answered all questions. The great Christian schoolmen called their main work *Summa*, which means entirety. It is different for modern scholars and thinkers; they fumble their way, seeking and experimenting; they can take no original premise for granted. For the ancients, on the other hand, the world was ready, completed. It was created by God and came from His hand, and God had given His children the ability to comprehend it. Therefore the study of the world, both human and natural, was a gateway to religion.

NO ONE LIKE MOSES

'The Guide for the Deluded' joined the ranks of those great mediaeval folio volumes, which gave the answer to every question, following clear, concentrated, systematic trains of thought. It left its mark on both Arabic and Christian thinking.

The book caused dissension among the Jews. Many thinking Jews received it gratefully; it opened locked doors and showed them prospects they had never dreamt of. The poet Jehuda Alharisi spoke for many admirers when he expressed it like this: 'Many Jews have risen to the heights of reason. Only to Moses was it vouchsafed to reach God.'

But as already mentioned, alarm and criticism grew, and even in Maimonides' own day there were bitter battles over his ideas. He answered many attacks gently and calmly. The great storm did not break until after his death; then all Israel was visited by a divine tempest.

Maimonides was one of the great men. Notwithstanding the fact that he started with supreme abilities and powers. What did he not overcome? He was *Nagid* in Egypt, governing and administering all the Jewish inhabitants in the country. In addition he sat as Judge in Cairo with the numerous duties this high office entailed. In the middle of all these different tasks he wrote his majestic works. As his fame grew, the whole Jewish world gradually turned to him and asked the great scholar for advice on all kinds of problems. If a false Messiah appeared in the Yemen, he had to give his opinion. If news came of new persecutions in Morocco or philosophical discussions in Provence, he wrote letters with advice and guidance. And all the time he poured forth occasional writings and letters.

On top of that he was a doctor. In this sphere, too, he was pre-eminent. In the sixteenth century his medical text-books were still considered fundamental. A contemporary Mohammedan said jokingly that if the moon had consulted Maimonides, it would have been cured of its spots when it was full and never wane again. It is certainly a fact that if serious illness occurs in Cairo's Jewish quarter today, the sick person is taken to the synagogue which is traditionally associated with Maimonides, and left to sleep there for one or two nights.

THE THREE RINGS

We have one of his letters which gives an idea how busy his day was.

'I live in the old part of Cairo, the king lives in the new, two sabbath miles away. Every morning I have to visit the king. If he or one of his wives or children is ill, I cannot leave the court, but must stay there all day. Next I have to treat everyone connected with the court when they fall ill. But even on the days when nothing special happens, I don't get back home until late afternoon, tired and hungry. In the ante-room of my house a mass of people sits waiting for me, Mohammedans and Jews, noblemen and common people, judges and officials, friends and enemies, all impatient. I get off my ass, wash and ask the waiting crowd to excuse me because I must eat a little first before I talk to them. Then the sick come in, one by one. I examine them and give them prescriptions for the medicines to cure their troubles. People come in and out of my house until late in the evening. Often I stay up till one or two o'clock in the morning discussing learned matters; I lie on the bed, dead-tired, giving advice and instructions. On the Sabbath it is the custom of the members of the community to come to me after divine service for instructions for the rest of the week.'

Maimonides did not reach threescore and ten. At the beginning of 1204 he died, tired and full of days.

There was national mourning; the Mohammedans mourned as well as the Jews; everyone understood that a great man had departed. At the funeral, the text about the ark of the covenant coming back to Israel from the land of the Philistines was read. His corpse was embalmed and taken to the Holy Land. There it has rested for 750 years in Tiberias on the shores of the Lake of Genesareth.

Perhaps there is something symbolic about the great son of reason's lying in the same familiar soil as the ancient prophets.

In spite of everything that separated them, they were of the same blood.

Every generation has conservative minds who are on their

guard against new ideas. They will not tolerate any attempt to alter the established order of things and are afraid of saying old truths in a new way. It might mean a step away from what was once established and prove dangerous; perhaps the dearest of their possessions might disintegrate or be destroyed. There were wide circles in the Jewish world which saw Maimonides in this light. Indeed his books and ideas invited criticism; they were frankly rationalistic and differed from the customary attitudes on numerous points. Soon after his death the dispute was in full swing and stretched from one end of the Jewish world to the other.

Maimonides had many supporters who looked on his books as a new revelation, but his opponents were constantly increasing. They called him 'the Jewish Aristoteles' and claimed that he had degraded religion to the status of philosophy's handmaid. There had been large Jewish communities in Provence and the south of France since ancient times. In many ways they played an important role in both Jewish and European cultural development. 'Anti-Maimonism' had its headquarters among them.

The battle raged for many generations and grew more and more bitter. The opponents used strong words about each other; one congregation excommunicated the other and was excommunicated in its turn; anathemas crossed each other. But worse still was to come.

At the time a Catholic Inquisition, composed of Dominican monks, was busy seeking out the last remnants of the so-called Albigensian heresy, which had persisted in Provence. One of Maimonides' bitterest opponents was Rabbi Solomon of Montpellier. He had the desperate idea that in the existing situation he and the Christians shared common interests; by and large their goal was the same. So he took the unheard of step of going to the Dominicans and saying outright:

'You must know that in our city there are many heretics and godless men, who have been seduced by the teaching Moses propagates from Egypt; he is the author of depraved philosophical books. When you root out your own heretics, you ought to extirpate ours at the same time and burn their harmful books.'

He showed Maimonides' books to the Dominicans and the hair rose on their heads when they read them. Imagine if such ideas should spread from the Jews to the Christians! As they might easily do, for the book was translated into Latin.

So the Inquisition went into action. Jewish houses were ransacked, the shameless books confiscated and publicly burnt.

This event shook public opinion; both friends and enemies of Maimonides looked on it as the blackest treachery for Jews to deliver Jews to their bitterest enemies. Curses were heaped on the unfortunates' heads and things went ill with them. One of the conspiracy was accused of perjury in the course of court intrigues and had his tongue cut out. His accusers triumphantly quoted a passage from the Bible: 'Their mouths turned against heaven, now their tongues trail in the dust!'

Another, bitterly regretted what he had done. He threw himself on the floor of the synagogue and admitted:

'Maimonides was right; his teaching is true and we were the liars.'

Then he went from town to town repeating his admission. He had made a vow to travel to the Holy Land, weep on Maimonides' grave and beg for forgiveness. He was unable to keep his promise, for he died before he reached his journey's end.

IX

THE CABBALA

THREE wise men were on a journey: a Mohammedan, a Christian and a Jew. They did not travel together, for each one liked his own route best. But finally they met, for eventually their paths joined. Here they saw a beautiful noblewoman sitting on a horse which stood with lowered head drinking from a fountain; around the fountain were five remarkable trees; never had the three men seen such trees. They bowed low to the lady and asked her who she was. She said that she was called Wisdom. Then they asked her to tell them about the wonderful trees in whose shade they were standing and the lady revealed the trees' secret to them.

The first tree had twenty-one blossoms; the tree was God and the blossoms the virtues He had not given to the world. The second tree with forty-nine blossoms stood for the created virtues. The third also had forty-nine blossoms; they were the seven great virtues and the seven deadly sins. The virtues were stronger than the sins, but if they did not fight against them, they would wither away. The fourth tree and its twenty-one blossoms stood for the seven created virtues, which must be united if truth shall prevail. And the fifth tree had forty-nine blooms, which stood for seven more virtues and seven more sins.

It was Raymond Lull, the remarkable Christian mystic, who told this legend and it is typical of Spanish mysticism in many respects. Firstly in its imaginative imagery; trees and blossoms are like human beings, except that they stand on a higher plane. Plants rise above the earth so that they are a joy to see, but men bow down to the earth in their search for fleeting pleasures. Trees bring forth leaves, blossoms and fruit in the order they are created for; they do not reject the laws of nature as men do. Therefore trees and blossoms can symbolize heavenly things.

But it is equally significant that the three great religions met at the fountain of mysticism. They did so in fact, for in this domain too, Spain was the land of the three rings. The Middle Ages was always an epoch of mysticism, in the Church, Islam and Israel, but nowhere so much as in Spain, which was ever the home of the great mystics.

Certain longings were nascent in the minds of mediaeval Spaniards. A few centuries later they produced the typical romantic adventurer, the brave man, who felt compelled to sally forth in search of distant lands, to open the doors to unknown worlds. But it is worth remembering that long before the heroes of the great voyages of discovery lived, their fathers, who were also fearless visionaries, had risked themselves in the mystic realms of the invisible world and the soul's wonderland had opened to them.

The soil was ready for mysticism in Spanish Israel; it was ploughed and harrowed, so that the seed could fall on good earth. And the sower came.

Minds were hungry for spiritual nourishment which would be more satisfying than the sustenance they had previously been offered. The philosophers, above all, Maimonides, had made God distant and cold; they had sublimated Him to a concept which only superhumanly equipped rationalists could grasp at all. They forgot that men are not all reason; they have a heart as well, with its own longings and urges. They robbed religion of its mysterious magic; they put abstract ideas and concepts in the place of vivid images and tales, which appealed to the imagination and opened the door to a world of dreams.

But there was something else. It seems to be a law that the conditions for mysticism are especially favourable when a people is struck by a great national catastrophe. Even in the old days, during the centuries just before and after the beginning

THE CABBALA

of the Christian era, misfortunes befell the Jews. The Maccabees' fight for freedom, the strict regimentation of the Romans, the devastation of Jerusalem and the Son of a Star's desperate uprising, cut the ground from under their feet. But when men lost everything else, they turned to God in their despair. Longing for his miraculous help became so great that deep impulses for mystical communication with him were revealed. And this ecstatic aspiration formed the seedbed for mystical conceptions.

The craving for mysticism, which is inherent in mankind, is surely part of the mind. In peaceful, prosperous times it grows silently, in hiding, and only the select few cultivate it. We can find it in the Jewish mentality throughout the ages; mysticism is never forgotten, but it is the times of catastrophe which make it flare up. And when the bloody persecution of the Crusades and the Almohades began, the mystic mentality was active again.

The word Cabbala means handing down, tradition; it is not the title of a book, nor the name of a person or single group of men, but is used as a collective designation for all the mystical teaching which put forth such luxuriant, and to modern level-headed men, completely incomprehensible shoots in those ancient days.

The name alone implies that what appeared was nothing new. The Cabbala is indeed tinged with age-old Jewish conceptions, but it is curiously intermingled with material from the most varied fields, many of them quite foreign to the classical Jewish faith.

Anyone who ventures into the bizarre world of the Cabbala starts back involuntarily when he sees the hotch-potch of far-fetched visions and wild claims it contains. Any reader who dislikes prolonged mental effort or being drawn into strange and occasionally gruesome territory, and needs to wrap his sensitive nerves in cotton wool for fear of bad dreams, had better skip this chapter. But anyone who enjoys or has a leaning towards the esoteric is welcome to accompany me in my attempt to penetrate this primaeval forest. It will not be long before we see both beauty and a flash of genuine genius. However, we must remember that the Cabbala, like everything else, must be understood on its own premises. So we must adopt a balanced, tolerant attitude and put on the historian's spectacles, as it were, which are necessary if we are to tolerate the exaggerations and much which seems to make no real sense. And we shall take our time so that we can have a good look round.

But before we enter the wood, we must begin—as always when we visit a foreign country—by learning a little of the language the Cabbalists spoke, otherwise we shall get nothing out of the journey.

The Hebrew language consists solely of consonants, twenty-two in all. Naturally there are vowels as well, but originally they were spoken, not written. The context decides which vowels shall be used. Sometime between the sixth and eighth centuries a method of simplifying reading by including vowel signs in words was invented. It was the work of the so-called Masoretes; the men who were responsible for handing down the Hebrew texts in the Bible's holy books. These vowels, which can be helpful to beginners learning Hebrew, consist of dots and dashes placed above or below the consonants. Consequently they are not an original part of the language, and in the New Hebrew spoken in Israel today, the vowels have been removed once more. Anyone reading Israeli newspapers and books has to make do with consonants.

Naturally this peculiarity can give rise to difficulties and misunderstandings; the meaning of a word is obviously largely dependent on the vowels it contains. But this uncertainty just suited the Cabbalists; it made it easier for them in their mystic urge to find hidden ideas behind the most commonplace words.

One further piece of information. The old languages of antiquity had no special signs for figures. It is well-known that Roman numerals are only letters, which have fixed values. Hebrew made use of the same method; each individual letter signified not only a sound, but also a number. Sitting with a word in front of him, it was easy for a man to add up the numbers of the letters. The total was the number of the word. Here we come up against a prime rule of the Cabbala; every word is a number. And the next rule says the same thing in another way; given a number, it can be re-transcribed and become a word whose letters add up to the number.

This is the method which is applied to the famous word in the Book of Revelation:

'Let him that hath understanding count the number of the beast: for it is the number of a man; and his number is 666.'

The number 666 stands here for a name which men either did not know or should not name. But it can be reckoned, if men can discover the letters which add up to the famous number. The history of the church is rich in examples of the deluded visions to which this one instance alone gave rise.

But it is possible to go a step further. There is nothing to prevent quite different words having the same number. The Cabbalist is always on the look out for them. Then he can change one word for the other. Obviously the meaning becomes quite different, but the number is the same, so in a way, no change has taken place. Vast territories open up. Imagine what hidden meanings can lie behind words once one begins to build up from them in this way!

But what is the point of all this? The idea is to find the secrets which are not explicit, but are there, nevertheless, for the man who has the key and can unlock the words, especially the words in the holy scriptures.

Anyone can read the words in the Bible; they yield a direct meaning. But behind them lies a deeper meaning, the real one which is concealing itself from the profane. The writing is like a lovely girl who hides her beauty from the eyes of strangers and only gives permission to lift the veil from her face to him who genuinely loves and admires her. In the same way the curtain of symbols hides the mystery behind the words and only the man who is inspired by God's grace can see into the revelation's depths.

When Moses received the tables of the Law from God on

THE THREE RINGS

Mount Sinai, the Lord ordered him to proclaim the commandments to everyone, but he also whispered his secrets in Moses' ear and said: 'The first all men shall know, but these things shalt thou keep secret.'

So the mystery was only for the initiate; it was what we call esoteric. The only person to whom Moses entrusted God's teaching was Joshua. And Joshua whispered it to one of the next generation. The hidden teaching about the creation could only be entrusted to one man's ears. The secret knowledge of the calendar which will tell the hour of the Messiah's coming and the mystery surrounding God's unutterable name were things which could only be said in a whisper. But the initiated could find the secrets behind the words.

When such great matters were at stake, we can understand why the Cabbalists used all their ingenuity to develop methods of numeral and verbal mysticism. Words and numbers could be combined in many ways and every time new sensational results were obtained. Let us have a look at two of the systems most frequently used.

The first is *Gematria*. It works quite simply by substituting words with the same numerical value for each other. In the account of the three angels' visit to Abraham on the plains of Mamre in Genesis we find the words: 'and, lo, three men . . .'. The numerical value of these four words is 701. But if we add up the numbers in the names Michael, Gabriel and Raphael, we also get 701. Therefore those were the angels' names! It was a very important discovery for the Cabbalists. They were always searching for the angels' heavenly names and no effort was too great so long as they could discover them. And here were the names hidden behind four everyday words. One more example: the value of the letter *shin* (sh) is 300. But if we add up the numbers in *ruah elohim*, God's spirit, we also get 300. So the initiated merely had to say *shin*, when they meant God's spirit.

Then there is the *Notarikon* system. In this the letters of a word are extracted and each used as the first letter of another word. In this way a whole sentence grows from a single word.

THE CABBALA

The first sentence in the Bible opens: 'In the beginning'. If Notarikon is now applied to the word, for it is one word in Hebrew, the result is: 'In the beginning the Lord saw that Israel would accept the law'. The whole of Israel's relation to the Lord lay like a hidden prophecy in the Bible's very first word.

The systems were many and varied. And not only that, but the individual systems could be built up and combined in a variety of ways, resulting in complicated cryptograms to which only the initiated had the key, in other words, the very same methods used in modern warfare both for espionage reports and operational secrets.

But there is another aspect of 'the technique' in the Cabbala we must know before we can go further. It was one thing to discover the hidden meaning behind the Bible's words, another to interpret it. Here the Cabbalists had to hand a highly developed refined art, which the rabbis had been masters of for centuries.

They had four methods of interpreting the Bible. The first was called *Peshat*; it was purely linguistic and straightforward; the next, *Derash*, showed the way to the content and the edifying or legal use to which it could be put. Naturally neither of these two interested the Cabbalists, they were too simple. But the next two could be used. One was *Remes*, which means suggestion. As far as it was concerned, the Bible's word and its stories were merely symbols of a deeper reality. Here imagination could run riot when it tried to get behind the words. The last method was *Sod*, secrecy. Behind every word and letter, indeed behind the Bible's minutest sign lay secret depths. It was the real mystical interpretation.

Now we really come to the point. The Cabbalists took the initial letters of these four names and put them together so that a brand new Hebrew word resulted; PaRDeS, i.e. paradise or garden. Here we have one of the central concepts in cabbalistic mysticism. The man who steeped himself in mystical practices and contemplation forced his way behind the curtain of secrecy and went into the garden.

THE THREE RINGS

Armed with this knowledge we have some of the most elementary pre-requisites for following the mystics in their strange experiences.

There were two parts of the Bible which the mystics particularly loved to dwell on. They were the creation and the prophet Ezekiel's vision of the Lord, surrounded by cherubs or glowing winged creatures sitting on his chariot. Throughout all ages, from ancient days up to the Cabbalists this ecstatic vision remained a mystery to ponder over. It was given its special name, *Merkaba*, which means chariot, after the chariot the Lord rode in. Men had to be extremely careful about entrusting Merkaba's secrets to others, because they set heavenly forces in motion. There are countless descriptions of this. Here are two of the oldest, which never failed to fire people's imagination.

Rabbi Eleazar ben Arak was riding on a mule with the renowned Rabbi Johanan ben Zaccai and asked to be initiated into Merkaba. The great master tested him first and put one question after another. Finally he found him worthy. Then he dismounted and sat on a rock.

'Master, why have you dismounted?' asked the disciple.

'Can I remain sitting on my steed, when my narration of Merkaba causes God's majesty to dwell in us, and the angels descend?' was his answer.

And lo, straightway fire fell from heaven; there was such radiance among the trees that they began to sing songs of praise and an angel cried: 'In truth, here are Merkaba's secrets!'

Another time two of the masters' disciples were out walking and said to each other: 'Let us talk about Merkaba!'

Scarcely had they begun, when a rainbow arched up over heavy rain clouds and angels came and listened to what they said, like people on earth listening to a wedding march.

When Rabbi Johanan heard what had happened, he said: 'Blessed be the eyes that saw such things happen. Truly, I saw myself in your company in a dream. We sat among the chosen on Mount Sinai and I heard a voice from heaven which said: "Go into the assembly hall and be seated with thy disciples among the highest ranks of the chosen."'

THE CABBALA

Fairly obviously these are descriptions of ecstatic conditions, in which the images flashing into the mind are perceived as reality, for even the blind see them.

It was dangerous to participate in such experiences. One young man was consumed by the fire which leapt up. A man had to be of age to withstand initiation.

'I am not old enough,' said one, when he was invited to participate.

Initiates confined themselves to indications; they only said the first word in a sentence.

The man who heard about Merkaba went 'into the garden'. There he saw the seven heavens with the teeming angelic host and the divine throne above the highest heaven. But first the bold aspirants had to be put into an ecstatic state. This was done according to carefully worked out rituals, with washings, fasts, burning prayers and songs. He could not climb into the heavenly chariot which began his journey until he had undergone this hallucinatory preparation. The chariot whirled up and up until in a blinding flash he looked on the innermost secrets which were otherwise impenetrable and invisible.

But a thousand dangers threatened the Merkaba rider on his journey. He had to be armed and equipped with amulets and seals with mystic names, which protected him and helped him to return alive from the garden.

But the creation was—if possible—an even greater mystery than Merkaba. One of Israel's greatest books, *Sefer Yezirah*, which means the book of creation, coming into existence, deals with it. With the exception of the Bible and the Talmud, no Jewish book is read and studied so much. All kinds of thinkers are in its debt; they have drawn on it, commented on it and used it; we can trace its ideas down to the eighteenth century. And *Sefer Yezira* was one of the two great books to set their mark on the Cabbala.

It was old when the Cabbalists read it, but not so old as it laid claim to be. For it stated that it originated with Rabbi Akiba, who lived in the days of the Son of a Star. But it was not the celebrated Akiba who had written it. He had only

THE THREE RINGS

rescued it from oblivion. No, the author was no less a person than Moses! Such claims cannot be taken literally nowadays; underpinning a book's authority by pretending that its author is a famous man is an old trick.

It also contained unusual ideas, some of them taken from paganism. For example, it tells of two disciples of Jehuda ha-Nassi, Rabbi Haninah and Rabbi Hoshaiah, who dedicated themselves to mystical speculations about the creation of the world and created a three-year-old calf every Sabbath eve. They did not use magic; the miracle was performed with the aid of the letters of the all holiest's name, which is only known by the consonants JHWH.

Such cock and bull stories arose from the element of magic, presumably the Egyptian black art, which had insinuated itself into and infected the Jewish mentality. But behind them lay ideas of the mystical powers which presided at the world's creation and could always be brought back to life to help the magician in his convulsive urge to perform miracles. We must remember that we are dealing with an oriental mentality with a leaning towards violence and dark esoteric ideas.

It is difficult for modern readers to take *Sefer Yezira* seriously. And it is almost impossible to penetrate its obscure style and bring its complete lack of a coherent line of thought into logical order. But gradually we see some great visions and ideas stand out in the wilderness. They were the matrix for the Cabbala—or to put it another way, from these flickering flames, sparks ignited men's minds and lit a fire which gave them warmth and showed the way to an incomprehensible and mysterious world.

The book speculates about the mystery of the world's creation. The source of everything is the word; 'the word is God', says *Sefer Yezira* outright. But the word is made up of letters. If a man knows the law of the letters and the forces which lie behind them, all riddles can be solved.

So the book delves into words and letters. There are twenty-two letters in the alphabet and ten numerals. The Hebrew for number is *sefirah*, plural *sefirot*. Altogether there are thirty-two signs, all stemming from God, and each of them with its task assigned by him. The ten *sefirot* are the most important, for God used them when he made the world. The fully developed Cabbala built the idea of the creation and the ten *sefirot* up into a mighty system which we shall have the opportunity to study in more detail later. Here we pause at the letters, for they told the initiated about the created world in all its infinite variety.

The twenty-two letters were divided into three groups: 'the three mothers', 'the seven double ones' and 'the twelve single ones'. Notice that the numbers are three, seven and twelve, which have always had a secret significance.

The three mothers are the three basic elements in the construction of the world; fire, which strives upwards, water, which seeks the depths and air, which forms a barrier between them. The number three can be found in many places. The year has three seasons: summer, winter and the rainy season. Man consists of three parts: the head, the body and the limbs.

Then there are the seven double ones. They are double, because they contain the antithesis between good and evil. There are the seven planets, whose influence is both good and bad. There are also seven days in the week, and man's head has seven gateways, which are open to both good and evil: two eyes, two ears, two nostrils and the mouth.

The twelve single ones are found in the signs of the Zodiac, in the months of the year and in man's twelve functions through his hands, feet, kidneys, gall-bladder, bowels, stomach, liver, pancreas and spleen.

These indications will serve to show how *Sefer Yezira* gropes its way in an attempt to investigate nature. It tries to discover the order and unity in life and trace the divine wisdom, as it is expressed in existence's conformity to the law.

These mystical ideas grew in exiled Israel for thousands of years. But they were confined to small, narrow circles and guarded as deep secrets. The average man had the rabbis and the synagogue. There he listened to the traditional exposition of the Bible and the Talmud. Unless he was one of the few absorbed in philosophy's remote incomprehensible speculations.

THE THREE RINGS

But when bloodshed and oppression came, none of this held good. In any case it is a fact that around 1200 mysticism burst forth with almost explosive violence, and spread like a forest fire. Normally mysticism only addresses itself to the individual or is worshipped in closed assemblies or conventicles. Now it suddenly became a popular religious revival.

To many it came as a liberation. It was as if a light which had been extinguished for a thousand years had been re-lit. Or perhaps they felt like a tree which is knitted together again after being brutally split when the nation was thrown out of the ancient land so suddenly and found itself in a cold and hostile world. Now communications with the lofty minds of those old happy days were functioning again. The treasure the sons of Judaea had brought with them to their new home in Spain, which lay hidden in the Bible and the Talmud, revealed itself and was read in an entirely new way. And both national life and poetry received new stimuli and blossomed.

In the year 1305 a man called Moses of Leon died while he was on a journey to his home in Avila. He was a writer and had attracted attention by dealing in copies of a book everyone wanted to lay their hands on. He claimed that it dated from the olden days, but that he had been lucky enough to find it. It sold like hot cakes. When he died, a rich man visited his widow and offered her a high price for the original. She had to confess that it did not exist. Once she had asked her husband about it and he had admitted that he himself had written the book, but that it was best to claim one of the great men of olden times as its author so that it would have a readier sale.

So runs the story of the book which became the Cabbala's bible; it was called *Zohar*, which means radiance. The question of its origin is shrouded in darkness and no one knows what role Moses of Leon, who for that matter was a competent but not very important writer, played in its sudden appearance. Most probably it is not the work of a single man, but the accumulated literary expression of the mystical dreams and ideas of changing ages. It had probably wandered from one mystic circle to another by devious routes and received new contributions and references to current events. In any case it is certain that it came at an opportune moment and released the ideas which were stifled in so many men's minds. Very soon everyone was talking about it and it spread like wild-fire.

It claimed, then—like so many books—to be very old; its author was supposed to be the renowned teacher Simeon ben Johai from the days of the Son of a Star. His authority was well worth resting on.

Simeon ben Johai was one of the disciples of Rabbi Akiba. When the master died a martyr's death, the Romans went in search of his disciple, and Simeon fled together with his son into the wilderness east of the Lake of Genesareth, where they went underground. This should be taken quite literally; every morning the two men stripped naked and buried themselves in the sand. In this way they saved clothes, since new ones were unobtainable in the desert. But when the hours for prayer came, they dressed again, covered their heads and said their prayers. They slept in a cave and drew water from a spring. Nearby was a tree with locust beans, which gave them a meagre supply of food.

Here they lived for many years. Simeon followed in the Master's footsteps and practised mystical exercises; he experienced ecstasy's boundless peace and disappeared into the invisible world.

Finally the hour of deliverance came. Simeon was given a sign. One day he saw a bird-catcher trap a bird in a net. The bird fought desperately to get free, but in vain. A mighty cry came from heaven: 'Caught!' But a moment later the bird escaped and swept up to heaven. Again the mysterious voice cried: 'Free!'

Simeon took this as a sign from heaven and he set off homewards with his son. Sure enough, when they finally met people again, they learnt that the Roman emperor who had driven him out was dead. To the end of his days Simeon ben Johai lived as a respected teacher in Tiberias, where he founded a school for mystics.

It was this legendary teacher who figured as the author of the *Zohar*. The framework of the book is the revelations he entrusted to his disciples. In true mystical style, it falls into two parts; the more general revelations, which formed 'the large holy collection', *Idra Rabba Kaddisha*, and the secret things, which were reserved for *Idra Zuta Kaddisha*, 'the small holy collection'.

Here the Cabbala unfolds in all its richness. It is like a blinding light which falls on, or rather floodlights all problems. Remarkable colours flare up and are extinguished again, profound beautiful words of truth, highly audacious images and comparisons, a fast flowing train of thought and wild confusion are jumbled together. No one can read this stimulating book and remain unmoved.

On the purely formal level the *Zohar* is an exegesis of the five Books of Moses. It is written in Hebrew, but large parts are in the Aramaic dialect, and the language changes with calculating subtlety so that the book's poetic strength gains thereby. This is the book which tells us about Jewish mysticism when it was at its zenith in the Middle Ages; in the *Zohar* all the different mystical trends converge and come into focus. We must be content with a few glimpses of the colourful world which radiates from the *Zohar* and choose one or two basic themes, its speculation about the creation and Israel's situation in the world picture.

Naturally everything has its origin in God and He is the distant one passing comprehension. No human idea or conception can give the remotest picture of God and words cannot express His being. He is 'En-sof', the Hebrew word the *Zohar* constantly uses for God, which means that He is without end. Nevertheless the *Zohar* tackles the impossible task of explaining why the finite world was created by an infinite God. In bold graphic images the book expounds the drama of the creation as emanations, radiations from En-sof. We remember that Solomon ibn Gabirol seized on the same solution when he was speculating about the mystery of the creation.

Now we shall need our knowledge of the Cabbalists' concept

of numbers, the ten *Sefirot*. They are not dead figures, but living beings; supernatural powers are concealed in them. It is not so extraordinary that the numbers contain mysteries, for God used them when the world was made! The infinite God radiated through the numbers and the world came into being. Each one of the ten *Sefirot* hid one side of God's being and was given a name which symbolized its function. Here is the whole story:

God's radiant light was concentrated in the first of the ten *Sefirot*, called *Keter*, the crown. *Keter* was so near God that it was beyond human comprehension, but with it the process of creation began. The next *Sefirot* radiated from *Keter*. That was the remarkable thing about them; they followed two by two and were male and female. It stated clearly in the account of the creation in Genesis that God created mankind as man and woman. Did not that mean that both sexes were in God? If so then the radiations from him must also come in pairs.

The next two *Sefirot*, which radiated from *Keter*, were called *Chokma* and *Bina*, male wisdom or strength and female understanding. From them in turn radiated *Chesed*, grace, and *Gebura*, might. The two were held in equilibrium by the seventh *Sefira*, *Tiferet*, beauty or tenderness. The essential part of the creation was completed with these six *Sefirot*. This tallies with Genesis, where it says that God created the world in six days. And the first word in the Bible, *bereshit*, in the beginning, can also be interpreted as 'He created six' if the right systems of numbers and letters are applied.

Now the emanations moved over into the earthly sphere. With *Nesach*, solidity, and *Hod*, glory, they continued to *Jesod*, foundation, and finally the last *Sefira* shone out, *Malhut*, the kingdom, which made up the total of the work of creation.

The Cabbalists had all this fantastic system constantly in view. Literally so, for they drew it in their books in the form of a man or a tree, with the different *Sefirot* coming down from above, from the head or treetop, and descending to the feet or roots.

Obviously this is only a general summary of the Cabbala's teaching on emanation; actually it was embellished with numerous details. But the main thing is that this world is a reflection of God, projected from Him and bearing His stamp. Through the ten *Sefirot* the world is in mystical communication with God; they are like channels between heaven and earth.

The human soul came down from above. Therefore it aspires to ascend and be united with God again. The path is via mystical exercises. The questing soul goes upwards step by step until in the last ecstatic stage it reaches 'understanding through love', where the Torah reveals its innermost secrets in a glowing vision.

But a man had to observe many rules in order to reach this ultimate stage. He had to sit motionless, with his hands between his knees, while he mumbled prayers and psalms. The mystic climbed up seven steps, each with its own colour, until he reached the seventh, which was colourless. There he lost consciousness. Simeon ben Johai describes it as follows:

'Once I went into ecstasy and saw a sublime ray of light which fell on 325 circles; in the midst of them something black was bathed. Then the dark point began to move towards the deepest place in the sea of light, where gradually all the brilliance concentrated. When I asked what this vision meant, I learnt that it was the forgiveness of sins.'

But the soul which does not strive upwards must remain on earth for ever. When its body grows old and dies, it gets a new body, later perhaps another and so on eternally until it finally proves worthy to return to heaven. That is the Cabbala's teaching of metempsychosis, also known as *gilgul*.

But there are a great deal of sinister aspects as well. For example, during the creation some sparks and remnants escaped and flew out into space. These *skaller* or *klippot* travel round and settle wherever they find room, in men, plants and stones, and animate their new abode. They are homeless beings or demons and the whole world is full of these terrifying creatures, from whom stem all evil, misfortune and disease.

However, the worst evil in the world is sin. When God created the world, everything was good; the upper and lower

THE CABBALA

world, God and man, were in harmony with each other. But the concord was broken with Adam's fall and a gap opened between God and man. And man who was created as a spiritual being to be in eternal communion with his creator was driven out of *pardes*, the Garden of Eden and now lives in exile, or *galut*.

But God did not forget His men and women; a part of Him, His *shekina*, or reflection, is still here. As our first mother Eve followed her child into exile, the *shekina* is here to share man's condition. It was the *shekina*, in the form of the pillar of cloud and the pillar of fire, which showed Israel the way in the wilderness. It stayed with Israel in good days and bad days, and accompanied them when they were driven from their country. As Rachel wept over her child, the *shekina* sorrows over Israel's degradation.

Israel lives in exile in the literal sense of the word, but in a figurative sense so does the whole world, since it is separated from God. Israel alone has the key enabling the world to return, for they have the Torah and consequently know the way to deliverance. If Israel gave up the Torah, the *shekina* would withdraw and God would hand the world over to perdition. But the more intensely Israel studies the Torah, the nearer is the salvation not only of Israel, but also of the whole world. Some day the hour of rehabilitation will strike, and then complete unity and harmony between God and the world will be realized again.

It depends on Israel. That is why the Cabbalists applied all their willpower to coming closer to God. Both their own and the whole world's destinies depended upon them.

Such is the system of the *Zohar* in very broad outlines. Naturally these sophistical fantastic speculations were coarsened and popularized when they emerged among the masses. The sublime part of the visions was cut out and gradually the Cabbala became a practical guide to living for the masses. It gave prescriptions and rules for daily life, laid down certain colours for clothing, recommended particular prayers and formulae as especially effective and taught names which had supernatural power.

THE THREE RINGS

As time went by, the Cabbalists devoted themselves to the study of nature in order to extract the secrets they could use. They turned to alchemy and astrology, and finally to occultism, sorcery and magic. The Cabbalists sold amulets and were masters of the black art.

So far did the movement, which began as a spiritual revival, degenerate, that we now know the word cabal as an expression for intrigues and plots, primarily the manipulation of human destinies, but also of—playing cards.

But before we let the Cabbala fade into the mist, we shall draw a portrait of one of the movement's most characteristic figures, an inspired enthusiast, who had absolutely no inhibitions, a dreamer, who was something of a prophet, but believed that he was the Messiah. For often a living man tells us more about a great movement—both good and evil—than a long theoretical explanation.

Abraham Abulafia lived a short, but stormy and eventful life in the last half of the twelfth century. He was born in Saragossa, but grew up in Navarre, where his father saw to it that he had a comprehensive education. The name Abulafia means father of health; the family was large and famous, and it still exists in Mediterranean countries.

Abraham's father died when he was an eighteen-year-old lad. That cut the last tie binding him to a settled existence. From then on he led a roaming life.

Significantly enough his first journey was to the Holy Land. His lively imagination dreamed of the fabulous river Sambation, behind which, according to legend, dwelt the ten lost tribes of Israel's people. Abulafia wanted to find the river and establish communications with his forgotten vanished brothers.

He only got as far as Acco. The country was devastated after the Crusades and conditions were so unsettled that it was impossible for a Jew, at least, to travel in Palestine. He returned to Europe. He lived for a time in Capua, where he eagerly studied Maimonides' 'Guide for the Deluded'. Abulafia always held the great philosopher in great esteem, but Maimonides could not slake the thirst in his heart.

THE CABBALA

He moved on and came home to Spain. In Barcelona he met the Cabbalists, and with that his fate was sealed. Here was everything he was looking for. *Sefer Yezira* made the deepest impression on him. In his agitated state he fell into ecstasy and saw visions: 'I saw strange pictures in my imagination and my thoughts were confused, for there was no one to show me the way; I felt like a blind man groping his way in broad daylight. An evil spirit pursued me and I nearly lost my reason.'

In his excited condition Abulafia read all the Cabbalistic books he could lay hands on. Gradually the light dawned on him and he constructed his own system. Every sign in the Bible, letters, numbers, dots, even the least little stroke was alive to him; they were symbols of divine reality. They hid secrets; the pulse of life itself beat in them. He worked on them night and day, changed them round, tried new combinations and sought to penetrate God's incomprehensible being. He mortified himself, underwent ritual procedures of a mystical nature, but mainly he pondered on the four holy letters in God's name, JHWH, or tetragrammaton, as it was called. Gradually he felt that he was filled with an invisible force; he worked miracles, frightening powers stirred in him and to his astonishment Abulafia realized that he was on the way to becoming a magician.

An inner voice told Albulafia to go to Italy. He was to convert the Pope, Nicholas III, to Judaism! He had long been preoccupied by the relationship between Judaism and Christendom. The Cabbala set him on the track. The first time he heard of the creation and the ten *Sefirot*, he was angry. Belief in such things might be the first step on a dangerous road. It might easily obscure people's belief in God's unity, which is the most firmly established axiom of all for a Jew. He mocked the Cabbalists and said: 'The Christians make God a trinity, but you make him tenfold!'

But gradually, as he penetrated deeper into the Cabbala, he realized that this similarity could be used. The Christians must realize that the trinity was hidden in the Cabbala. So he set himself the goal of turning the Pope into a Jew.

THE THREE RINGS

Things did not go at all according to plan; the audacious venture nearly cost the exalted visionary his life. The papal court made its preparations. When Abulafia set foot on Italian soil he was arrested and taken to Rome. The scaffold was already built, but the night before the execution, the Pope had an attack of apoplexy, and the execution was deferred. In this extraordinary way the Jewish enthusiast was forgotten, and after twenty-eight days in prison he became a free man.

The next stop in his stormy career was Sicily. There Abulafia reached the zenith of his career. He proclaimed himself the Messiah! God had revealed to him 'the end of exile and Israel's deliverance'. It was to take place in 1290, only six years away. Gullible souls acclaimed him.

But now the Jewish authorities took a hand. Letters of warning poured in from great teachers and Abulafia had to take the road again. This time he hid himself in a little island near Malta; he was so compromised that he had to find an out-of-the-way refuge. There we lose track of him; we only know that he died in 1291.

Abulafia was a most unusual man. Few had his gift for enthusiasm and enthusing others; he literally infected them. And it was he who gave the Cabbala its visionary stamp. Nor was he like the venal candidates for the post of Messiah. They were often more or less conscious swindlers or psychopaths. Actually it was remarkable that he had an appeal for the many; he was by no means a man of the masses, but addressed himself to the few, mainly intellectuals.

And he tried to bridge the gap with the church. Behind the bizarreness of his clumsy attempt to convert the pope lay a genuine longing for fellowship which would reach across the gulf created by the difference in creeds. There were many people like him in all three religions in those days; lonely men met in longing for fellowship; more people came together through mysticism than were separated by it.

The time came when the church discovered the Cabbala. The great humanists of the Reformation were struck by the Cabbala's writings and studied them avidly. Through them

THE CABBALA

many of the Cabbala's mystical ideas penetrated Christian circles. But that has no place in this history.

So we leave the Cabbala, but let us pause for a moment and listen to one of Abulafia's poems. In its imagination and ecstasy it gives a glimpse of the beauty and power inherent in the Cabbala in its great age.

> Praised be his name,
> increased in beauty his might,
> praised in snow-clad peaks,
> praised in streams of flames,
> praised in clouds of honour,
> praised in radiant palaces!
> Praised be he who rides above the heavens,
> raised by myriads and legions
> with the mystery which hides itself in flames!
> Praised be the thunder's voice,
> praised by the lightning flash!
> Jordan utters praise,
> the deep utters praise,
> the waves of the deep thunder his praise,
> praised by the One,
> the one man on the throne,
> by every soul,
> by all creatures
> into eternity's eternity!

X

THUNDER IN THE NORTH

THE Catholic church counts Innocent III as the greatest of all its popes. When the thrilling papal election of 1198 was concluded, it turned out that he, the youngest candidate, had been elected. Some shook their heads because of his youth, but the cardinals who had voted for him, waited to 'find the cup in Benjamin's sack'.

It was there too. In the very short span allotted to him—he died in 1216—he raised the church's might higher than ever before or since. This restless, active man, who was equipped with an iron will and a uniquely acute intelligence, was perpetually at work. He smashed self-willed kings, he poured out excommunications and finally Europe bowed to Rome.

The times were dangerous for the church. In the south of France the Albigensian heresy had seized nearly the whole population and it was supported by powerful princes. The Pope called for a Crusade against them. Scarcely had the summons gone forth when the same scenes took place as at the first Crusade. Warriors flocked from all countries in Europe, either to fight for the faith, or seek adventure and win booty. This 'internal Crusade', as it was called, developed into a veritable war of extermination, which ravaged the smiling towns of southern France. Thousands of men were massacred and the land was turned into a wilderness.

We have already heard of the flourishing Jewish life in Provence, one of the great cultural centres, where the treasures of antiquity hibernated, until Europe was ripe enough to

THUNDER IN THE NORTH

appreciate them. The church suspected the Jews of being accessories to the heresy, and not without reason. The movements for Christian reform, forerunners of the Lutheran reformation, undoubtedly received instigation from Judaism. The mere existence of men, who refused to accept the church's central dogmas, were an invitation to doubt and gave a boost to free thinking. The Crusade crushed the Jewish communities in Provence during indescribable scenes.

The great Pope's policy as regards the Jews is the blackest point in his life. After the great Crusade the Jews in Western and Central Europe lived in permanent insecurity, but with Innocent III the great period of darkness began for Israel.

'Thy word is God's word, but thy deeds are the devil's deeds!' This was the greeting a bold Roman dared to shout at the Pope. And with reference to Innocent III's treatment of the Jews what he said was true. He was the first Pope who not only refused to protect them, but actually persecuted them.

In his first letter about the Jews, he confirmed all his predecessor's severe measures against them. Admittedly he added: 'Although the Jews' false belief cannot be suspected enough, they must not be suppressed excessively when they are living witnesses to the true faith.' But his hostile attitude was soon revealed. 'The Jews' doors stand open to criminals and they mock the Christians for believing in a crucified peasant.' Therefore, like the fratricide Cain, they are doomed to wander over the earth as vagabonds and exiles, and hide their faces in shame.

The peak was reached at the famous Fourth Lateran Council in 1215, the meeting which has kept a permanent place in history, because it confirmed the Catholic doctrine of transubstantiation in the sacrament of communion. The Council introduced the badge of Jewry. All Jews over thirteen, both male and female, had to wear a visible badge on their clothing showing their fellow-citizens that they belonged to the despised people. Usually the badge was a circle several inches across, of yellow felt or cloth, sewn on to the clothing on the chest or back. In other words, it was shaped like a coin and may have

THE THREE RINGS

symbolized the thirty pieces of silver Judas received for betraying Our Saviour. Or perhaps it resembled the sacred host. The Jew refused to participate in the communion, now he was forced to wear its image next to his heart! In England the badge took the form of two tablets. In some places the Jew had to wear a special hat in addition; it was red and had a high pointed crown, or else it had two horns on top.

Anyone not wearing the badge was subject to severe penalties; the mildest was for the informer to be given the clothes from which the Jew had dared to remove the badge.

Once the avalanche was under way, it gathered momentum. In Crete Jewish houses had to be marked; it was the custom to stone the Jews at Easter time; they were forbidden access to the public baths except on the day when they were reserved for prostitutes. In Cretan towns, the Jews were forced to act as hangmen; the gallows was set up in the Jewish cemetery—and so on and so on in an endless succession of evil inventiveness.

The justification for the badge of Jewry was that the Church wanted to prevent mixed marriages or loose sexual relations between Jews and Christians. Obviously a badge could not stop two people falling in love, but it was supposed to serve as a warning to the Christian lover, so that he or she knew who their partner was. As times grew worse the authorities acted far more severely; the penalty for intermarriage was death.

But the real intention of the badge of Jewry goes much further. It was the mark of Cain, which was branded on the Jew's forehead. He belonged to a pariah caste and was cut off from the society of other men; he was degraded to solitude and contempt; everyone could recognize him and spit on him.

The Jews had long been isolated; they were not allowed to practise several callings. But now isolation entered its decisive phase, which three hundred years later led to the ghetto,[1] once again on papal initiative.

---

[1] The origin of the word *ghetto* is unknown. Most probably it comes from the Italian *geto*, iron-foundry. The first ghetto was set up in Venice in 1516 near a cannon factory. There is also a possibility that it is simply the ending of another Italian word *borgetto*, a diminutive of *borgo*, town.

But the Lateran Synod was not content with the badge of Jewry. Several of the old Visigothic measures affecting the Jews were refurbished and put into force again. The council stated most emphatically that Jews must not hold public office. And during Easter week they were forbidden to appear in the streets, so that they could not revile Christ crucified. A completely new regulation was that Jews had to pay a tenth of their property to the church and measures were also promulgated to protect Christian borrowers from Jewish creditors.

Two great institutions became permanent after the Crusade in southern France and the important synod, and both had fateful influences on the destiny of the Jews. They were the Dominican order and the Inquisition.

The new monastic order was called after its founder, Domingo. The monks were to be preaching brothers; the whole world was their parish and soon in their black cowls they ranged far and wide in every land where heresy or different faiths persisted. They were known as the watchdogs of the church and popular wit turned the name Dominican into *'domini canes'*, the hounds of the Lord.

They lived up to their name; the order, driven by a most militant spirit, became one of the church's mightiest organizations. Its main centre was the house of Saint James in Paris and a chapter general governed its machinery, which had wide ramifications.

These mendicant friars were free of all earthly ties, so that they could go to work implacably. At first they concentrated primarily on heretics, but later, as the latter were rooted out, they turned their artillery on to the Jews. Many compulsory converts had slipped back into their old faith, and the Dominicans were constantly on the watch for imaginary or genuine attempts by the Jews to win proselytes.

Their foremost instrument in the hunt for heretics or Jews was the Inquisition. The word means investigation and originally it was a sort of court of enquiry which handled cases of heresy. Even during its early days in the south of France the Inquisition was known for its harsh methods. It used informers

THE THREE RINGS

and accepted anonymous charges as important evidence; it conducted examinations under torture and pronounced hasty sentences which were usually death sentences. The condemned men were handed over to the secular authorities who lit the fire at the stake. A few centuries later the church militant found widespread use for this gruesome weapon in Spain.

But first we shall see how the hurricane began to blow over the European Jews. To the Spaniards it was for many years still only a distant storm in the north, whose thunder re-echoed faintly beyond the Pyrenees.

Easter eve in Norwich, England, in 1144 was a fearsome affair. The bloody corpse of a fifteen-year-old boy was found in a wood outside the town. His name was William and he was apprenticed to a furrier; he had suffered from epilepsy and had presumably fallen and died during an attack. But people began to whisper that his was not a natural death. Some Jews had kidnapped the innocent lad and murdered him as a reminder of how their fathers had killed Christ at the first Eastertide. The authorities refused to take the matter up; the rumour was too ridiculous.

But some monks believed in the story and took great pains to spread it. In addition they could point to the statement of a converted Jew, Theobald of Cambridge. He said that the Jews met every year or every other year somewhere in Europe and drew lots to decide where a Christian boy should be sacrificed next Easter. Last year the meeting had been held in Narbonne and the lot had fallen to Norwich.

The people of Norwich had long been irritated by the prosperity of their Jewish neighbours. Consequently they found it easy to believe the rumour. The sheriff did his best to warn the Jews, but the agitation was too great. Many Jews were murdered; the rest had to leave house and home, and flee.

Now the dead boy was a martyr. He was called Saint William. After all he had given his blood for Our Saviour. Although the church did not sanction his canonization, the corpse was exhumed and buried in state. Miracles happened at his grave and it became a favourite place of pilgrimage.

This was the usual accusation of ritual murder against the Jews, which reared up in all its horror; the suspicion which is as old as the Jewish people in dispersal and has always clung to them like a shadow, namely that the Jews use the blood of outsiders, preferably Christian children, in their rituals and do not stop at murder to procure it.

As early as Josephus we hear ridiculous stories about the Jews fattening up a Greek boy, i.e. a heathen, every year. They sacrificed him at Easter, tearing out his entrails and swearing eternal hatred for all Greeks.

The case of William of Norwich was the first appearance of the rumour in the Middle Ages, but afterwards cases followed in rapid succession. In 1171 the accusation led to the whole community of Blois in France, including seventeen women, being burnt at the stake. None of the countless curious onlookers attending the execution forgot that when the flames closed over the condemned they sang a Hebrew psalm. It was a favourite psalm in the synagogue. Known as *Alenu*, it was the Jews' proudest challenge to the heathens.

At Valréas in Provence a little girl of two was found dead in the moat one Ash Wednesday. She had wounds on hands, feet and forehead, exactly the same places where the crown of thorns and the nails had wounded Christ. A short while before she had been seen in the town's Jewish quarter. That was adequate evidence. The leading Jews were put on the rack; under agonizing tortures they confessed to anything, including that every year at Easter it was their custom to kill a Christian child and drink its blood, a practice they had learnt from their Spanish brothers. The list could be continued indefinitely; it leaves a long bloody trail throughout Jewish history.

Accusations of ritual murder have proved tenacious of life. Right up to the present day they continue to flourish. As late as 1913 there was a sensational trial in Kiev, the so-called Beilis case, which in all its horror attracted the attention of the whole world.

THE THREE RINGS

Accusations seldom came from above, from the authorities or ecclesiastical officials. On the contrary they normally did what they could to suppress them. The emperor himself disapproved of courts of enquiry and the result was always that the indictment was found baseless. Princely edicts stamped the stories as fables; even the popes spoke against them. But they were like weeds which spread their seed on every wind and there were always willing minds where they could proliferate.

For the rumours smelt of blood, and once the thirst for blood is aroused, it is not easily quenched. Then there was another thing which awaked slumbering distrust. No one really knew about the Jews; they kept themselves to themselves, so that people felt there was something secret and frightening about them. Their way of life and customs were unfamiliar and strange; they were different. So one could expect the worst of them.

If a Christian happened to peer into a Jewish home on Easter Eve, he saw that the family drank four beakers of red wine. And if he caught some broken sentences, there was probably something about the red colour having to do with blood. The ritual was supposed to remind them of the blood which countless Jews had shed when they gave their life for their faith. And popular Jewish tradition knew that it also symbolized the blood of the children in which the leprous Pharaoh bathed. For Pharaoh—according to legend—had used the blood of 150 Jewish babies every day for his bath! From ancient times blood had had the reputation of being able to cure leprosy.

There were other things which had a mystifying effect. The Jews took a good deal of trouble to see that the Easter bread, the so-called matzo, was completely pure and unleavened. So they surrounded the baking with many ceremonies which were unintelligible to outsiders and consequently awoke fresh suspicion. What was more natural than to compare this Jewish matzo with the wafer the church used for communion. And at communion one received both the body and blood of Christ! After the Lateran Council had laid down that the bread and wine at communion really changed into the flesh and blood of Christ, it was a short step to suspect Jews of stealing a host at Easter. They made Christ suffer again by piercing and mutilating him!

An atmosphere of horror and suspicion hung over the towns in which Jews lived. It only needed a spark to blow the gunpowder barrel into the air.

And there was no lack of sparks. As soon as anything inexplicable and evil happened, it was the Jews' fault. Fires did terrible damage in the cramped, inflammable mediaeval towns. Who started them? The Jews, of course. The heretics had learnt their dangerous knowledge from the Jews. If the enemy invaded the country, especially if it was the heathen, the Jews had allied and conspired with them. At Easter the atmosphere was oppressive and tense.

But nothing was so dangerous for the Jews as the great epidemics.

In 1348 the Black Death came to Europe. It was the greatest disaster which has ever struck mankind; the most frightful disease the world has known. The epidemic came from the interior of Asia; it reached the Black Sea ports by the caravan routes and was brought to Europe by sea. It was given its sinister name, because the sufferers went blue-black; the mortality rate was enormous and the pestilence spread from country to country with explosive force. In the course of the two or three years during which the pest raged, it removed a third of Europe's population; whole towns, indeed whole provinces, were depopulated.

But the spiritual disease was worse than the pest. People became senseless with fear about the incomprehensible disaster; they believed the most fantastic rumours about who was responsible for the Black Death. Naturally mass hysteria turned against the Jews.

They had poisoned wells and fountains, and summoned up the pestilence. No one remembered that the Jews themselves

THE THREE RINGS

drank from the springs they were supposed to have poisoned and that the pest naturally did not spare them. But suspicion of the poisoners was nourished by the incontrovertible fact that mortality was lower among the Jews than among the others. People were blind to the fact that it was connected with the customary Jewish way of life. Strict laws had accustomed them to moderation in both food and drink; there was much less drunkenness among them and even more important, they observed hygienic rules and had an organized medical service.

But the people had heard so many old wives' stories about babies who were tortured to death and hosts dripping blood that reason had no effect on them; mass psychosis seized them as rapidly as the disease.

The pest first arrived in Spain and the south of France in the spring of 1348. Here there was no antisemitic hysteria. Perhaps it was connected with the bill proclaimed by the exiled Pope of Avignon in which he forbade the people to persecute the Jews because of unconfirmed rumours. But soon there were other places where people procured 'proofs' of their suspicions.

The Duke of Savoy had some Jews seized and put on the rack. One of them, a doctor called Balavigny, went insane with pain and confessed everything that the torturers wanted to hear. A Jew had come to Toledo with plans showing how to eradicate all the Christians with one blow! The plans were on a world-wide scale; poison would be sent to all the Jews and wells poisoned. The poison was composed of dried and crushed snakes, frogs and scorpions, and mixed with host dough and Christians' hearts!

Here was proof; the fire at the stake was lit and the smoke rose to heaven, while masses of Jews were burnt. None of them accepted the offer of being baptized and saving their lives.

The Jews in Switzerland were broken on the wheel and burnt in hordes. But in Germany, which has always been the land of mass-psychosis, the fear of the Jewish poison burst through; it was like the hydrophobia which follows the bite of a mad dog. In Germany flagellants went from town to town. They were people rendered senseless by fear; they whipped themselves, they stood in the street and mutilated themselves; some of them even castrated themselves while onlookers stood helplessly by. On the psychological plane this masochism sprang from the same source as Jew-baiting, i.e. *Schadenfreude* or pleasure in pain.

Some towns kept their sanity and the authorities protected the Jews. But only for a time; soon the flames flared up, first in sick minds, then at the stake in the square. Wherever we look in these times of terror, we find the same spectacle, inflamed crowds wallowing in blood and screaming persecuted men falling and dying. At Colmar visitors are still shown the 'Jews' hole' where the Jews were driven into a trap and murdered. Every evil instinct combined. This was the simplest way of all to lay hands on one's promissory notes and mortgage deeds, and here were money chests for the emptying.

A faint gleam of involuntary comedy appears in Strasbourg. The people found something in the synagogue which they looked at in amazement. It was a ram's horn, a so-called *shofar*, which was blown at the Jewish New Year, *rosh hashana*. The citizens did not understand what it was for; they thought it was a kind of bugle blown by the Jews when they wanted to betray the town to the enemy! To commemorate this evil, which had been so luckily averted, the magistrates cast two bronze bugles after the same model. They were blown daily at midnight as a permanent reminder to the townspeople of the Jews' treachery, and a warning to Jews in transit to leave the town as quickly as possible. For four centuries the signals of hatred for the Jews rang through Strasbourg night after night; they did not cease until the time of the great revolution.

The Black Death was a time of terror. The epidemic killed millions, but it also demoralized the survivors and that was even more serious. Only the Jews themselves remained unaffected by the spiritual plague, with all its newly wakened animal instincts.

There is one picture which recurs over and over again in these years of horror and etches itself so indelibly on the memory

THE THREE RINGS

that we feel sickened; the contrast between those who trampled the defenceless to death under the sign of the cross, who broke them on the wheel, drowned and tortured them, and the Jews who faced death singing psalms from the Bible and wore their prayer stoles when they hurled themselves into the flames to avoid compulsory baptism.

There is some secret hidden in this people which goes through fire and death, and always rises again like a phoenix from the ashes. Not without reason is its typical symbol a burning bush, which is in flames but is never consumed.

XI

CASTLES IN SPAIN

THE black storm-clouds which circled above the European Jews and time after time poured vials of wrath on them, took a long time to blow southwards and scale the Pyrenees. When the time came, however, the catastrophe was complete; the Jews were literally extirpated. But for a variety of reasons, the development was late and was prolonged for centuries.

Principally because two great opponents faced each other there and long preserved a certain equilibrium. History repeated itself from the first days of the Visigoths, when the Aryan kings and the Catholic church both had to reckon with the Jewish minority and take some notice of it. Now it was the Christian kingdoms and the Moors in Andalusia who struggled for power. In the light of this all overshadowing conflict the Jews were allowed to live. As we shall see, the kings found good use for them. Not until Granada fell and the last Moorish prince was driven into exile did the victorious Christian regiments bow to the church's age-old craving and cut the Jews down, now that they were no longer any use.

But it was also connected with the fact that the Moors had created a culture which did not differentiate too sharply between creeds. The air in Spain was tempered by breezes which breathed mutual esteem, respect and friendship. Great Christian kings inherited Abd al Rahman III's majestic tolerant government and continued the tradition. King Alphonso VII of Castile, who recaptured Toledo, was called 'the king of two faiths', i.e. the Christian and the Jewish. He

THE THREE RINGS

and many of his successors took Jews into royal service. For many years Moors, Jews and hidalgos lived peacefully side by side, at first in Mohammedan Cordoba and Granada, later in Christian Toledo.

True, the foundations of the Jewish golden age in Spain were fragile and tottering; everything depended on the unstable moods and whims of the princes, but it lasted a long time and one can search the whole of mediaeval history without finding a parallel to it. So the Spanish Jews succeeded in defying the stupid decrees of Innocent III and the Lateran Council, and avoiding the restrictions which made life miserable for their fellow Jews in the other European countries.

The fortunate lot of the Spanish Jews played its part in preventing the demoralization of the rest of the Jewish people in Europe. The Jew in France and Germany felt persecuted, branded and degraded, but Spain revived his courage and the thought of Cordoba, Toledo, Seville and Barcelona enabled him to hold his head up again. We call beautiful but impractical visions castles in Spain. The European Jews also had wonderful Spanish castles to dream about, except that they were not vague utopias, but proud reality.

At the time, then, the Spanish Jews lived in an atmosphere of happiness and gaiety. Life was rich, bright and free; the great poets' work overflows with wit and everyday life was full of laughter and friendship.

So far there is nothing particularly remarkable about this; the Jewish mentality has always been illuminated by sunbeams of light and laughter. But during these happy centuries we see the laughter kindle and the bright wit develop, free of most of the restrictions which hemmed it in or threatened it elsewhere.

And this side of the Jews life in Spain is so important that we can catch a glimpse of laughter in even the darkest pages of this book; perhaps at times it is almost crushed, no more than a faint hint of melancholy, bitter humour, but it is still laughter.

Anyone who wants to understand Israel must have a feeling

for Jewish humour. It would be quite wrong to imagine that the Jew allowed his mind to be darkened or his optimism crushed by the sea of suffering and adversity he and his people had gone through. Normally we would expect a people which was homeless and persecuted for millennia to have developed a sense of melancholy and tend to lapse into self-pity and whining. But the opposite happened, the Jew has preserved a wonderful gift for humour and developed a light elegant wit far more than other peoples.

The Jew belongs to an ancient people and he has sailed the seven seas of misery since he was Pharaoh's thrall in Egypt. This harsh destiny has stripped him of illusions and forced him inexorably to be a realist. So tragedy and comedy merge in Hebrew wit; the Jew himself calls it 'smiling through tears'. He smiles to win the courage to mourn. But his wit is not cynical; he prefers to smile *with* people rather than *at* them. He uses the foil, not the sabre, in his satire.

And best of all he likes to smile at himself and his own people. The Jew is a great self-ironist. But he always has a didactic aim, for the Jew is an inveterate schoolmaster and moralist. Mockery and sarcasm are expedients intended to illustrate and improve, preferably employed in an unexpected way. You think that he is tickling with a straw, but discover that he is aiming at the mind. He makes his opponent laugh. The victim only discovers that the shaft points at himself when it is too late.

Jewish wit has deep sources; it is connected with the most central thing in life, God. Humour and gaiety are the keystones of piety. Even in the Bible the sources of laughter flow. Everyone knows how humour flashes from many of its pages. We remember—to take but one example—the prophet Elijah in the great scene on Mount Carmel, when he mocks the prophets of Baal. They had called on Baal from morning to evening, but there was not a sound in reply and they began to dance and leap on the altar. Then Elijah says to them: 'Cry aloud: for he is a god; either he is talking, or he is pursuing, or

THE THREE RINGS

he is on a journey, or peradventure he sleepeth and must be awaked.'

But we shall hear two examples of the traditional stories the Spanish Jews told each other. They are selected at random, but they show the sensitive lovable method the old narrators used. They did not make people shriek with laughter, but they brought a twinkle to the eye and made the listeners be introspective, reflect and—smile.

A man had two wives, one young, one old. The young one wanted her husband to look younger and she pulled out all the white hairs on his head. But the old one wanted him to look as old as she was and pulled out the black hairs. The result was that the man was bald.

Here is another story which has a sharper point:

A widow lived in the Holy Land with her two daughters; she was poor and all she owned was a small field. She had to borrow to have the field ploughed. One neighbour lent her his ass, another his ox. But the rabbi came and warned her: 'Thou shalt not plough with both ox and ass!' When she was ready to sow, he came back and quoted the great law-giver again: 'Thou shalt not sow two kinds of seed in the same field!'

The corn grew and autumn came. She reaped and put up the sheaves. The rabbi came and warned her that she must leave the rakings behind and let the corners stand. That was the sheaf for the poor.

Then she garnered the corn in her house, but first she had to deliver the priest's share, both the first and second tenth. She gave way obediently and did everything she should. But she realized that she was not earning enough daily bread for herself and her daughters in this way. So she sold the field and bought two sheep instead. She could live by selling the wool and lambs they yielded.

As soon as the first lamb was born, the indefatigable priest appeared and quoted the law again: 'Give me the first born as the Lord hath said.'

Finally the time came when she was to clip the sheep. The priest popped up: 'It is written: Give me the wool from the shoulder, the cheeks and the belly.'

In her despair the poor woman burst out without thinking: 'Rather let the animals be dedicated to the Lord!'

Scarcely had she said the fateful words when the priest interrupted: 'Then they belong to me, for the Lord has said: Everything holy in Israel is thine.'

And the widow and her daughters stood by in despair and watched the priest go off with the last things they owned.

But the stories could also tell of love and romance.

There is a law which orders a Jew to divorce his wife if they have been married for ten years without having children. Once upon a time a man lived happily with his wife; they loved one another dearly, but unfortunately they had no children.

When ten years had elapsed, they went to the rabbi and put the case to him. He advised them to have a banquet on the last night before they parted. The woman would be entitled to take home with her something she was very fond of as a reminder of the happy days when she was married.

They did so. The wife prepared a magnificent meal and amid laughter and gaiety she kept on filling her husband's beaker with sparkling wine.

This naturally ended with his getting drunk and falling into a deep sleep. She ordered the servants to carry him to her father's house and put him to bed. There he slept like the dead till next morning.

Finally he woke up and looked at the unusual surroundings in amazement. His good wife came and sat on the edge of his bed, and said with a smile:

'I did what the rabbi asked me to and took the most precious memory I had. It is you, my darling, for I simply can't live without you.'

The man was deeply moved and promised that they would never part.

A few days later they went to the rabbi, told him what had

happened and asked for his blessing. He gave it them, and it must have been a powerful blessing for before the year was out they had a baby.

The Spanish Jews had doors and windows wide open to the whole world. Their horizon was quite unrestricted; they only knew isolation by name. It was the order of the day for strangers to come from distant lands and ask for hospitality. They could always rely on finding a bed ready for them in the synagogue's guestroom. They were welcome; it was one of the natural duties to show hospitality and visitors brought news from the great uneasy world. A gust of information blew into the Spanish Jews' homes and there was something to talk about next day.

They had become a mixed flock with the passage of time, when one thinks back on it. Wandering preachers and scholars had new ideas to propound and they could not stop talking about them. Then came the so-called mendicant students, poor young men, who had studied at some great academy and were now on their way to the next. Perhaps they had even been driven from their school when it was captured by the Crusaders or the advancing Mohammedans. Most often the new arrivals were merchants or craftsmen who had travelled long weary miles to find customers or work, and they brought new customs and methods with them. Itinerant singers settled and taught the people their songs; pious pilgrims had been to the Holy Land and told incredible stories which made the heart glow with longing for the lost country; exalted mystics aroused wonder with their accounts of miracles or a newly-emerged Messiah, so that fresh fuel was added to the inextinguishable dream of Israel's bright future, which shone above grey humdrum existence and made the sad reality easier to bear.

No matter where the Jews looked in the world, they found fellow-countrymen; they were everywhere and thousands of invisible bonds bound them to each other. This made the Spanish Jews cosmopolitan and gave them a world-wide horizon. But they were not content to sit at home dreaming of what lay beyond the blue horizon. Many of them also journeyed forth into the wide world. For the Jews had a chance which no other people had at the time. It was this circumstance which made them a pivot on which the whole world culture hinged in a decisive hour. But in order to understand how it happened, we must stop a moment and consider the world as it was at the time, 600–800 years ago.

Two mighty blocks opposed each other, armed to the teeth: West and East, Christianity and Islam. Europe was united. In spite of deep divisions and countless national and social differences, it was welded into a block. One language, the Latin of the church, was the bond which linked the Christian peoples and gave them the basis for a common culture, one religion, dictated by the universal ruling church, and one faith to which all bowed and crusaded for. Opposed to Christianity was Islam, which was even more closely united.

But there was one great difference between then and now. Today men from the Near East at once recognize Occidentals as their teachers when it comes to technical skill, economic methods, business ability and medical science. It may well be that he despises the religion and morality of the West, but he admires and wants to learn everything else.

Then it was just the opposite. It was Islam's great age. The West both admired and feared the East; they knew full well that the stronghold of science and learning was in Islam. During the Crusades, Christendom had felt the strength of its brilliant military organization, and tried to copy it, as words like admiral and arsenal remind us.

But it was not only the technique of war which they were tempted to imitate. The Western mentality was about to awake after sleeping for centuries and longed for the spiritual treasure Islam guarded.

Such was the stage on which the Spanish Jews eventually played a part which set in motion the forces by which the present-day world was created.

The international tension between East and West naturally set up an iron curtain between the two spheres of interest. It was impossible for Mohammedans to travel in Europe and Christians were regarded with suspicion if they ventured into Mohammedan countries; they risked being sold as slaves or losing their lives. But the Jew was tolerated in both camps. Admittedly he was subject to certain restrictions, but apart from that he could travel freely without anyone interfering in his affairs.

He had one more advantage. Wherever he went, East or West, he found brothers who made him welcome and looked after him. The unity of the world's Jews extended over frontiers and seas, and made them one people, whether they came from the East, Africa, Germany or Spain. They had a common tongue, Hebrew, which no one else understood, but the local Jews also knew the national tongue and could act as interpreters.

That was how the Jews became the great intermediaries of the Middle Ages, linking the peoples of the other two religions. We could say that the Mother, Judaism, from which both Christendom and Islam had sprung, tried to reconcile and carry messages to her two quarrelsome rival daughters.

The main importance of these Jewish middlemen was in the sphere of economics and international trade. They were merchants and during Islam's great period all the trade between the countries was in their hands.

Actually the Jews' strength does not lie in the economic field. Perhaps that sounds strange, for we tend to emphasize his natural leaning for trade and say that the Jew is a born merchant. He was not so in Biblical times. Then Israel lived in mountain country, yet there were trade routes down in the valleys, and still the Jews did not share in the traffic. Every house produced what it needed, food, clothing, timber and tools; only luxury articles had to be bought from itinerant foreign merchants. The simple fact that no Jewish money was minted until the time of the Maccabees shows how small their trade was. The Israelite's ideal was to rest in the shadow of his fig tree—and preferably the tree should not bear more fruit than the family required, so that he would not have to sell it!

CASTLES IN SPAIN

As late as the Talmudic period the Jew looked askance on trade; a famous passage in the Talmud says: 'The less trade, the more Torah!'

It was the Jews in dispersal, the perpetually wandering exiles who were first forced to turn to trade; later they acquired a taste for it and gradually developed a great ability for it. Jews were spread over the whole Roman Empire as early as the first century A.D. They lived in towns and preserved their distinctive mark; their religion was a universal, not a parochial faith. As a unique element in the Roman Empire they protected themselves and hung together, and that was a sound basis for commercial relations.

But the Jews only became businessmen on a large scale under Islam. Amusingly enough, an example of big business from that distant time has been preserved. When the Colossus of Rhodes, one of the seven wonders of the world, fell in 653, a Jewish merchant bought the massive ruin and took the stone blocks away on 900 camels. And it was not long before Jewish merchants had a practical monopoly of trade between East and West.

In 847 the Postmaster-General in Baghdad wrote a 'Book of Routes' in which he described the routes taken by Jewish merchants on their far-ranging journeys. He relates how good they are at languages; they speak Arabic, Persian and Greek, but they also know the languages of the Franks, the Andalusians and the Slavs. They sail over the 'western sea', i.e. the Mediterranean, to Egypt. There they load their goods on camels and take them to Suez, whence they sail across the 'eastern' or Red Sea to Arabic ports; from there they voyage further to India and China. Another of the routes goes to the Syrian ports, thence to Baghdad by caravan through the desert and then down the Tigris by ship to the sea, after which the way lies open to India and China again. They also used the great caravan route across the whole of North Africa from Morocco to Egypt, continuing to Baghdad via Damascus and right through immeasurable Asia to China. And lastly they knew the way across the Balkans, north of the Black Sea through

THE THREE RINGS

the land of the Chazars and on to the caravan routes through Asia. These merchants were not called *Radanites* for nothing, a word coming from the Persian 'rah dan', he who knows the way.

They brought wares back to Europe from the Eastern countries, mostly spices and perfumes. There was a good market for spices, so that the winter's salt cod and the Lenten dried fish might have a little flavour, and perfumes were useful in the dusty, cramped towns with poor or non-existent sanitary installations which stank out the corridors and rooms. The *Radanites* brought a measure of refinement to coarse European manners.

Practically speaking all luxury goods came to Europe from the Orient: cotton, silk, velvet, damask, satin, muslin for clothes; for furnishing houses carpets, tapestries, mattresses, divans; fruits and vegetables such as figs, lemons, melons, rice, spinach, asparagus, new varieties of flowers, roses, lilies, tulips, jasmine, precious stones, all kinds of spices, pomades, cosmetic articles, dyestuffs and above all, medicine. Lists have been compiled with thousands of words for everyday objects which come from oriental tongues; they are like so many witnesses of the richness which the oriental countries sent to Europe. There was a tremendous advance in mutual trade with the advent of the Crusades, but for centuries before it was the Jewish *Radanites* who monopolized this international trade. Many different factors contributed to the speedy breaking up of the networks, but they began it. And Moorish Spain was the starting point and the natural centre for the whole trade.

But the *Radanites* and their successors did not merely carry wares from East to West; they also brought ideas and thoughts with them. Many folk-tales, adventures, songs and proverbs flowed via them into the European mentality; they also introduced chess. As businessmen, they needed numbers and accounts, and they transmitted our knowledge of the Arabic decimal system and the use of zero[1] to Europe. They learnt

---

[1] In the Middle Ages the Arabic word for zero, *tzipha*, was used. The English zero and the word cypher also come from it. I mention this as a simple example of the influence of Arabic culture.

CASTLES IN SPAIN

astronomy and calculated astronomical tables, not only for investigating the movement of the stars, but also for navigation. So gradually the first seeds of modern mathematics, on which the whole superstructure of modern cultures is based, came to Europe.

As soon as the first Arabic caliphs had consolidated their victory they set store by making the wisdom of the ancient world available to their people. As we have already seen the works of Plato, Aristotle and many other great thinkers, writers and scientists hibernated in Syrian translations. The Nestorian Christians in Syria were always strong in philosophical thinking and they prepared the translations. When Islam was in full flower at Baghdad, the translations were done into Arabic and spread through the mighty Arabic empire to Syria, Palestine, Egypt and via North Africa to Moorish Spain.

There the people of the West went to school. Jewish scholars translated the books into Hebrew so that the Jewish schools dotted round Europe could use them. Here again the Jews in Provence played a special role. Provence bordered on Spain and at certain times it had been politically associated with the Christian kingdoms in northern Spain; the distance from country to country was never long. From Hebrew the books were translated into Latin, so that the Christians could imbibe the ancient knowledge and wisdom. The books literally flew across the countries and many Greek, Arabic and Jewish books were standard works in Europe's Christian universities and had a revolutionary influence on European thought and culture.

Christendom and Islam met on the Spanish peninsula. Gradually, step by step, the Moors were forced back southwards. But behind them they left their language, their literature and their culture. So it happened in Toledo, for example. But long before the Moors came, Jews lived in the ancient city. They had adopted the Arabic language and imbibed all the brilliant culture from the days of antiquity. From them Christianity acquired its new wisdom.

In terms of modern statistics, perhaps all this does not cut

THE THREE RINGS

very much ice. Mediaeval knowledge did not carry much weight in itself. Its researchers did not work in experimental fields and consequently added little to the store of human knowledge.

Nowadays, a single year probably provides us with more material than the whole period between the years 800 and 1500, which we consider as the Middle Ages proper.

But the ability to think remained alive; the urge to fumble one's way to the unknown never quite died. Had it not been for the Spanish Jews, Europe could easily have perished culturally and stiffened into a deadly monotony and orthodox conservatism, as happened in China.

These people carried the old and new cultures, and were middlemen between East and West. In the real sense of the word the Jews were the first Europeans.

The Spanish Jews felt that they were free; the disease of slavery never plagued their minds. They knew that they had lived in the country long before the Christian church came into being and they were free men when the Christian kings' forefathers hid themselves in mountains and caves.

We know a good deal about them, for masses of documents have been preserved, both royal missives and replies, or *responsa*, from famous rabbis, i.e. detailed considerations and answers to questions about the various problems of everyday life. From these yellowing papers rises a picture of a people's daily life in all its nuances and conditions. But the main line through all the confusing details is constant, that the exiles by the rivers of Castile and Aragon felt like fellow members of a people which goes far beyond geographical boundaries and right back to a divine origin. It filled them with pride and dignity.

In reality they balanced on a see-saw for centuries. Two powers each took their own way, the church and the king. The church continued to look on the Jews as a challenge. They were descendants of Cain, branded and sentenced to bear the guilt of the crucifixion for ever. Therefore, they were part of the divine programme of revenge and eternal retribution, and witnesses to God's sacrifice for man's salvation. Canon law went systematically about the task of reducing the Jews to degradation.

In this respect the kings were remarkably little affected by the church. Naturally as devout Christians they shared the church's attitude and at times helped the church, although most unwillingly, to enforce the canonical decrees. But their general policy was determined by practical considerations. The Jews simply represented a source of revenue, which the monarch inherited along with the country. If he took care of them and protected them they were a source of prosperity.

This was the keystone in the Jews' political status in Spain. Much could change, the course often travelled in zig-zags during the different phases of the reconquest and opposing currents clashed, but the kings' attitude to 'their' Jews was surprisingly stable. The kings gained such great advantages from the Jews, that they could turn this factor to account by threatening to emigrate if they were subject to undue interference.

So the Jewish community achieved rights and privileges which in many respects put them on the same footing as the nobility; for more than five hundred years each individual community was assured far-reaching self-government based on royal letters, so that they could base their lives on Jewish law and tradition.

Such a community was known as an *aljama*, the usual Arabic name for a Jewish community in a town or village. Every *aljama* included all the Jews in the locality; they elected their officers and handed over the running of the town to them; they dealt with economic conditions, the purchase and sale of landed property, the prices of meat and wine, poor relief, the administration of the synagogue and schools, and especially the levying of taxes and administration of justice.

If we study the taxes in detail, we notice at once that the king raised a surprisingly large part of his income in the Jewish *aljamas*, a disproportionately high percentage in relation to the number of inhabitants. Naturally, like other inhabitants, they had to pay taxes to the general government of the kingdom,

THE THREE RINGS

to the court and the law courts, to the army and navy. But extra taxes were levied for all kinds of purposes; the Jews paid for the dowry at royal weddings, the king's extravagant gifts, usually valuable horses—once, in fact, they paid for a menagerie. The king had the right to levy thirty dineros from every Jew, man, woman and child. The amount was supposed to remind them of the thirty pieces of silver Judas received for his betrayal, and expiate it. The king frequently needed extra revenue for the suppression of rebellion or wars by land or sea —and the Jews had to pay up. It was said of Aragon's navy that 'the whole world trembled when the eagle of Aragon prepared to fly'. But it was Jewish money which paid for it. The last great war against Granada which gave the impetus to the ejection of the Jews, was largely financed by Jews in the form of massive extra taxes and loans, in other words, a veiled form of confiscation. The Jews paid for the king's journeys to foreign countries, the wine and corn for the court's table; in Saragossa the Jewish butchers daily delivered all the meat the court needed—as a gift.

The Jews were hemmed in by taxes. When they went through the city gates or crossed a bridge, it cost a toll. There was a tax on the everyday necessities of life; flour, bread, fish, meat, clothes and shoes. The authorities insisted on being bribed; 'in every town we are forced to bribe noblemen and magistrates, we pay annual contributions to the judges so that they may be our shield', it says in one place.

The lawcourt was called *beth din* and was steeped in Jewish tradition. As a rule the judges were medical men, but with a legal teacher to guide them; they judged exclusively according to Biblical and rabbinical law.

The severest punishment was excommunication, *cherem* in Hebrew. It was a fearful weapon with devastating consequences. The excommunicated man was completely boycotted, both socially and religiously. No one could come within eight feet of him; he could not enter the service of a Jew or have a Jew in his service. If he entered the synagogue, divine service stopped abruptly. If he died while still excommunicated, he was allowed burial, but only with a stone over him. Pronunciation of sentence was a terrifying ritual. The ram's horn, or shofar, was blown; lighted lamps were put out and fearsome anathemas were read out.

The Jew had a predilection for gruesome striking ceremonies. If a man had to take an oath, a cock was put on a bier, lights were extinguished, ashes were strewn beneath his feet, the shofar sounded, and children cried out in fear, while the oath taker was led before the ark containing the Torah, to swear.

The greatest crime was informing. It was the cancer in Jewish life and they showed no mercy to informers, who indeed betrayed the whole people. Punishments were inhumanly harsh; for example stoning to death at the most holy hour on the Day of Atonement or opening the criminal's arteries as he stood over his own grave. These severe punishments must be considered in connection with the state of emergency in which the Jews always lived. In such circumstances the *beth din* was really a court martial which made summary brutal judgments.

Otherwise, the Jewish legal system was marked by a calm, painstaking feeling for justice and in many respects formed a contrast to the semi-barbarian practices which were general in the Middle Ages. It is characteristic that in the thousands of cases we know, we never find a Jewish judge accused of bribery. Normally it was the custom to include an entry called 'bribery and other expenses' when making out the accounts for a legal case.

Inside the *aljamas* great insistence was placed on the fact that no Jew could use the civil Christian legal system. The Jews asserted clearly and bravely that 'the national law is not our law'. And it was considered a great religious sin if a Jewish creditor took his brother Jew before a Spanish court to recover an outstanding account.

The majority of Jews lived in the towns. In Spain—in contrast to other countries—they could own landed property. Several Jews had large estates and plantations. But out in the country it was difficult to find the ten men required to form a community. Nor were the conditions safe; the risk of attack

THE THREE RINGS

was great and then who would help the victim? So the Jews sought refuge behind the sheltering town walls and lived near each other.

In the towns there were Jews in every kind of profession, from the highest to the lowest. We have information about numerous high officials in the kings' service; the intellectual sphere teemed with Jews, mainly doctors, but also jurists, teachers and rabbis. Many were craftsmen; armourers—the famous Toledo swords come to mind—jewellers, parchment makers, to name only a few of the ordinary trades. And as a curiosity, but one which helps to illuminate the Jews' all-round developments, they were the lion-tamers in the royal menageries.

The Jews of Barcelona were known as craftsmen who made wonderful gold and silver embroidery. And there is something ironic in the thought that the ecclesiastical pomp and brilliance at *autos-da-fé* was usually the product of a Jew's imagination, and assembled in his workshop! Another delicate craft was cartography and the making of nautical instruments. The island of Majorca was the centre of cartography, which was exclusively in the hands of the Jews. They were the men who drew the maps and constructed the instruments which helped the great discoverers to find their way across unknown seas.

Mediaeval Europe was solidly organized. In the towns merchants formed guilds and craftsmen unions. This was the best way of safeguarding their interests. Among other measures they also did so by excluding Jews from their unions. But even in this respect the Spanish Jews were better off than their brothers north of the Pyrenees. The kings intervened and saw to it that the doors were not closed to their Jewish subjects or at least that they were entitled to form their own guilds and unions. Right to the last they preserved a certain economic standing. Immediately before their expulsion Jewish merchants travelled by land and sea under the protection of Ferdinand and Isabella.

The Jews primarily asserted themselves within the economy. And just as they had assisted the advent of new ages in the sphere of ideas, they marked an important milestone in the development of Europe's economic history.

We have already heard about the travelling Jewish merchants, the *Radanites*, who were pioneers of international trade between East and West. There was little ready money in their day and all trade was barter. But the *Radanites*' successors, the large-scale Jewish merchants, especially in Spain, pioneered the way for the modern monetary system.

Europe's development called for immense capital. The kings were nearly always at war; they needed vast sums of money. And grandiose building went on; new towns, churches, monasteries, castles, harbours and ships, which even today tower up as so many monuments to the creative imagination of those distant days, as it took shape in brick and stone. But it cost money. Without money it was impossible to equip the army, build a fleet and crusade against the people of the crescent.

But where were kings, nobles and church to raise the money? It was a mediaeval dogma that 'money does not beget money'. Everything else creates something new; a house gives shelter, a field grows, clothes keep people warm. But money is unfruitful, it neither grows nor multiplies. It is a useful convenient means of exchange; it is easy to keep and does not perish, but it does not create. As Thomas Aquinas put it, one cannot sell a thing which does not exist.

In modern terminology we distinguish between usury and interest. Interest is the reasonable charge paid by the borrower; usury is a higher percentage than the law or general opinion allows. But the Middle Ages looked on the two things as one; all interest was usury. This was not only an economic theory, but also a religious doctrine which the church wanted carried out to the letter. Canon law put usurers on the same plane as whoremongers and murderers; they were excluded from communion and could not be buried on consecrated ground.

The Bible also forbids usury; we find it prohibited in the Books of Moses, the Psalms and the Prophets. The Talmud follows suit and says: 'He who loans money at interest, is like he who sheds blood.' That was how seriously both the church and Judaism regarded this problem. How could a solution be found?

The Bible only prohibited accepting interest or usury from other Jews; it said nothing about heathens, i.e. people with a different faith! The church had a similar attitude. The Jews were outside canon law, therefore the prohibition did not affect them, and the rabbis allowed Jews to accept interest from non-Jews, in this case the Christians! With that the path was cleared and the Jews were recognized as money-lenders people could turn to when cash was needed to build, travel or wage war. We may smile at the sophistry involved. In reality the strong forces driving development along could not be stopped, so that some kind of a compromise solution had to be found. And this was the answer.

Interest was naturally high when the only security was the borrower's word. But the risk was correspondingly great. As a rule the lender had to use legal means to get his money back; repayment was often in bad or clipped money; if the borrower died, his heirs were not obliged to recognize the loan; the times were uncertain and the Jews' position even more so; judges had to be bribed and so on *ad infinitum*.

But the kings protected the Jewish money-lenders carefully and actually had them in the hollow of their hands. They imposed swingeing—brand new!—taxes on them; a third or a fourth of their income belonged to the king. If a Jewish capitalist died, the king took the whole of his property. From this point of view the Jew's property was ultimately the king's; in reality the Spanish kings were the country's usurers, they merely used the Jews to do their dirty work. Popular wit did not christen the Jewish money-lenders 'sponges' for nothing. They absorbed the country's money, but the king squeezed the sponge dry over his treasure chest. If a Jewish usurer was baptized, the king demanded compensation from the church! For then he could no longer continue as a money-lender and the king lost a source of income. So the Jews helped to consolidate the royal authority and make it independent of other

CASTLES IN SPAIN

powers in the kingdom. This was the impetus to the development which gradually broke down mediaeval uniformity and pioneered the way for national states.

Obviously in this way the Jews only came into contact with the *élite* of the community. The common people tilled their soil or practised crafts, but the Jewish bankers had nothing to do with them. But the major part of the economic activity which flourished in these centuries was set in motion on Jewish initiative. To name but one example, the great financier Aron of Lincoln was behind the construction of no less than twelve Cistercian monasteries in England, as well as St Albans Abbey. Not to mention that Jewish capital made the Crusades possible.

Naturally the church looked askance on all this traffic and envied the Jews their *de facto* monopoly. Gradually it found a way of pushing them out of the market. Christian banking firms were set up in Italy, especially in Lombardy. They accepted disguised interest, calling it payment for loss and damage, or repayment overdue. Popular wit was busy again and talked about the 'pope's usurers'. Lombard Street in London, where the great banks are situated, is named after them. After the Black Death they got the upper hand of the Jews and dominated the money market.

A reputation for usury has hung over the Jews to our own day. In reality they were forced to deal in money, when other solutions—outside Spain in any case—were closed to them. So it came about that they laid the foundations of the capitalist system which supports the modern world today.

The Spanish Jews could live where they liked in the towns. Many built their houses in Christian neighbourhoods; we even known examples of Jewish houses which lay in the shadow of a Christian church. But on the whole they preferred to live close to each other; it was both safest and most practical. And gradually in every town and village the Jewish quarter, or *juderia*, grew up, surrounded by strong walls and carefully guarded gates. It was attractive in the *juderia*, with its frequently imposing houses hidden in orchards and vineyards. The Jews

THE THREE RINGS

also took care of the sanitary conditions, in which respect they were head and shoulders above their neighbours.

The synagogue was the biggest building in the *juderia*, rising high above the neighbouring houses. But not *too* high. It was not allowed to compete with the Christian church whose spire towered up to heaven outside the walls of the *juderia*. A patch of wall above the door was left unwhitewashed as a reminder of fallen Zion. In the same way a corner was missing or a section unpainted in private houses. As long as the temple lay in ruins, no house could be completely finished. Israel should always remember what she had lost, and no happiness could be entirely unclouded. The people had no political hope, but the dream of Zion gave them consolation in gloomy days.

For the Jew, life is a unity, something integral. All the mass of trivia of everyday life are connected and are governed by his faith. We might say that life absorbs religion, or perhaps it is rather religion which absorbs life. This was shown in the most literal way in the synagogue. It was not exclusively reserved for divine service, but had wings for guests, the law-court, the school and social welfare.

In the synagogue everyone shared their sorrows and happinesses with one another. There the young were married and newly-born boys circumcised. There they wept over the dead and complained about family disputes. There was gossip and rumour; they felt like one big family and were very prone to look through each other's keyholes, and were not averse to making business deals in the middle of the reading of the holy texts. But suddenly all the humming babbling sounds ceased. A martyr's roll of murdered Jews in one remote country or another was read aloud and mournful song united all the agitated voices.

Jewish home life has always been rich and varied. Their religion calls for attention to many small details. On Friday night when the sabbath began, the man of the house put a lock on the kitchen-range so that no one could light a lamp or a fire on the holiday. But first he had been to the market to buy the delicacies to make the sabbath festive. It could take a long time, for the fish merchants used to take advantage of the situation and put up their prices before the sabbath. But when the shopping was done, he hurried triumphantly home to show his wife the booty. Then he helped her to clean the kitchen utensils and cutlery, lay the table and put out the sabbath candles so that the holy eve could be celebrated as it should.

The Jews are often depicted as especially sensual. But anyone studying the family life of the old Spanish Jews does not receive confirmation of this impression. They set great store by self-control and demanded respect for sexual life. The scripture uses the relation between man and woman as an image of God's relation to his people, and the mystics used the most intimate pictures when they painted man's love for God in strong colours, and thereby raised physical union so high that it reminded people of the union with the eternal.

The first duty of the communal authorities and above all, the court, was to supervise the purity of family life and the chastity of the single. The law was very rigorous on this point. A husband's unfaithfulness was severely censured, but even suspicion of a wife resulted in divorce. For marriage was so sacred that it was nothing less than blasphemy to break it. 'Marriages are made in heaven', is a quotation from the Talmud.

Chastity was regarded as one of the greatest virtues, and since marriage was a sure haven, care was taken to marry young people early. 'It is the duty of every Jewish man to take a wife in his eighteenth year, but he who does so earlier is praiseworthy. Yet no one should marry before he is thirteen', it was written. There was no room for romance or sentimental love; the parents picked the partners, and the two proud parents made all the necessary arrangements. We are unused to this way of arranging things, but it is a fact that Jewish home life was attractive and rich, and the home was the Spanish Jew's sanctuary in the most real sense of the word. Even if there was no love before the marriage, there was never a sign of unfaithfulness afterwards.

'The world is based on three things: study, worship and

THE THREE RINGS

doing good.' That is an old Jewish saying and consequently the *aljama* took care that the children had as good an education as possible. When a boy was five years old, his parents sent him to school. During the first hour he began to learn Hebrew. The sacred letters were written in honey on a blackboard. The boy lapped them up, while he uttered their names; the word of the law should be sweet in his heart.

In his first year at school the boy learnt Jewish subjects, but gradually instruction was extended to rhetoric, medicine, poetry, mathematics and as the crown of the other branches, philosophy.

'Every Israelite is under an obligation to reserve a time for reading both morning and evening, whether he is poor or rich, healthy or ill, young or old; even the beggar who roams through the streets must do so.' That is a Spanish quotation from the fourteenth century and shows that the Jews were rightly called the 'people of the book'.

Throughout, books played a large part in the Spanish Jews' life. We have heard how great patrons took the greatest pains to procure books. It was not right to refuse when someone wanted to borrow a book. Once a rabbi imposed a fine on a man because he had refused to lend a student one of his books. Since this did not work, the fine was changed to a daily fine to be paid until he complied. A student was entitled to break in and steal a book the owner had refused to lend him!

And we have some charming instructions as to how books should be treated:

'Look after your books, cover the shelves with a fine cloth and protect them from moisture and mice. Compile a complete list of them; check over your Hebrew books once a month and your Arabic books every other month. Write down when you lend a book and strike it out when you get it back.'

Here are the rules for reading:

'Work together with a friend; pay attention to what you read and understand everything before you go any further. Use mnemonics; read only one book at a time; use only tasteful, well-bound books which are written on good paper. You should sit and read in a room with fine furniture, your eyes shall look on lovely things so that you come to like the work. There shall be beauty always in your books and your house. You shall not pore over the books in silence nor read aloud or sing when you are studying the Bible. Teach yourself by teaching others. Read out of love of wisdom; read at fixed times and never say: on such a day and at such a time I will read for a while. If you have worked by day, then read by night. The path to wisdom is through prayer. Ask God to give you the knowledge you seek.'

But learning and reading were only one side of life; we have a list of the most important things men must set store by:

'These things are like a tree which yields us its fruit in this life, but whose trunk remains standing until the world to come; to honour your father and mother, practise good works, regular reading morning and evening, hospitality to strangers, to visit the sick, give the bride a dowry, follow the dead to the grave, be devoted in prayer and create peace between a man and his neighbour.'

Here good works come before study, and that was the actual order in which things were placed; good works and piety were the pillars on which the community depended. Maimonides said: 'I have never heard of a Jewish community which did not have a poor-box.' Here is a story which is characteristic of the Jewish way of thinking:

'The richest man in the town was dead. Although he had been thrifty, he went to heaven, where there was a big street with fine shops and wares whose like he had never seen. He went in and bought many good things, and tried to pay for them with a cheque as had been his wont in his native town. But the assistant could not accept it and said that there was no cover for it in the bank of heaven.

'You have no money to your credit here.'

THE THREE RINGS

In confusion the newcomer asked: 'Why not? I am the richest man in town.'

The answer came: 'No, you are not. For here in heaven we only own what we have given away.'

Such was the importance of good works. Maimonides edited a list of its different forms, like a staircase which one descended step by step. The highest is to put the poor in a position to help themselves. But those who attempt it are not all equally successful. Maimonides begins to describe the steps. On the topmost step is he who does good without knowing whom he helps, and without the poor person knowing from whom the help comes. Then comes he who gives and knows whom he helps, whereas the latter does not know his benefactor. A little lower stands he who gives without knowing the recipient, but the latter knows the donor's name. And then comes he who gives without being asked, but both parties know the other's name. A step lower down stands he who gives when asked; then he who gives willingly, but not enough. And on the lowest step of all is he who gives and grudges doing so.

But it is as much a duty to share in others' happiness as it is to mourn with the afflicted. So a bride should be greeted with song and flowers and gay speeches, even if she is old and ugly. There is a cheerful smile in this favourite epigram: 'All brides are beautiful, all the dead are devout!'

It was a long time before the badge of Jewry was introduced into Spain. The church did what it could to force it through, but had long been unsuccessful. As a result there was no profound difference between Jews and Christians. They spoke the same language, their names sounded the same and there was no difference in their clothing, not even in the aristocracy. Spanish noblemen, Jewish merchant princes and statesmen vied in luxury and brilliance. They had countless Moorish slaves and wore expensive raiment, silk and furs; their wives were covered with jewels, they rode on superb racehorses, they owned country houses and game preserves. The authorities in the *aljama* were often afraid that the wealthy Jews would arouse envy and stir up the evil instincts of the Spanish masses.

Social differences in the *juderias* were not so deep as in the Christian community. At one extreme they lacked nobles and warriors, at the other serfs. The virtues which counted when judging men were learning, piety and prosperity; here the man who applied himself with talent and energy could easily rise up. This was the class from which the kings summoned their diplomats and financiers; here too were found the industrious scientists and outstanding doctors, who made their names famous.

Nor were there any visible barriers dividing Christian and Jewish merchants, who traded freely with each other. Christian builders built houses for Jews and Jewish craftsmen worked for Christian employers. Jewish lawyers often represented Christian clients in the civil courts and Jewish brokers were middlemen between Christian and Mohammedan merchants.

All these daily contacts naturally created an atmosphere of mutual respect and tolerance. In spite of moments of irritation for religious reasons they led to frequent friendships. In spite of all ecclesiastical prohibitions, we often hear of Christian and Jewish families being on friendly terms, exchanging gifts on holidays and following each other's happinesses and sorrows with friendly interest.

Two of the Middle Ages' greatest Jews frequently put this tolerant attitude into words and it is worth while recalling two quotations. First Maimonides:

'Christ's teachings and after him Mohammed's strivings to bring everything to perfection and fill the world with the message of the holy scripture. When the Messiah comes all will turn back from their misguided courses'.

Then comes Jehuda ben Halevi:

'God's wise providence with Israel can be compared to a grain of corn which lies in the earth. It looks as if it turns into earth and water, and rots and vanishes, so that it is no longer recognizable. But in reality it is the grain which changes earth and water. The days follow each other, the grain sprouts and rises step by step and finally has a stem and ears. So it is with the Christians and the Mohammedans. The Law of Moses has changed those who came into contact with it, even if they have apparently rejected it. These religions are a preparation for the Messiah we await. He is the fruit of the seed which once was placed in the earth, and all mankind will one day become fruits of God's seed, and all become one mighty tree.'

These two Jews spoke about Christendom and Islam in this way at a time when the crusaders were ill-treating their fellow-Jews and the Almohades were laying waste Israel's communities with fire and sword.

But we also know examples of Christian kindness to the Jews. In one town, market day was changed from Saturday to Monday, so that both Christians and Jews could use it. Another time we hear of a knight who removed the cross from his cloak so that the Jews he knew could also greet him.

In spite of everything, a similar spirit existed on both sides. There were hearts which beat in time, so that neither prejudice nor persecutions could divide them. Admittedly good will could not alter the course of the current, but that it existed at all was a hopeful sign.

But the Catholic church prevailed in the end. It never retreated, for thousands of years it neither tarried nor swerved from its course for one minute. It wanted one thing only, to gather all men into its fold. The church and mankind must be one. If anyone ventured to oppose this desire to rule in heaven and on earth, that stubborn character must be reduced to impotence and contempt, or be exterminated. It was deadly serious to the men of the church that the gospel of love should be drilled into the hearts of those who did not want to accept it because they knew another way to heaven.

The conversion of the Jews figured prominently in this missionary programme. There was something mysterious about Israel which the church could never leave alone. After all they had—according to the Christian faith, too—a divine future, and—as Pope Gregory IX put it—'the Jews are the guardians of the Law; the proofs of the Christian faith's truth lie hidden in Jewish archives.' The same Pope wrote: 'We greet converted Jews with special happiness, because we hope that when a branch from a wild olive tree has been able to produce fine fruits, it may do so all the more when it is grafted on the holy trunk.'

But the most important thing was that the church considered the conversion of the 'remnant of Israel' as a necessary prelude to Christ's second coming. And all means were lawful to expedite this event.

To be sure the church's official point of view since Gregory the Great's day had been that baptism should be voluntary. But zealous impatient priests were seldom satisfied with that. It did not need much to fan the minds of the masses into a flame. For centuries they had their ears stuffed full of anti-Semitic propaganda. The Jews had crucified the Saviour and bore eternal guilt. They killed Christian children and maltreated the sacred host. Their blood was black and rotten, and they had a loathesome smell which only baptism could remove. They poisoned wells and caused diseases; they were usurers and battened on the poor. And they were rich. Just think of plundering their houses!

Then pogroms raged, Jewish houses went up in flames, the fire at the stake was lit and once more the Jews were faced with the choice of baptism or death. It also happened now and then in Spanish towns, although it was a rare occurrence before the fourteenth century.

The new converts were not to be envied. They cut themselves off from the future. As a rule they were individuals; the family seldom followed suit. And the others regarded him as the outcast of the family. Children shunned their fathers; if he died, no one mourned. The humiliation he brought on them held suitors back and his daughters stayed at home unmarried.

The priesthood came to their aid: 'A new plant shall not only be strengthened with the dew of learning, it shall also be

THE THREE RINGS

nourished with timely gifts', they proclaimed. But their new brothers were rarely enthusiastic about them. As a rule, too, it was the black sheep who sought the church. If anyone had sinned against the law of the *aljama* and was liable to severe punishment for blasphemy or whoredom, baptism was a sure refuge. Many of them showed their real colours by turning violently against their former people. They cherished hatred for their old friends out of vengeance or to justify themselves. We shall meet some highly gifted and learned renegades who became dangerous enemies of the people they had left.

But there was one thing more the church had to watch out for. It feared most of all that the Jews would win proselytes. It was long, long ago since Israel had suspended active missionary work. But it frequently happened that Christians began to take an interest in the Jewish faith. There was something about the Jews' life which attracted them. It is a known fact that if a religion is blackened enough there will always be people who begin to ask whether there is something in it, precisely because such sharp arguments are used against it. In the archives of the Inquisition we find a surprising number of documents dealing with Christians who sought out solitary remote Jewish communities and asked for shelter under the wings of Israel's God.

The punishment was swift and merciless. In 1227 a priest was executed at Oxford because he had gone over to Judaism. The church was so afraid of the Jewish infection that they used both confiscation and death to attack the proselyte and the *aljama* which had dared to receive him. As a result the circumspect Jews held back.

The end-product of all these complicated feelings and ideas was the canonical decrees, which definitely drove a wedge between the Jews and other people. The Jews were to be shunned by Christians. They could not hold any sort of authority and it was therefore forbidden to appoint them as officials. Marriage between Jew and Christian was punishable with death; the Jews could not walk the streets when religious processions went by; they must not be trusted as doctors or apothecaries; no Christian might live in the same house with them or serve them as nursemaid or foster-mother; it was forbidden to bathe with them, break bread with them and sit at the same table during mealtimes; the bonds of friendship must be broken.

Now we shall hear how things went when this spirit began to spread in Spain, which had been the country with the three rings for so long.

XII

RECONQUISTA

WE followed the great Pope Innocent III, who called for the Crusade against the Albigensians in southern France and assembled a vast army of crusaders from the whole of Europe. When the bloody work was accomplished, they looked round for new tasks and adventures. They soon found a happy hunting-ground in Spain.

For long ages the myth of the Christian reconquest—the *reconquista*—of Spain had re-echoed through many countries. In castles and towns throughout Europe strolling troubadours sang about the adventurous war between the cross and the crescent which had already lasted for five hundred years. They used bright colours, describing the distant country with towering mountains, rushing rivers and radiant cities, where Christian knights in their thousands performed heroic deeds against the heathen. There the devout could fight for the holy faith and enterprising mercenaries take beautiful women and win golden treasure to take home to a poor castle in some corner of Germany or France.

In this very year the Christian kingdoms in Spain gathered their forces for the decisive battle with the Almohades, who had held sway for so long in Andalusia. With great diplomatic skill King Alphonso VIII of Castile had formed a coalition of the kingdoms of Castile, Navarre, Portugal and Aragon.

This King Alphonso was already something of a legendary figure. Throughout his long reign he had deliberately taken Jews into his service. He himself fell in love with a young Toledan Jewess. People still sing about the lovely girl, Rachel, also called Fermosa, which means the favourite, for whose sake the king 'forgot wife, people and kingdom' for seven years and carried on an open love affair with her. This burning folly ended in bloody tragedy, when the bitterly wounded queen aroused the mob to attack the Jews and Rachel was murdered.

But there were solid facts behind the romantic stories. King Alphonso had given 'his' Jews stable conditions, but they also had the privilege of paying for them. The king extracted enormous taxes from them and they had to arrange financial operations on a hitherto unheard of scale so that the treasury could pay for the preparations for the holy war against the Moors.

Now crusaders streamed over the Pyrenees to join the campaign. In Toledo they tried to repeat their treatment of the Jews in Provence. They made a sudden attack on the *juderia* and began to murder and loot. They very soon learnt that such things were not tolerated in Spain. The Castilian knights intervened and repelled them vigorously. This happened in 1212. The year is remembered in Spanish history for in it the Christian army met the Almohades at Navas de Tolosa and won the decisive victory in the long religious war.

Deserters had captured a mountain path for the Christian high command from which the enemy could be attacked in the rear. The whole company of Christian knights was led over this path under cover of darkness and when day broke thousands of armoured knights thundered down the mountainside. They swept everything aside like a flood tide and mowed down the Moorish chieftain's bodyguard, twelve hundred camel-borne negroes, the bravest warriors North Africa could send in aid.

The battle sealed Spain's fate. A few decades later the royal banners of Castile and Leon flew above the mosque in Cordoba, once the proud capital of the glorious Caliphate. It was not long before the King of Castile also hoisted the red cross flag over the Giralda at Seville and the King of Aragon conquered Valencia. From now on Moorish dominion was reduced to the kingdom of Granada in the farthest corner of Andalusia.

THE THREE RINGS

Strangely enough the Moors managed to keep a footing there for several hundred years. The kingdom was confined to a small coastal strip with the city of Granada as its capital, together with a few small towns, but it was easy to defend. Southwards lay the sea and the way was open to help from their co-religionists in North Africa; to the north the snow-clad peaks of the Sierra Nevada barred the way, their steep narrow passes were almost impassable.

Granada was literally teeming with inhabitants. Tens of thousands of Moorish exiles had left the lost provinces and sought shelter in the last Moorish state. They were some of the most capable people in the whole of Spain and were extremely active economically, giving the Lilliputian state a vast amount of capital. Arts and crafts and trade flourished, bringing the country fame and wealth. And Granada was lucky enough to have a long line of skilful, flexible diplomats on the throne. They understood the art of the balance of power and played Mohammedan North Africa off against Christian Spain in masterly fashion. They sacrificed small frontier towns with complete cynicism and threw them to the wolves, sometimes in the north, sometimes in the south. Granada herself remained permanently free from the ravages of war and even reaped economic advantages from the eternal border warfare.

During these last two centuries Moorish art put forth its finest blooms, the wonderful buildings in the Alhambra stand as eternal witnesses to the Arabic sunet. Here one can study the horseshoe arches and the fantastically slim columns; here the arabesque is developed with staggering virtuosity and the stucco of the stalactite-like ceilings displays extraordinary patterns. But the overwhelming luxuriance also proclaims that here was a culture in its last stage; its dissolution had begun. One of the three rings was on the point of disintegrating.

The other two rings still shone and vied in brilliance. The Spanish Jews entered their most powerful period, but only superficially. The literary and philosophical golden age stopped short with Maimonides, but long afterwards Jewish skill and prosperity flourished. For the time being no one noticed that

RECONQUISTA

the great ebb had begun. But anyone who sees the events in clear perspective cannot help noticing that Jewish life was starting to become a golden shell which lacked its noble contents. When the days of dissension came, it could no longer be concealed.

The Spanish kings scoffed at the Lateran Council's anti-Semitic decrees. They needed their Jews to be able to wage war, mainly against the heathen, but they were also constantly feuding with each other, which likewise cost money. In addition, Jewish capital was needed to build up the newly-won provinces. When King Ferdinand of Castile, who was nicknamed the Holy, entered Cordoba, the city's Jews hailed him as a liberator; for centuries they had been forced to hide their faith from the Almohades. Now they handed the king a golden lock for the town gates with the Hebrew inscription: 'The king of kings unlocks the door, the earthly king enters'. And King Ferdinand acknowledged the gift by giving them back their former *juderia* and three mosques which were converted into magnificent synagogues.

Time after time the church protested against the kings' open contempt for the canonical decrees and the pope sent pressing exhortations to show obedience to the church. But none of Castile's changing kings thought seriously for a moment of losing the wonderful sponge the Jews were in their hands. It absorbed the country's money and the kings squeezed it dry over the ever empty treasure chest. The kings of Aragon did likewise, even summoning Jews from other countries where they were less well off. The list of Jewish financiers, diplomats and doctors grows longer and longer.

In Toledo Jewish scientists were particularly distinguished as astronomers or astrologists (in the Middle Ages the two names covered the same field). The cantor in Toledo's biggest synagogue, Isaac ibn Cid, compiled the famous 'Alphonsine tables' of the movements of the stars, which the great discoverers later used for navigation.

Gradually the ecclesiastical protests against the kings' pro-Jewish policy became so sharp that they were forced to make

THE THREE RINGS

certain concessions. But they did it so cunningly that they confined themselves to assisting on the theoretical front and helping the church to conduct theological discussions with Jewish rabbis to disprove the Jewish faith.

It did not look very dangerous. But theories usually lead to practice and it was to prove that the discussions became one of the sparks which sent the powder barrel into the air.

Jews have always liked discussion. The cleverest of them think quickly, their repartee is swift and surprisingly dangerous; not for nothing has their intelligence been sharpened on the whetstone of the Talmud since time immemorial. And naturally Jewish tradition teems with amusing and striking examples of rhetorical fencing. This is one of the stories which gives a good idea of the method:

'Who created heaven and earth?' Abraham asked his father Terah.

The latter pointed to one of his effigies and said: 'This image is our God.'

When Terah had gone, Abraham decided to see if it was true. He had a cake of fine flour baked and put in front of the god. It did not eat the cake. Then Abraham had another cake baked, this time of even finer flour. But it was not eaten either, and when the god neither ate nor said anything Abraham was angry; he set fire to all the divine images in Terah's house and burnt them.

When Terah came home and saw what had happened, he asked Abraham: 'Who did that?'

'They quarrelled and then they burnt each other,' was Abraham's answer.

'You fool,' scolded Terah, 'how can you believe that images which can neither walk nor eat can do that?'

Then Abraham answered: 'How can you leave the living God and serve gods who can neither hear nor see?'

But Nimrod heard what Abraham had done and summoned him: 'Don't you know that I am God and rule over the whole world? Then how dare you burn my images?'

RECONQUISTA

But Abraham said: 'If you really are God and rule the world, why do you not make the sun rise in the west and set in the east? Why don't you tell me what I am thinking about now and what I shall think in the future?'

Nimrod said: 'You must worship fire.'

'Why not water which puts out fire?' answered Abraham.

'Then worship the water.'

'Why not the clouds which absorb the water?'

'Let be, worship the clouds.'

But Abraham was not finished: 'Rather let me worship the wind which drives the clouds away.'

'You can worship the wind.'

Abraham was still not tired. 'A man can walk into the wind or build a house which gives him shelter from it.'

Now Nimrod could go no further; he had his servants bind Abraham—but God stepped in and freed him!

And here is an example of a discussion between a Jew and a heathen in the days of the Emperor Hadrian and the Son of a Star.

The heathen asks the Jew: 'If your God is almighty, why does he not destroy the false gods?'

The Jew answered: 'Why should the sun and the moon and the stars perish because a few fools worship them?'

'Yes, but there are many sacred images he could destroy without damaging anyone.'

'Then neither stolen seed which is put in the earth could sprout nor a child which is conceived in whoredom be born. No, the world goes its way according to the laws God has decreed. Transgressors meet their reward later.'

The tone was different when Jews and Christians began to wrangle. It was bitter and sarcastic as when members of a family quarrel, but for the time being it had no more serious consequences than the smoke in the kitchen usually involves. For the Middle Ages were a time when two opponents could debate objectively and peacefully, and have mutual respect for each other. We have several examples of ecclesiastics who felt inferior to learned, witty Jews, and sometimes the latter even dared to criticize the church's dogmas.

The turning point came with Pope Innocent III. He imbued the church with the spirit of the Inquisition, and the Dominicans pursued their merciless crusade against everything which deviated from the church's teaching. Now public discussions became veritable pitched battles between two deadly enemies. The Dominicans had a flair for publicity and arranged the debates like real theatrical performances, big public shows, at which the king and all the personalities of church and state sat in the royal box and the front row of the stalls. They were simulated tournaments in the fashion of the time, but the Jews were fated to suffer defeat in advance, with the whole people present to witness their humiliation. Innocent fencing scenes became deadly earnest. One party encountered the enemy in armour, with heavy, sharp weapons, the other was uncovered and had only a wooden sabre to defend itself with.

To be quite sure of victory, the Dominicans were fond of putting renegade Jews in the first rank. They nosed out learned, intelligent Jews who had suffered spiritual shipwreck for one reason or another and been sheltered by the church. As often happens, some of them became extreme fanatics in the new faith; they seized willingly on opportunities to humble their former brothers. They went through the Talmud and Jewish liturgy with a fine toothcomb to find weak or ambiguous points, and they squeezed them inexorably to find quotations which could be represented as 'blasphemous' or as slanderings of Christian dogmas, or Jesus himself.

Both parties prepared themselves zealously when they undertook such tournaments. Learned theologians, both Christian and Jewish, wrote handbooks in which arguments, questions and answers were systematically arranged, so that a man could quickly find what he needed in the heat of conflict. Some of these guides still exist, so that we can follow the discussions closely.

Naturally, the Jews at once found material for attack in the

Christian doctrine of the Trinity and God's mother. They also asked to whom Jesus was calling from the cross when He complained: 'My God, my God, why hast thou forsaken me?' Was He asking himself for help, for after all He was God? And why had He not come four thousand years earlier than He actually did come to free mankind from original sin after Adam and Eve? Then He would have made hundreds of generations happy which now had to suffer the torments of hell. And—continues the argument—how can you Christians claim that the Jews are scattered throughout the world as a punishment because their forefathers surrendered Christ to an agonizing death? If Jesus came into the world to save mankind by His suffering and death, the ancient Jews had surely only acted as He would have wished by letting Him die. Why should their successors suffer then? Looking at the matter closely, they had done Him a good deed.

There are countless examples of witty, subtle intelligence in this art of fencing. A priest asked Rabbi Nathan why there were no bells in the synagogue. The Rabbi took his Christian opponent to the fish market. A few miserable street traders stood outside offering their stale fish to the passers-by in loud voices. But when they entered the actual fish market and came to the stalls with good fresh fish, there was no one shouting.

'There you are,' said Rabbi Nathan, 'the man who has good wares to sell does not need to advertise, the wares sell themselves. That is the reason we Jews can dispense with bell-ringing!'

Another priest asked Rabbi Nathan: 'Why did God reveal Himself to Moses in a burning thorn bush? Why did He not use another tree?' And Nathan answered: 'Because it is impossible to carve a cross from a bush of thorns!'

The first of the great public disputations took place in Paris at the court of Louis IX. It ended with twenty-four waggon-loads of Talmudic writings being ceremonially burnt. The next was held in Spain in the royal castle at Barcelona, the capital

THE THREE RINGS

of Catalonia, on July 20, 1263. It became the classical example of a disputation. A fanatical renegade Jew, brother Pablo, met the greatest name in Judaism at the time, Rabbi Moses ben Nahman.

When brother Pablo was baptized, he entered the Dominican order and became one of its most celebrated agitators. He travelled through Provence and Catalonia, preaching; people called him an apostle and one of his specialities was challenging rabbis to disputations. His favourite trick in these debates was to prove Christian dogmas from the Talmud! Naturally this attracted attention and Pablo's brother monks saw a choice instrument in him. Finally they had managed to persuade King James of Aragon that this man could open the Jews' eyes.

This King James was one of Aragon's great kings. He it was who reconquered Valencia; the exploit earned him the name of Conqueror. He ruled for more than sixty years and had both protected his Spanish Jews better and squeezed more out of them than any other Spanish king. He realized perfectly well that to convert them to Christianity might be an expensive jest, and he was certainly none too keen on the experiment. But King James had reached the age when the devil a monk would be and his confessors acquired more and more power over him. Whatever the reason, the king agreed to arrange the disputation in Barcelona.

Rabbi Moses ben Nahman is one of the few great Jewish names after the golden age had gone. He was tremendously popular and celebrated; so much so that he not only had his name transcribed into Greek, Nahmanides, but the people also contracted—as they had with the great Maimonides or Rambam—its Hebrew letters to Ramban; his nickname was to recall that of his great predecessor!

Throughout his long life he lived in his native town of Gerona and worked—again like Maimonides—as a doctor and legal teacher; finally he was appointed chief rabbi of Catalonia. Nahmanides was one of the conservative theologians; his respect for the results of earlier generations was boundless: 'we

RECONQUISTA

bow to them; even if their word does not always convince us, we must yield to it.' But the Cabbala's mysticism also found a friend in him and with his great authority he studied it—but not without reserve and critical glosses.

Until he was seventy he had lived quietly and peacefully in Gerona, surrounded by his family and numerous pupils. But his peace was rudely interrupted when he received a message from the king to go to Barcelona and defend his faith at a disputation with brother Pablo.

The royal palace was the setting for the brilliant drama. It teemed with courtiers, knights, bishops, priests and monks. The black-clad Jewish Rabbis did not cut much of a figure among the elegant red, yellow and blue costumes and gem-studded weapons. But when the verbal battle took place, even the most fanatical opponents had to bow to Nahmanides' wit and learning.

He fully realized the risk he ran, so he secured a promise of freedom of speech from the king. The subjects of discussion were the usual ones: whether the Messiah had already come, or whether He was to be expected; whether He was born of Jewish parents or had a divine nature. Nahmanides claimed that the prophets had foretold that the Messiah would introduce an era of peace, but that it certainly had not come yet.

'It is written that the peoples shall forge the sword into ploughshares and no one shall learn to fight any more. What if you, Lord King, and your knights were forced to leave your art of fencing on the shelf now?'

The high point came when Nahmanides turned directly to the King and said:

'You, Lord King, are the son of a Christian man and born of a Christian woman. All your life Christian priests have hammered one thing into your brain, a conception which is absolutely contrary to everything reason, nature and the prophets foretell: that the creator of heaven and earth shall become flesh and blood in a Jewish mother's womb, undergo a normal pregnancy, be born a baby, grow up and be handed over to the enemy, condemned to death and finally rise from

THE THREE RINGS

the dead to return to his divine state. Such conceptions are incomprehensible to us Jews; all your rhetoric is in vain. On this point our ways part, never to meet again!'

In the midst of the discussions Nahmanides scored a point with his rapid brain. Brother Pablo said that the doctrine of the trinity was so deep a mystery that not even the angels could fathom it. Nahmanides riposted like a flash: 'In that case you can scarcely hold us responsible for finding this mystery incomprehensible too!'

That is a glimpse of those discussions in the olden days which it still topical today in every conflict between the two religions. But Nahmanides' daring speech caused irritation at the time, especially in the Jewish quarter of the town. The Jews knew only too well what they could expect if the Dominicans had to avenge a defeat.

So Nahmanides suggested bringing the disputation to a close after four days. The king agreed and paid Nahmanides many compliments before he left. He had never heard so brilliant a defence of a wrongful case, he said. As usual both parties proclaimed themselves the victors. And the Dominicans had power behind them. The outcome was that Nahmanides was forced to leave Spain. He spent his last days in the Holy Land; he gathered a new circle of pupils around him at Acco. But he was tormented by homesickness; in one of his letters we find these moving human words:

'I left my dear ones, deserted my house. At home I had sons and daughters; once they were sweet little babies and sat on my knee. I left my soul behind with them; my heart stayed with them and my eyes seek them.'

The disputation in Barcelona had far-reaching consequences. The Dominicans realized that propaganda must be changed; now it was the general run of Jewish people who mattered, not the intellectuals. Decrees were issued laying down that all Jews, men and women, had to put in an appearance and listen to Christian preachers. And the Dominicans took no risks. Monks stood at the entrance and checked that the Jews had not stuffed cottonwool in their ears and others went round poking people with sharp sticks if they looked like falling asleep. Dominican monks also made a point of breaking into synagogues in the middle of a service. They planted a cross in front of the ark containing the Torah and forced the community to listen to what they preached. The net spread around the Jews and it was difficult to find a hole to slip through.

In 1413 the greatest disputation of all began in Tortosa. The attendant pomp and ceremony was on an unparalelled scale. Even the pope—admittedly only a so-called pope; there was a dispute for the papal throne—was present. The disputation dragged on for one year and nine months, a genuine marathon feat of rhetoric.

But then the darkness of night had already fallen over the Spanish Jews. In 1391 injustice became the order of the day for the Jews in Spain.

It had to happen some time; every trend in the developing situation pointed to it. The Jews had mighty enemies. Both the nobility and the growing middle classes felt threatened by them, and the church had preached against them for centuries. The only remarkable thing was that the catastrophe had not come much sooner. In every other European country the Jews were wandering through the valley of the shadow of death. In 1290 they were driven out of England. France banished them in 1306. A few years later they were given permission to return, but in 1394 they were chased out of the country definitively. It is one of history's inexplicable freaks that Christian Spain, which crusaded against the Saracens for centuries, should be the great exception. But now the last grain of sand was running out of the hour-glass there too.

Finally the ecclesiastical reactionaries felt strong enough to strike the decisive blow. They found their standard-bearer in the Archbishop of Seville himself, Ferrand Martinez, a fiery fanatic and Jew-baiter.

This firebrand lavished accusations against the Jews all over the country. The Jews had taken over the real power in the kingdom; tax collectors piled up mountains of gold; the king was their obedient tool who spread their evil teaching and would soon turn the churches into synagogues. The only salvation was to extirpate them and raze the synagogues to the ground; they had been breeding grounds for poisonous propaganda for long enough!

The masses got the message although the royal authorities did what they could to hold them in check and the pope himself forbade violence. But now the avalanche had started and nothing could stop it. In Seville the mob stormed the *juderia* and murdered 4,000 Jews. The riots spread from town to town. In Cordoba and Toledo and Burgos the Jewish quarters were in flames and thousands of corpses lay strewn in the blazing ruins and streets. The bloody tidal wave reached Barcelona and crossed the sea to Majorca. The large Jewish community which had done so much for scientific and technical progress was annihilated.

Until now Spanish Jews had been spectators, watching from afar the fate which befell their brothers in other European countries without giving a thought to the possibility that similar things could happen in smiling Spain. History repeats itself. Around the turn of the last century the French and German Jews sat in the security of their snug homes and heard about their fellow Jews suffering agonies in the pogroms. At the time no one could imagine the fate which awaited German Jewry in the 1930's and French Jewry in the 1940's. But it is impossible to set bounds to spiritual contamination; this was as true in 1933 as in 1391.

The Spanish Jews were not brave martyrs. Naturally there were many who chose death before baptism and gave their lives for their faith. But by far the greatest number gave in and accepted baptism. Now the fact that the great majority had started a process of spiritual degeneration could no longer be concealed. They had become half Spanish and allowed themselves to absorb a foreign culture. Such things frequently happen when people are well off materially speaking— prosperity and progress make the bold front crumble. It was unthinkable for them to accept the degradation which hung

RECONQUISTA

over them; they tried to continue as Jews—if they got off with their lives.

For now canon law was to be enforced to the letter. Jews could only live behind the walls of the *juderia*; they had to wear the badge of Judaism and wear hideous clothes; they could not cut their hair or beards, they could not—it is frankly impossible to enumerate the endless paragraphs, each of which meant a spit in the face for the Jews.

So they gave in. Even if—as people said—their tears blended with the baptismal water, they went to the font. But if these compulsory converts, the so-called *Marranos*—a nickname which means swine—had dreamt of the fate which awaited them and their children, they would certainly have chosen death or tried to flee from Spain in time.

The events of 1391 were called the 'Holy War'. The method proved its worth; tens of thousands of Jews were taken into the fold of the church. New bigoted priests and bishops leapt into the front line and continued the battle. Once again Jewish renegades showed their zeal.

Bishop Paul of Burgos was a baptized rabbi who tried to be more catholic than the pope himself. Even more virulent in his hate was Joshua of Lorca, who when he was baptized had been given the resounding name Geronimo de Santa Fé, i.e. Hieronymus of the holy faith; he was catholic standard-bearer at the disputation in Tortosa.

But worst of all was Vicente Ferrer, a gloomy Dominican, who went through the whole of Catalonia and Aragon, surrounded by shrieking flagellants, and preached 'holy hate' against the peoples with different faiths, Moors and Jews. With cross in hand he burst into synagogues in the middle of the service. He was flanked by a threatening mob who added their own weight to the threats. In Toledo he dedicated the synagogue on the spot to the immaculate virgin, Santa Maria la Blanca.

Now the state authorities began to put the brakes on. The kings were dismayed when they saw their income vanishing away. The special Jewish taxes had almost disappeared. The taxpayers were either christened and consequently exempt from payment or they sat among the ruins of their houses, workshops or warehouses without a penny to bless themselves with. It was necessary to give the Jews a breathing-space so that they would be able to pay up again. No one likes killing the goose which lays the golden eggs. A more pleasant period set in, in which the Jews were allowed to reorganize and the severest decrees were modified.

In any case every culture needs some peace to thrive. The stormy time set its mark on the Spanish Jews who remained true to their hereditary religion. Literature is always the straw in the wind which shows the direction of ideas and thoughts. And most of what we possess by Jewish authors from this time consists of apologia or bitter blunt attacks on the Christianity which had been so hard on them.

Naturally the church and the Christian community accepted the new Christians with joy. They had bowed to the word of truth and were a living witness to the church's triumph. Many of them were distinguished people, the richest, most refined and most cultivated—in other words those who had most to lose and so were the first to give in. For the time being there were not so many. It seems to be a rule that so long as there are not too many Jews in a community, the people find it easier to tolerate them.

So the new Christians saw the doors open to them and they soon merged with the Spanish aristocracy; it was not long before the majority of distinguished Spanish families married into newly converted Christian families. Many were businessmen of long standing; they made new connections, while holding onto the old ones and money flowed into their coffers. They started fortunes, bought property and soon filled high offices. And now the Jews were not satisfied with civil offices, because the church's doors stood open to them. They penetrated deeply into the Christian hierarchy, sitting as bishops or controlling the financial affairs of monasteries. The Jewish family of Caballerio from Saragossa included among its members a bishop, a vice-rector at the university, the minister

RECONQUISTA

of finance in the Kingdom of Navarre, the vice-chancellor of the Kingdom of Aragon, the speaker in the Cortes, which corresponds to our parliament, a high court judge and—a much talked-about anti-Semitic writer. The example is by no means unique.

But these happy days were short numbered; the reaction soon set in. The more there were of these capable people, the more Spaniards found themselves forced out of jobs they had counted on. And the new Christians not only took over new jobs, they kept the old ones as well and held key positions as administrators of taxes and state finances, and they were willing to act as money-lenders. A distinguished nobleman must have gone white with rage when he found that he could no longer beat his usurer when the interest was too exorbitant. Now the usurer himself was a grandee!

It was at this time that the opprobrious word *Marrano* appeared and was used instead of new Christian. Christian Spain had done all it could to bring the Jews into the church. Now they had partially succeeded, but gradually a frightful suspicion arose. Perhaps the enemy was far more dangerous inside the walls than he had been outside? Had the renegades sneaked into the Christian fortress so as to be able to blow it up the better?

It was clear that by far the most *Marranos* were only Christians in appearance. They were baptized, they went to the priest to get married, they went to mass and confession— like good catholics. But behind this external pretence the old existence went on unchanged. When they left the church with a newly baptized child they hastened to wash the holy water off.

At home they carefully observed their ancient ceremonies, as far as possible. Anyone who stood on top of a tower on a Saturday could count the *Marranos'* houses. No smoke came from their chinmeys because the *Marranos* lit no fires on holy days. A *Marrano* told his circle of acquaintances that unfortunately he could not stand leavened bread. All the year round he ate unleavened bread to be protected in Easter week. The *Marranos* used to circumcise their new-born babies. They hung together and helped each other; when they were colleagues in the business world, they preferred to marry other *Marranos*. During this time the old word *anussim* also cropped up again. We met it in Maimonides' time when it was used of Jews whom the Almohades forcibly converted to apparent acceptance of Islam. Now the *Marranos* felt like Christian slaves. They were Israel in the thrall of Egypt and were entitled to deceive and exploit their Christian neighbours.

Once again the pulpit began to re-echo with Jew-baiting sermons, this time not against genuine Jews but those who had sneaked in to sanctuary. The Spanish community was divided on the question of the *Marranos*. That was when the theory of 'pure blood' was launched. Iberian blood was superior; Jewish and Moorish blood inferior. Newly appointed officials were required to produce Aryan certificates. There is nothing new under the sun. Liberal circles counted a *Marrano* as one of them and were eager to destroy the barrier between true Spaniards and newly converted Jews. But naturally they had the short end of the stick.

There were towns where the tension was released in regular battles. Fanatical mobs stormed the houses of the *Marranos*. But they had weapons and defended themselves. Sometimes they actually conquered, but as a rule they had to yield. Then it meant death and fire. There was no salvation for them in baptism. It was out of the question, for they were baptized already!

It did not take much more to bring things to a head. In Cordoba a religious procession was passing through the streets. Suddenly a rumour spread that a *Marrano* girl had emptied a chamber pot out of the window and soiled the image of the holy virgin! The mob went berserk on the spot. The massacre only stopped when they could find no more victims. But such violence was not confined to Cordoba. The disease spread from town to town. The *Marranos* were murdered and their houses burnt and plundered.

The closing chords of this melancholy symphony of destiny begin to sound.

RECONQUISTA

For long centuries Spain had seen the three rings sparkle. Christians, Moors and Jews had lived side by side. They had mutually inspired and fertilized each other; their different cultures were woven together into a beautiful, richly coloured tapestry. Throughout the darkness of the Middle Ages Spain had shone like a burning torch.

The country had the distinction of holding back when other European countries were celebrating wild orgies at the expense of their Jewish guests.

But now the goal was reached. Finally we see Spain abandon her restraint and hasten to make up for lost time, outdoing the others in severity against Jews and Moors. The old Visigothic spirit awakes and advances with the motto: One faith, one state, one religion.

It is the *reconquista*; not only the country, but also peoples' hearts must be reconquered. The people shall fuse into one, if necessary from the heat of the blazing fire at the stake. The obstinate must be driven out.

The stage is set for the last act.

Isabella the Catholic makes her entrance.

XIII

ISABELLA

ISABELLA was a long-legged eleven-year-old girl with red hair, a pretty round face and big, light blue eyes when she first visited her half-brother King Henry IV at the court of Castile.

A sensation had happened. Everyone knew that the degenerate, extravagant and flabby king was sexually impotent—and now the queen, the gay, cheerful Juana of Portugal, had given birth to an heir, a little girl, after eight years of childless marriage. A young nobleman, Beltran de Cueva, handsome as a Greek god, had come to the fore at court. He became the king's favourite and the queen's lover. The former favourites found themselves out of the king's good graces, which were reserved for the new rising star. Foremost among them was the Marquis of Villena, who had ruled the king with a rod of iron and amassed an enormous fortune which made him the most powerful man in Castile.

A weak king and a court which is a battlefield for rival ambitions cannot rule a kingdom properly. Castile, then, was on the point of dissolution at the time. Justice was knocked down to the highest bidder; law and order did not exist outside the fortified castles and strong powers of the towns; the kingdom lay open to looting knights or robber bands, and everyone grabbed whatever he could lay hands on.

The young red-haired princess—the colour was a legacy from her English forefathers of the house of Plantaganet—had lived unnoticed in retirement in a castle, together with her mother and a younger brother. There she stayed, engrossed in her books, receiving education in the noble arts which a well-born girl of those days was expected to master. She was well-read, proud of her royal birth, strong willed and clear-sighted, and her spiritual mentors had been lucky enough to instil her with a wholehearted, almost fanatical devotion to the secrets of the faith and unconditional submission to God's will as she found it in his holy catholic church. Today we would undoubtedly call her a bigot. But in her kingdom, bigotry was a shining virtue—and for that matter still is today in Franco's Catholic Spain.

The royal castle towered up, based on a high cliff overlooking the almost waterless Manzanares; it had grown up around Madrid's ancient Moorish fortress. The Alcazar was perched up there like an eagle's nest on its inaccessible peak; its small windows flashed in the sun like bird's eyes out to the distant snowclad summits of the Guadarrama shining in the sun. For centuries the spacious patios in the castle with their slender columns and halls hung with Gobelin tapestries had seen all too much of Castile's history and terrible dramatic events.

But never had the scene been so pregnant with evil, as when the court met one spring day in the castle chapel and the newly born baby princess was christened. The courtiers set their mouths in complaisant smiles, but their raised eyebrows contradicted their amiability, and behind gloved hands they whispered the nickname which never left the little princess, Beltraneja, after the man who was presumed to be her father.

The drama's protagonists were grouped around the font. There stood the king, red-haired and hirsute, with feeble gestures and weak features, the handsome Beltran who was responsible for everything, Villena, who had already decided to crush the child he was now acting as godfather to, and the eleven-year-old Isabella who successfully concealed the fact that young as she was, she saw through them and realized in her inner mind the possibilities that opened up for her. Only Isabella's confessors knew her secret thoughts—and he who could hear her burning prayers which she whispered for hours on end.

THE THREE RINGS

A hotch-potch of intrigues and humiliations for the king followed the christening. A commission was set up to investigate his ability to have children. Once he declared on oath that he was Beltraneja's father, but the next time that he was not. Villena raised the flag of rebellion, but rapidly made peace with King Henry again. One of the conditions was his brother's marriage to Isabella.

But it was far from her ambitious dreams to marry an upstart, nothing in the world would force her to such a humiliation. When the triumphant bridegroom rode forth to fetch his royal bride, his path was crossed with poison; in a roadside inn he suffered an agonizing death. We do not know whether Isabella was an accomplice. She would not have hesitated to sanction the deed; she was not one of those who shrank from causing others suffering if she saw that it was inevitable.

Isabella withdrew to the convent of Santa Clara at Avila. She was now seventeen and far more mature than her years. Events had sharpened her judgment, now all she was waiting for was the right moment. But no one knew her as she was in her heart of hearts. Villena and his fellows needed a royal personage for their plans. They counted on a girl so young being a willing tool in their hands and offered her the crown of Castile. Villena gauged her brother's shame and unworthiness, and naturally kept silent about his real plans.

But it was not part of Isabella's plans to weaken respect for the crown which she suddenly saw within her grasp. It had been wrested from the heathen through seven hundred years of holy war; the *reconquista's* high minded religiosity had endowed the wearer of the crown with divine sanction. It would be sacrilege to insult the crown. Isabella's hour had not yet come. She wanted to use the crown to sway noblemen and princes like Villena. So she refused.

Instead all the intrigues were directed towards getting her married to the right man. There was no lack of suitors; there were English princes, Portuguese princes, the King of France's brother and the heir to the throne of Aragon, the young prince Ferdinand.

ISABELLA

Isabella struck out most of the list, they suited Villena's plans too well, moreover one of them, the French prince, was described as a little weakling with skinny legs and watery eyes. And this devout princess was a warm-blooded girl; the man she wanted had to be quite different from her impotent half-brother.

It began as normal girlish falling in love, with a man she had never seen. Ferdinand had been praised to the skies by the people Isabella had sent to have a look at him and collect information. He was about her age, tall, strong and lissome, with great gifts. Suddenly it dawned on her that no one else fitted in so well with her plans. Her intention was to crush the noble tyrants who had brought anarchy on the country. The army of Aragon would make her stronger than any other alliance.

The wily old King Juan of Aragon, Ferdinand's father, also had his ideas. Aragon's future lay at sea, but France was a dangerous competitor when Barcelona's red and yellow banner was to be carried against the heathen Levant. Aragon was a poor country, but once united with the greater and richer Castile, everything would be possible. Without the slightest scruples, King Juan discarded his eldest son for the benefit of the younger Ferdinand. He was prepared to do anything to make Aragon great.

But Villena saw through both Isabella and Juan, and was stricken with panic. By making fantastic bribes he managed to arrange a lightning engagement between Isabella and the King of Portugal. But then Isabella had already secretly betrothed herself to Ferdinand and she gave the Portuguese envoy a polite refusal. Villena was furious and Isabella was in danger of her life. At the time nothing was easier to get rid of troublesome monarchs. But she had the heart of a lion as well as the cunning of a snake. And no one was as skilful at invoking a man's admiration and help. A handful of gallant knights escorted her to the strong city of Valladolid, where she could feel safe.

But there was no time to lose. Messengers in disguise hurried between Ferdinand and Isabella. An imposing cavalcade of Aragon's personalities rode openly on the high roads to the

THE THREE RINGS

King of Castile. No one noticed a modest group of four merchants who hastened to Valladolid by devious mountain passes. Their servant was a fair-haired youngster, handsome and dashing. He was Ferdinand, hastening to his bride. If he had fallen into Villena's hands, it would have been all up with him, but he arrived safely.

One of history's great crossroads was passed when the Bishop of Valladolid married Isabella and Ferdinand. The two kingdoms became one; Spain was united.

Naturally there was still a lot to be done. But step by step everything was arranged. King Henry was poisoned and died according to plan. Villena arranged Beltraneja's engagement to the rejected King of Portugal. He invaded Castile with a strong army and everything seemed to collapse for Isabella. But summoning up their last remaining forces, the armies of Castile and Aragon were victorious. Villena was killed. And now towns and castles opened their gates, as Ferdinand and Isabella took possession of their kingdom. The Catholic Kings (*Los Reyes Catolicos*) as Isabella and Ferdinand were called, ruled Spain from the Pyrenees to the Pillars of Hercules. Little Moorish Granada was the only blemish of heathendom on the cross's reconquered country.

By one of the strokes of fate Isabella and Ferdinand were the two greatest political geniuses of their time. Although barely twenty-seven they had acquired experience and won back the kingdom. And never had Spain seen such a beautiful queen as when Castile paid homage to Isabella. In scarlet brocade, with her golden crown outshone by her red hair, she rode on a snow-white horse which was decorated with gold flowers on its withers, caparison and saddle. Fourteen noblewomen followed her in gaily coloured skirts, half burgundy-coloured velvet, half green brocade, and their head-dresses were shaped like crowns. Knights and noblemen surrounded her, and Ferdinand rode by her side on his charger, armed with his lance, the proudest knight in Spain.

Isabella was definitely the greater personality of the two; her disposition was full of both dignity and sweetness, as everyone

ISABELLA

felt who came into contact with her. Her striking religious humility and devotion won the men of the church. There is no reason for doubting her genuineness and good intentions, but she shrank from no methods of achieving what she believed was right. Nor should we think that she loved cruelty for cruelty's sake, although she never shrank from it when she found it necessary.

There are enigmas in Isabella's nature which are only clarified when we learn that her mother was insane. After her husband's death she lapsed into melancholy religious mania, a legacy several of her successors had to bear. And Isabella lived in strict isolation in her childhood and early youth, shut up in a convent where all her surroundings filled her with mystical religious exaltation.

During seven hundred years of war Christian Spain had gradually won back the kingdom for the cross. It felt as if it was the leader of a divine mission to re-establish the cross's dominion all over the earth. And had not saints in shining armour, wearing the cross, appeared in the sky and proclaimed the victory of God's own army, and relics and talismans assured success? Mysticism and aspiration for martyrdom filled the spiritual climate in Isabella's first impressionable years. She herself, a saint-like neurotic, who incidentally was both genius and queen, fully shared Castile's national role.

There was one man who fostered and fed the growth of these feelings in her young impressionable mind, a burning soul who did not know the meaning of compromise, Isabella's confessor, the Dominican Tomas Torquemada.

As the queen's confessor and spiritual mentor he never stopped telling her of the ruler's holy duty to uproot the weeds of heresy, both root and branch. No ruler could be happy if he or she did not ruthlessly harry heretics, heathens or sceptics for the sake of God's honour. The whole of the Dominican Order's pride and arrogance was combined in Torquemada, and of Isabella he fashioned a weapon of steel, ruled by a heart of both ice and fire, which he constantly egged on to pitiless combat. Isabella could equally well have uttered the words actually said by her great-grandson, King Phillip II, that come what may he would never be king of heretical subjects. Ferdinand was just as despotic and ambitious as Isabella, but his methods were different. He wanted to make united Spain great and powerful. He also saw that religious unity was necessary if he was to wield a sharp weapon. But Isabella's exalted mysticism was foreign to his temperament. He was a man of action. He never kept an oath longer than it paid him to; he blithely changed his convictions when it was profitable and piloted his way between opposing interests. He was the born cynic, who even made use of things sacred.

The religious minority in the country had no idea what consequences the union of absolute monarchy and clericalism had in store for them. Both Jews and *Marranos* hailed the marriage of Ferdinand and Isabella, and the country's unity with undivided sympathy. The *Marranos* observed that Ferdinand had cultivated friendship with *Marrano* families and that Isabella had surrounded herself with Jewish advisers. Moreover, the distinguished tax collector, the Jew Abraham Senior of Segovia, had given invaluable assistance during the dynastic negotiations which preceded the marriage.

Ferdinand had high ambitions. Barcelona was to be the mistress of the Mediterranean. But he realized that he must first follow his Queen on a Crusade and cleanse Spain of the last plague of heathendom in Granada. It could easily be the beginning of christianizing the Levant.

The Catholic Kings' ideas coincided on the subject of the *Marranos*. Ferdinand needed money. He discovered that the people in Spain with the most ready money were precisely the men whose orthodoxy was open to attack. If he seized the opportunity he could be rich beyond the dreams of avarice. Isabella had the same goal as Ferdinand, but she lacked his greed. If she could extend Christ's kingdom on earth, crush His enemies and raise the cross high, so that the kingdom was cleansed of heathenism, she would win the honour she strove for. The methods they employed were widely different, but they wanted the same thing; and they reached their goal.

ISABELLA

Both Isabella and Ferdinand put pressure on the pope to obtain a bull proclaiming the establishment of a combined court of inquiry and tribunal in Spain, an Inquisition with extraordinary powers to examine and punish *Marranos* who secretly clung to their former faith. The negotiations dragged, because the Spanish monarchs wanted it laid down that the fortunes they expected to extract from the victims of the Inquisition should not go to the church but clink in the royal treasury. Finally the pope gave in and issued the fateful bull in 1480. Isabella still held back for two years before she dared take the final step. But in 1482 she established the Inquisition in Seville, which was the *Marranos'* stronghold.

The *Marranos* were taken in their beds. They had indeed heard unpleasant rumours that something was afoot, but they preferred not to believe the worst and—like the German Jews in the 1930's—allowed themselves to be misled by unrealistic hopes that the storm would blow over and that all was not lost. They were soon to find out how illusory their dreams were.

The Dominicans organized the affair. Every possibility had been thought of and they had made careful preparations. Their thoroughness is reminiscent of the Gestapo's—even if the motives for persecuting the Jews were not the same.

An instruction was drafted which all the officials of the Inquisition had to comply with. In it there was a list of characteristic features which they should pay attention to when they were in search of *Marranos*. It was suspicious if someone changed his clothes or did not light a fire on Saturday and other Jewish festivals, if he laid his hand in blessing on his child's head, if he omitted 'Glory be to the father and the son' when reading the Psalms and even if a dying man turned his face to the wall in his last moment. The hunt for heretics was on; it was the duty of every Christian to denounce any suspicious persons whose tracks he came upon.

Torquemada was the master mind of the Inquisition. He was the humblest man in the kingdom, therefore his zeal knew no bounds. And he became the mightiest man in Spain, because

THE THREE RINGS

he was master of the Queen's conscience and filled Ferdinand's money bags.

Torquemada directed the Inquisition's activity. A period of grace was announced in every town. All penitents could assemble before the court within thirty or forty days and confess whether they had cherished secret sympathy for Judaism. Then they would get off with paying a fine—a severe one, to be sure —towards the costs of the holy war against Granada. When they walked in procession through the streets in their penitents' shirts, they would count as 'reconciled with the church'. Those who waited to report until after the expiry of the period of grace had their whole fortunes confiscated and were condemned to life imprisonment.

But anyone who ventured into the proximity of the Inquisition was forced to denounce everyone he suspected of 'Judaizing tendencies', as the mighty Dominicans put it. If it was not done rapidly and voluntarily, the rack was there to help; it had a special gift for making tongues wag.

The prisons were soon filled; the prisoners were packed together in cramped subterranean cells. The food and drink, doled out in niggardly amounts, were awful; sanitary installations were non-existent so that the captives lay in their own and others' ordure; the stench was indescribable. Day and night demented heart-rending screams came from the torture chambers. Here the *élite* of the town met in surroundings which were brutally different from those they were accustomed to. For the *Marranos* belonged to the upper classes; they were intellectuals or rich, refined men in important offices. Now their limbs were stretched on the rack, and trembling and senseless with pain they stammered out all the confessions their tormentors required.

Every week the fire at the stake blazed. The condemned, clad in penitential garb, were led through the streets of the town in ceremonial procession. The most distinguished people in the country were waiting in the biggest square, often with the king or queen at their head, to watch the solemn *auto-da-fé*, as the execution was called. (The words mean an act of faith.)

They sat on a lofty tribune, so that they could follow all the details. The aristocracy had their own seats and the common people filled the square in teeming crowds. A royal personage had the honorary task of lighting the fire.

The only punishment permitted was to burn the heretics alive; it was called 'putting to death without shedding blood'. As a special favour those who repented at the last moment were tortured before the fire at the stake was lit. Not even the dead could rest in peace. If a man died on the rack or in his cell, his corpse was burnt. Dead people who had long rested in the earth and were now denounced as sympathizers with the Jews were exhumed and burnt, and their fortunes confiscated.

The Inquisition began in Seville and had its headquarters there, but it was not long before it had branches in other towns. The country was stricken with panic and terror. Deputation from all over the kingdom came to the king or queen with humble petitions to have the terror stopped. The pope himself intervened and wrote that the decrees against the *Marranos* sprang not from 'zeal for the faith or solicitude for curing souls but from covetousness!'

But nothing could halt the Inquisition—Isabella's heart was afire with zeal and Ferdinand watched the *Marranos*' gold flowing into the treasury in streams. Isabella's submission to the men of the church knew no bounds. It was at this time she acquired a new confessor; Torquemada had enough to do running the Inquisition. In his place came Father Talavera. The first time Isabella went to confess to him, he ordered her to kneel like the other penitents. She reminded him that it was customary for royalty to sit beside their confessor. But Talavera corrected her severely and said that his seat was God's seat, before which everyone, without exception, had to kneel. Then the queen knelt before him—and later she praised Father Talavera for his zeal.

In Aragon there was agitation against the Inquisition. The Aragonese had the reputation of being stiff, stubborn and severe. It was said that an Aragonese mother who had born a child hammered a pine cone into its head as soon as it was born. If the pine cone split into pieces it was a sign that he was a good Aragonese. If his head shattered, it did not matter. The lad was not worth anything!

The Inquisitor in Aragon was called Pedro Arbuez. He was the most zealous of all and abolished even the customary period of grace for penitents. In Aragon everyone who was suspected was immediately imprisoned, put on the rack until he confessed and led straight to the stake.

But Arbuez's terror led to counter-terror. He was well aware that conspirators were after his blood and he never ventured into the street without armour and helmet. Nevertheless the *Marranos* got him. Early one morning Arbuez entered the empty church to hear mass. At the very moment when he knelt at the altar, three masked men crept from their ambush between the columns and stabbed him. Naturally the result was fresh arrests and many fires at the stake.

The first fire was lit at Seville a few weeks after the introduction of the Inquisition. It was followed by countless others both in Seville and all over Spain. Naturally the Dominicans were not satisfied with *Marranos*. All heretics ought to be eradicated. Long after the *Marranos* were reduced to insignificance, the Inquisition continued its gruesome work. Heretics were burnt in Spain as late as 1756; the last fire was lit in Portugal in 1826. There is no doubt that the Inquisition helped to undermine Spain's power and contributed to the country's great period of decline. It rooted out many of the best and most liberal minds, and the cleverest leaders. And the cowed people trampled on them and reduced them to dependence and spiritual death.

But in its first phase it concentrated on the *Marranos*, not the genuine Jews. In its ways the Inquisition's attitude to unbaptized Jews was a remarkable example of religious tolerance. They were actually treated better than the recently converted *Marranos* and their successors. If a *Marrano* or an ordinary Spaniard dared to express even the slightest suggestion of doubt about the Immaculate Conception or the Holy Ghost, he was liable to the stake. But his neighbour the Jew,

ISABELLA

who neither believed in the Immaculate Conception nor admitted that there was a Holy Ghost, went free; no one did him any harm, at least not directly.

But the Jews' turn came too. The Inquisition realized that they would never overcome the *Marranos* so long as there were Jews in Spain. The numerous *Marranos*, who clung to Israel's faith in their hearts, received the spiritual nourishment and encouragement they could not do without in the *juderias*, naturally in deepest secrecy. But the Inquisition knew everything, it had eyes in every street and house.

Drastic steps were taken against this traffic. It was forbidden to frequent the company of Jews and the royal authorities even tried to remove them from certain towns where their presence was especially dangerous. But Isabella soon saw that only a radical operation would work. The Jews must be banished.

But not yet. So long as the war against Granada was not won, she needed the Jews. Without their money no victory over the last Moorish town on Spanish soil was possible.

XIV

GRANADA

FOR centuries the King of Granada had ruled Andalusia from the romantic castle of the Alhambra. The little kingdom of Granada was one of the world's happiest countries, or at least could have been. The people were numerous, industrious and clever; trade, shipping, horticulture and industry flourished and the standard of living was high. But there was constant political unrest; petty tyrants seized power and had to relinquish it again. This sapped the country's strength and gradually it was reduced to a province which was tributary to its powerful neighbour, Castile.

Naturally, it was only a question of time before this last Moorish foothold in Spain could be liquidated. Isabella had planned to employ the full might of the Kingdom to win back Granada for Christ. Only then would the *reconquista* be accomplished and Spain united.

A war may be inevitable. But there must preferably be some incalculable accident or other to start it. In 1481 some impetuous Moorish warriors from Granada overpowered a Castilian border fortress. Isabella and Ferdinand seized avidly on the excuse and the war was rapidly in full swing.

The Christian Kings knew that this was their great chance. So they made scrupulous preparation. They fetched mercenaries from distant lands; it was the first war in Europe in which mercenaries proved superior to locally recruited soldiers. Armaments were bought in various parts of Europe, the new iron canon for example, while ships brought big cargoes of gunpowder from Sicily. Spanish armament manufacture was

GRANADA

productive, now its capacity was stretched to breaking point; the best lances, swords and crossbows of the period flowed in a steady stream from workshop to armament depot.

The campaign got under way. The way over the Sierra Nevada was barred by frontier fortresses which were almost impregnable. But one after another had to yield. The battle was hopeless for the Moors. As early as midsummer, 1482, they could see, from the twin castles on the sister cliffs in Granada, the Alhambra and the Albaicin, the villages burning in the beautiful *huerta*, while the inhabitants fled before the Christians' lust for vengeance.

Treachery lurked behind the walls, and overt splits weakened the warriors' arms and made their hearts insensible. Harem intrigues, personal jealousy and revenge were more important than the war against the Christians. The king, the weak, indecisive Boabdil, saw anarchy spread.

But the rumour of the holy queen, who went to war against the heathen, flew round Europe, and knights from France, Italy, England and Portugal went to Spain to share in the honour of the battle.

Town after town was conquered. The victors rescued Christian captives from pestilent underground dungeons; full of incredulous joy they saw the irons cut from their crippled hands, while tens of thousands of Moorish captives were driven forth to slavery under the lash of the whip.

'I pluck the pomegranate seed by seed,' said Ferdinand. The pomegranate, of course, is named after Granada; it is very juicy and full of countless small seeds. Grenades are also called after it. The small iron shot they contain are like the seeds in the fruit.

Every week the kingdom of Granada grew smaller and smaller. The wretched Boabdil's dominion was based on ever weaker support; people whispered curses on his name in the narrow alleys. Outside the walls, hate and war, inside treachery and ambushes. The pomegranate tree was going to redden before it fell.

But Granada held out longer than anyone had dreamt

THE THREE RINGS

possible. It had brave warriors; the town was situated on inaccessible heights and the Christian army had long troublesome lines of communication. Ferdinand grew tired of the war; he went away for long periods to supervise more important interests. But Isabella was indefatigable. This war was a crusade she was waging for God's honour.

And she held out. The actual siege could not begin until the spring of 1491, i.e. after ten years of war.

The Christian camp lay just outside Granada's strong walls and towers. Tales of the fabulous queen's conduct in her camp shine through all the centuries which separate us from those days. The tents were of silk, splendidly and extravagantly decorated; everywhere billowing banners and crosses raised on high were to be seen. The queen rode on her white war horse, which had a flying mane and was bedecked with a velvet cloth which brushed the ground. Isabella wore damascened armour and royal purple; cardinals, bishops, princes and grandees swarmed around her. She was continually on the go; she had a thought for one and all, she encouraged, she consoled, she ruled.

Every morning when the sun's first rays strewed gold over the white peaks of the sierra, the queen and the whole army, from the highest prince to the lowest serf, knelt before the golden altar in the camp, while the cardinal of Spain conducted the mystery of the holy mass.

One summer night in 1491, a fire broke out in the camp and everything burnt to the ground. Isabella raised it again, but this time of stone, not tents. She called the new town Santa Fé, the holy faith, its streets were so laid out that they formed a cross. The defenders' courage fell when they saw from the walls how quickly the new town shot up. They were certain that the Christians had magic powers. And in Santa Fé the queen solemnly swore that there she would stay, summer and winter, until Granada was hers.

Granada was cut off from all communication with the outside world. The crescent's desperate warriors dreamed of a mass outbreak for victory or death. But Boabdil had lost his

GRANADA

courage and given up all hope. In deep secrecy he began to negotiate with the Catholic Kings.

It leaked out: the rumour of the fateful news was whispered from house to house. Ten thousand furious Moors raced up the steep streets to the Alhambra and called on Boabdil to deny the report. The king received them in the brilliant royal hall. Hopelessness and despair lent him an oratory he had never possessed before. In glowing words he expounded how hopeless the situation was; there was no way out but surrender—the main thing being to win as favourable terms as possible.

Stunned with grief they realized that he was right. With bowed heads and tears streaming down their cheeks they left the lovely palace they were soon to lose.

On January 2, 1492, a splendid procession rode out from Santa Fé to set the crown on Isabella the Catholic's victory. Isabella, surrounded by the knighthood of Castile and Aragon, rode on her white horse by Ferdinand's side towards the gates of Granada. They were followed by the flower of the victorious army. Isabella stopped on a height near the town walls to look out over Granada's towers and minarets, and up at the twin sister castles which her heart had yearned for.

It was the greatest moment of her life. Islam's last town in Spain lay in her hands, now worship of the false prophet would disappear from the land into which it had infiltrated nearly eight hundred years ago.

The trumpets sounded. The gates opened and a mourning procession moved slowly up to the group on the height. Boabdil rode on a black horse, his swarthy face was lowered and his almond-shaped, tear-stained eyes downcast; his bulging snow-white haik only half concealed a green turban, embroidered with golden ornaments.

When the defeated king neared his conquerors he made a gesture as if to dismount from his horse and hurl himself in the dust. But Ferdinand was clever enough to avoid this ultimate humiliation. While Boabdil bowed low in the saddle, Ferdinand accepted the heavy keys of the city and handed them over to the queen.

THE THREE RINGS

Four days later Granada was cleaned up and decorated; monks sprinkled holy water everywhere and made the city ready to receive the Christian Kings. The steep narrow avenue from the Triumphal Gate to the Alhambra was flanked by Spanish soldiers. Only a few dark-eyed Moors looked on in despair from behind lowered shutters when the knights of Castile, Aragon and Leon followed the king and queen up to the castle.

When they reached the Alhambra, the Spanish royal flag floated in the light breeze high up on the top of the lofty Comares tower. At the same moment a golden cross was hoisted above the flag, the symbol of the triumphant faith. A thousand heralds shouted: 'Granada, Granada for Queen Isabella and King Ferdinand!'

When the Cross shone high above her, Isabella dismounted. Together with her whole army she knelt in the dust in all her finery and thanked the rulers' God for the victory. Choirs intoned Christian songs of praise in all the recently purified mosques.

Accompanied by a few servants and his masculine mother, Boabdil stole out of the city and rode up to a little town in the mountains which the victors had allotted to him. When he reached the last mountain top from which he could see the Alhambra, he stopped. At that very moment the red cross flag was hoisted on the tower. Boabdil burst into tears. But his mother did not spare her unfortunate beaten son. She merely said: 'Yes, weep, weep like a woman over the city you were too weak to defend like a man!'

Since that day the peak has been called *el Ultimo suspiro del Moro*, the Moor's last sigh.

During the months preceding Granada's surrender people in Santa Fé had noticed a man who merely went his way and waited. He was tall, red-haired, with bright healthy-coloured cheeks, his eyes were pale blue with a faraway look, like that of seamen who are used to watching the sea. Although he was barely forty, his hair was greying for he had gone through many years of troubles and constant difficulties. The unknown was not a warrior, only a petitioner who waited patiently until the

GRANADA

princes had time to listen to his plans. The dapper courtiers made fun of him and only a few knew what he had in mind. He was a dreamer and not many believed in the visions he had. And worst of all he was a foreigner: it was said that he came from Genoa.

He was Christopher Columbus. Now the whole world knows that after long delays he eventually achieved his wish and that the Catholic Kings outfitted his small fleet, which sailed on August 3, 1492, to discover the sea route to the Indies, but reached America instead. But very few people realized what role the Spanish Jews also played in this turning-point in the history of mankind.

Columbus was fond of casting a cloak of mystery over his past; he found it wise to imply in veiled terms that he came of noble stock. But acute researchers have tried to track down his origins. They have reached the conclusion that his was a *Marrano* family, but that Columbus did his best to conceal the fact.

In any case one thing is certain, that his name—Colombo or Colon—was frequently borne by Jews. It is equally certain that Columbus left a legacy to a Jew in Lisbon in his will. More pertinent is the fact that his writings showed a marked Biblical influence and that his signature, which is difficult to read, is reminiscent of Hebrew characters. And it is decisive that his son expressly stated that his father was of royal blood in Jerusalem. The last claim was the usual method employed by Spanish Jews at the time, when they wished to boast of their high birth. Not much is left of the generally accepted view that Columbus was the son of a weaver in Genoa. The traces point rather in the direction of an *aljama* in one of the Spanish countries.

Be this as it may. It is far more important to emphasize the help and understanding he received from a small group of *Marranos* and Jews. First and foremost from the two tremendously influential Spanish statesmen and financiers, Isaac Avravanel and Abraham Senior, but also a member of the distinguished Caballerio family, whom we have already met.

THE THREE RINGS

They were the men who persuaded the queen to reject her former councillor's attitude to Columbus and they raised money for the expedition.

Quite a few of the crew were Jews and the first European who set foot on American soil was the interpreter Luis de Torres. He was a *Marrano*, baptized a few days before the expedition sailed from Spain.

But none of the great voyages of discovery would have been possible without the new improved nautical instruments. The shape of the quadrant, the so-called Jacob's staff, which was used for taking the heights of sun and stars, was invented by a Jew; it was the Jews in Majorca who drew the charts and Jewish astronomers had worked out the astronomical tables which made possible navigation on the open sea.

The last-named were compiled by the celebrated Abraham Zahuto, and not only Columbus, but also Vasco de Gama and Magellan navigated by them.

Incidentally there is an amusing example of how Columbus made use of Zahuto's tables in a tight corner. Together with some of his sailors he was stranded on Jamaica; his ship was wrecked and Columbus had to wait until help came. The Indians refused to bring the Spaniards food, but Columbus knew that there would be an eclipse of the moon a few days later. He invited the Indians that very night and made a speech in which he informed them that the Spanish God was angry and would punish them by putting the moon out. And when the crescent actually began to vanish and finally disappeared completely, the primitive Indians were naturally seized with terror and promised him and his crew everything they wanted.

The Catholic Kings' borrowed room in the Alhambra still smelt of delicate Moorish perfume when Isabella and Ferdinand signed the edict, on March 30, 1492, saying that all Jews must leave Spain within four month's time.

With his usual care and imagination Torquemada had prepared public opinion for this thunderbolt. A couple of years before the police had searched the luggage of a travelling *Marrano*, Benito Carcias, and been lucky enough to find a host!

GRANADA

The poor sinner was put on the rack at once and his confessions followed according to plan. One night he had met five other *Marranos* and six Jews in a cave. Together they had crucified a Christian boy, whom they had just kidnapped in the town of La Guardia. They had drained his blood and torn the heart out of his breast.

A few days later they were together in the cave again. This time they practised black magic with the heart and a host, and dedicated the inquisitors and the catholic faith to Satan. The most serious of all was that it was not a private conspiracy; all the Jewish communities in Spain had entrusted them with the frightful task. Obviously the decisive proof was lacking; it was impossible to produce the boy's corpse. And all the confessions were made after terrible tortures. But the twelve criminals were condemned as a matter of course and ended their days at the stake.

Now popular feeling was aroused, everyone was beside themselves with fear, petitions streamed in to the king and queen asking for protection against the Jews. The result was the edict of banishment which sealed the fate of the Spanish Jews.

They felt as if the very earth was opening beneath their feet. The edict meant that they would be uprooted from the country where they had lived and worked for more than a thousand years; they must leave everything they owned behind and wander poor and naked into a dangerous hostile world.

The Jews had not expected the catastrophe; it came like a bolt from the blue. And they had had good grounds for feeling secure. Had not their two most outstanding men, Abraham Senior and Isaac Avravanel, sat on the king's council and helped it to win Granada? It is strange to think that on one side of the council table sat Torquemada and on the other two Jews. From the former flowed exhortations to the army, while the latter raised the equally necessary money. But the Jews did not give in without great resistance; they did everything to stop the unbelievable happening.

Isaac Avravanel was in his fifties when misfortune struck him. He was the last of one of the oldest and most celebrated

THE THREE RINGS

Hispano-Jewish families; the family had lived in Seville since time immemorial. During the 'holy war' of 1391 his grandfather had to flee to Portugal. Both he and Isaac's father had administered Portugal's finances and reached high office.

He himself was a fine writer, as well as a philosopher; he is counted as one of the last philosophical thinkers of mediaeval Judaism. And the King of Portugal used and respected him as the outstanding financial genius this talented man in fact was. He himself describes his happy life in Portugal as follows:

'I lived a carefree life in the famous city of Lisbon, mother of all Portuguese towns. My father had filled the house with artistic treasures, God blessed me and gave me wealth, honour and all the happiness a man can desire. In my house I assembled all the important men, we rejoiced over books, good cheer, over wisdom and piety. I worked happily in King Alphonso's court and under him the Jews lived freely and without care.'

However, the new king, Juan II, was a savage despot. He introduced trials for high treason and executions. At the last moment Avravanel was warned and escaped over the border with his persecutors on his heels. He had to leave his wonderful library and his great art collection behind, but his life was saved. In Castile he settled in Toledo, but was soon summoned to the court, and a new brilliant career was under way.

Together with Abraham Senior he hastened to the Alhambra when news of the edict reached him. The two Jews were given audience and begged the monarchs to withdraw the fateful decision. They both knew what money meant to Ferdinand, so they offered him a really astronomical sum in return.

However, Torquemada, had thought of everything; such an offer was also included in the far-sighted Dominican's calculations. In the middle of the negotiations he burst into the palace with a crucifix in his hands and screamed at the royal pair:

'Judas Ischariot betrayed Christ for thirty pieces of silver. Are you setting a price of thirty thousand on him? Here he is, sell him!'

He threw the crucifix at the queen's feet and stormed out.

GRANADA

Now there was no changing things. Royal heralds went round Spain and announced that the Jews had three months to settle their affairs, after which they had to leave. Every Jew who was found in Spain after the expiry of the period of grace was condemned to death or—baptism.

The period of grace was so short that it was impossible for the Jews to get a reasonable price for their property. A house was given up for an ass, a vineyard was exchanged for a few yards of cloth. There was no point in selling for ready cash, because they could not take it out of the country and letters of credit would be useless abroad. Rich families saw themselves reduced to beggary.

The Dominicans seized the opportunity and pestered the desperate Jews to go over to Christianity. Only a few obeyed the exhortation. But among them was Abraham Senior. Both Ferdinand and Isabella were godparents at his baptism. Isaac Avravanel, on the contrary, followed his fellow Jews into poverty and exile. For the second time in his life he had to leave everything behind him.

Even when prepared for the journey, the Jews delayed till the last moment. They waited to follow each other. For in days of misfortune the Jews are not individualists, but a people who accept fate's blows together.

On the last three days they lay down by their fathers' graves and bathed the gravestones with their tears. And they adjured *Marrano* friends to look after them when they had gone. Some of them took the stones with them.

Most of the exiles made the long journey to Portugal. Many sailed from the ports; they hoped to find refuge in Italy or a North African town. But at the time—as now—it was difficult for Jewish refugees to find a country which was willing to accept them. Ships might sail from port to port, while famine and epidemics thinned out the unfortunate passengers. And it was the captains who made use of their opportunities and sold them as slaves.

Things went even worse for the refugees who went to Portugal. They had obtained the promise of asylum for eight

THE THREE RINGS

months against a heavy payment. When the period expired as many as possible were shipped away. The majority of them sailed to certain death.

But death is not the worst evil which can befall mankind, as those who remained behind and the whole of the ancient Portuguese Jewry learnt. King Manuel of Portugal married Isabella's eldest daughter. The Catholic Kings looked on the union sympathetically; perhaps at some point they could unite Portugal with their kingdom so that the whole Iberian peninsula would become one country. But they laid down the inevitable condition that King Manuel first 'cleansed' his country of the Jews.

He decided to pay the price and in 1496 issued an edict that all unbaptized Jews must leave his kingdom. But the Jews were worthy citizens, he preferred to try and force them to be baptized. Then he promulgated the terrible law that children should be taken from their parents and forcibly baptized. Indescribable scenes took place. Mothers threw themselves into the sea with their children, fathers embraced their youthful sons in farewell, but in the middle of the caress stuck a dagger into their hearts and then killed themselves.

Only 20,000 Jews refused to be forced. They gathered in the port of Lisbon to emigrate. They never embarked. Soldiers declared that they were the king's slaves, and monks sprinkled them with holy water and certified that they were baptized.

King Manuel did one good thing. He gave the Portuguese *Marranos*—and they became numerous all of a sudden—religious immunity for twenty years, during which period the Inquisition could not touch them. This respite was made use of; the *Marranos* learnt how to organize themselves and systematize their secret life according to the Jewish faith. They succeeded so well that there are still survivors of the ancient *Marranos* in Portugal.

As the centuries passed, many of them naturally left the country. They sought the same routes as the few who escaped during the great uprooting. Holland, England and France received them and communities grew up in Bordeaux, Amster-

GRANADA

dam, Hamburg, London and many other places in Western Europe. Their members were called the Portuguese Jews; their traditions and rituals have roots back in the Iberian peninsula. They nurtured some of European culture's greatest names, Spinoza and Disraeli, to name only two examples.

By a remarkable coincidence the date for leaving Spain was fixed for August 2, 1492. The day fell in the same week as 9 Ab, the day commemorating Jerusalem's destruction.

And the day after, August 3, 1492, Columbus sailed on his first voyage to America.

On almost the same day Isabella made Spain a world power, on whose empire the sun never set, and planted one of the seeds causing the tragic decline which finally made the country a target for Europe's witty leaders. For example, when Spain lost Portugal and the Netherlands, and the satirists compared her to a hole with the inscription, 'The more is taken away from it the greater it is!'

When Isabella drove the Jews out of her kingdom, she cut off a large and valuable part of the country's middle class, industrious, intelligent, useful people, intellectuals, craftsmen and merchants. Later Spain also lost the exiled Jews' *Marrano* brothers. The Inquisition rooted them out or they fled.

And while Spain's might rose to the heights, it was hollowed out from within. One fine day there was a landslide in the Spanish Empire. England and Holland took over a large part of it. They were the very lands the most intelligent Jews had fled to.

The curtain fell on Moorish dreams and the thousand-year-old Jewish drama, and the Spain which had blossomed for so long as the country of the three rings, dried up; she sank into apathy and stiffened into trivial orthodoxy.

XV

AHASVERUS

THE porter in Pontius Pilate's house in Jerusalem was called Kartafilius. When Jesus was led out through the door on the first Good Friday, he gave Our Saviour a push and said mockingly: 'Make haste, Jesus, why doest thou walk so slowly?'

But Jesus turned and looked at him severely. 'I go, but thou shalt wait until I come.'

And the story continues that since Our Saviour's words Kartafilius cannot die until Jesus comes again. Every time he lives to be a hundred, he is smitten by an incurable disease and falls into a swoon. When he awakes, he is suddenly thirty years old again.

So runs the oldest version we know of the myth of the wandering Jew. Later Kartafilius became Ahasverus and his romantic destiny has tempted countless poets and story-tellers. They have treated his life in poems, plays and novels and reproduced what the Church said was his crime and punishment, and used his eternal wandering in ever new symbols. Some saw in him the image of the Jews' destiny, others the image of the whole of mankind, the perpetually restless and striving man who never finds peace in life. And his fate always aroused sympathy mixed with fear; for he suffered the worst punishment of all, not being able to die.

Like the parable of the three rings the story of the Wandering Jew became one of the folk tales which clothed an idea with flesh and blood, and therefore began eternal wanderings itself and became as immortal as the man it tells of.

AHASVERUS

People had seen Ahasverus with their own eyes or they knew someone who had met him or heard of him. There was not a town to which a wandering Jew did not come now and then. He looked different from most people. He spoke with rapid loquacity in a strange, incomprehensible tongue; his clothes were worn, his eyes melancholy and apprehensive; weariness and despair could be read in his features. He disappeared again without anyone noticing; suddenly he had gone—but an impression of something strange and unpleasant remained, a gust of wind from the homeless people.

They were Jews who had left their homes. Perhaps they had never had one or they had seen their nearest and dearest murdered and their house go up in flames, while they only saved their lives by hasty flight. Now they wandered mile after mile in cold and storms; they felt at home everywhere and nowhere; they were eager to learn new things and knew everything they could make use of.

For the Christians Ahasverus became the type of the eternally wandering people. In the olden days the way led from Jerusalem to Babylon, and from Babylon to Spain. But they did not find a permanent home there either. So they continued the journey to Turkey or North Africa or northwards to Holland and thence to Poland and Russia. Everywhere the Jew was in transit; he was always a bird of passage.

But wherever he went, he had his own faith with him. It was as if he listened to the Jordan's rippling stream or the Euphrates' billows every day. He always differentiated between himself and everyone else; he built up the law's high fence; only behind it could he breathe freely. He looked out from it and dreamed of the glorious deliverance some time in the far distant future and the voyage home to the promised land. From his nightmares and dreams he could make a substitute for everything he had lost; inside he was free and looked down on everyone else from above.

The last Moors were driven out of Spain ten years after the Jews. They vanished, were absorbed by other peoples or simply went away. They left their traces behind them; their palaces and canals remain as memorials of the men who built for eternity; we know their philosophy and literature and adventures; they helped to create present day Europe via Jewish middlemen. But they themselves vanished like rain which is swallowed up in North Africa's deserts in a flash.

But the Jews survived, they remained Jews and they have never forgotten the proud memories of their Spanish golden age. They still speak the Spanish dialect *Ladino* which they took with them; it can be heard in Amsterdam, New York, Istanbul and Jerusalem.

There was always 'a remnant' which the prophets spoke of and which never died. There was 'a remnant' after the banishment from Spain. The Spanish Jews themselves were 'a remnant' from Babylon, as Babylon's Jews were 'a remnant' from Judaea.

This hard core always survived, the core which held fast to Israel's God and obeyed his commandments. The great men Solomon ibn Gabirol, Maimonides and Jehuda ben Halevi, were not the first who kept the torch burning through the endlessly long night. They received the lighted torch from the nameless common people, the persecuted, the despised, who clung to their faith in the one God in small undecorated synagogues, the God to whom a thousand years are as a day and whose arm is always ready to save.

There shone visions, there streamed the brook, so that the restless were calmed and found peace in that which passeth all understanding.

Ahasverus wandered onwards from Spain. He found new resting places, but only temporarily. Once again he had to take the long weary road.

Judaea, Babylon, Spain, Holland, Poland, Russia. They are milestones on two thousand years of wandering.

But today Ahasverus is on the move again and on his way home to Judaea again. Perhaps the world will yet see in our time Israel gathered in its ancient land.

Then the ring will be completed.

The first of the three rings.

INDEX

Abd al Rahman and Abd al Rahman III, 39–45, 58–9, 61, 72, 169
Abraham Abulafia, 154–7
Abraham ibn Ezra, 21, 110–15
Abraham Senior, 222, 233, 235–7
Ahasverus, 240–2
Albigensian heresy, 135–6, 158, 198
Aljama, 181, 183, 190, 192, 196, 233
Almanzor, 46–7, 88
Almohades, 91–2, 118–20, 123, 139, 199, 201, 214
Almoravides, 90–2, 98
Alphonsine tables, 20
Alphonso VII, King, of Castile, 89, 92–3, 169, 198–9
Anussim, 121, 214
Ashkenazic Jews, 19
Averroës, 119
Avicebron, see Solomon ibn Gabirol
Az Zahra, 44, 52, 64

Badge of Jewry, 159–61, 192, 211
Badis, 67–8
Barcelona, 21, 155, 170, 184, 208, 219
Beltran de Cueva, 216–17
Black Death, 165–7
Boabdil, 229, 231–2

Caballerio family, 212, 233
Cabbala, 81, 139–57
Cadiz, 23
Charlemagne, 40
Charles Martel, 37
Chazars, 52–8
Christopher Columbus, 232–4, 239

Cid, El, 89, 93
Clermont, Synod of, 83, 86
Cordoba, 20 and *passim*
Count Julian, 34–5
Count Roland, 40
Covadonga, 37–8
Crete, 160
Crusades and crusaders, 16, 73, 82–8, 106, 110, 123, 139, 158, 174, 178, 199

Decameron, 11, 13
Disraeli, 239
Dominican order, 135–6, 161, 204, 208–9, 211, 221, 224, 226, 237

Emek Habaha, 82

Ferdinand, 93, 184, 218–20, 223–5, 228–32, 234, 237
Fons vitae, 79–80
Fourth Lateran Council, 159, 161, 164, 170, 201

Granada, *passim*

Habus, 66–7
Hasdai ibn Shaprut, 48–52, 55–9, 61–4, 69
Heinrich Heine, 110

Innocent III, 58–9, 170, 198, 204
Inquisition, 135–6, 161–2, 204, 223, 227
Isaac Avravanel, 235–7
Isabella, 93, 184, 215–27, 228–34, 237–9

THE THREE RINGS

James, King, of Aragon, 206–8
Jehuda Alharisi, 21, 115
Jehuda Halevi, 21, 57, 94, 98–111, 193, 242
Jekutiel Hassan, 74
Jews, Jewry, Judaism, *passim*
Juan II, King, of Portugal, 236
Juderia, 20, 187–8, 193, 199, 201, 210–11
Jusuf, 90–1

Kartafilius, *see* Ahasverus

Lessing, Gottfried Ephraim, 11, 13
Lucena, 91–2, 94, 98–9
Lull, Raymond, 137

Mahbereth, 62–3
Maimonides, 93, 105, 116–36, 138, 154, 191–3, 200, 206, 214, 242
Majorca, 27–8, 184, 210
Manuel, King, of Portugal, 238
Marranos, 211, 213–14, 222–7, 233–5, 237–9
Menahem ben Saruk, 62–3
Mishna, 126–7
Mishne Torah, 127–30
Moors, *passim*
More Nebukim, 130–1, 133
Moses ben Hanoch, 59–61
Moses ben Maimon, *see* Maimonides
Moses ben Nahman, *see* Nahmanides
Moses ibn Ezra, 94–7, 99, 107, 111
Moses of Leon, 148
Musa, 35

Nahmanides, 206–8
Nicholas III, 155

Pedro Arbuez, 226
Phoenicians, 23–4

Radanites, 178, 185
Reccared, King, 30
Roderick, King, 34–7

Samuel ibn Nagdela, 65–70
Sancho the Fat, King, of Leon, 51–2
Santiago de Compostella, 87–8
Saragossa, 74
Sephardic Jews, 19
Solomon ibn Gabirol, 69, 73–81, 94, 100, 108, 115, 150, 242
Spinoza, 239

Talavera, 225
Tarik, 35–7
Tertullian, 26
Toledo, 20 and *passim*
Torquemada, 93, 221, 223–5, 236
Tortosa, 209
Tota, Queen, of Navarre, 51–2
Tower of Hercules, 35–6

Urban II, 83

Vespasian, 22–3
Villena, Marquis of, 216–20
Visigoths, *passim*

William of Norwich, 162–3

Zionid, 110
Zohar, 148

For Product Safety Concerns and Information please contact our EU
representative GPSR@taylorandfrancis.com
Taylor & Francis Verlag GmbH, Kaufingerstraße 24, 80331 München, Germany

www.ingramcontent.com/pod-product-compliance
Lightning Source LLC
Chambersburg PA
CBHW050630300426
44112CB00012B/1734